The Quality Improvement Glossary

D0792477

Also Available from ASQ Quality Press:

The Quality Improvement Handbook
ASQ Quality Management Division and John E. Bauer, Grace L. Duffy,
Russell T. Westcott, editors

Quality's Greatest Hits: Classic Wisdom from the Leaders of Quality
Zigmund Bluvband

The Quality Toolbox
Nancy R. Tague

The Executive Guide to Improvement and Change
G. Dennis Beecroft, Grace L. Duffy, John W. Moran, editors

Business Process Improvement Toolbox
Bjørn Andersen

*From Quality to Business Excellence: A Systems Approach to
Management*
Charles G. Cobb

*The Change Agents' Handbook: A Survival Guide for Quality
Improvement Champions*
David W. Hutton

*Making Change Work: Practical Tools for Overcoming Human
Resistance to Change*
Brien Palmer

Principles and Practices of Organizational Performance Excellence
Thomas J. Cartin

*Customer Centered Six Sigma: Linking Customers, Process
Improvement, and Financial Results*
Earl Naumann and Steven H. Hoisington

The Certified Quality Manager Handbook, Second Edition
Duke Okes and Russell T. Westcott, editors

*To request a complimentary catalog of ASQ Quality Press publications,
call 800-248-1946, or visit our Web site at http://qualitypress.asq.org.*

The Quality Improvement Glossary

Don Siebels

ASQ Quality Press
Milwaukee, Wisconsin

American Society for Quality, Quality Press, Milwaukee 53203
© 2004 by ASQ
All rights reserved. Published 2004
Printed in the United States of America

12 11 10 09 08 07 06 05 04   5 4 3 2 1

Library of Congress Cataloging-in-Publication Data

Siebels, Don, 1946–
    The quality improvement glossary / Don Siebels.
        p. cm.
    Includes bibliographical references.
    ISBN 0-87389-619-X (alk. paper)
    1. Total quality management—Terminology.   2. Quality control—
    Terminology.   I. Title.
    HD62.15.S574   2004
    658'.003—dc22   2004006839

ISBN 0-87389-619-X

No part of this book may be reproduced in any form or by any means, electronic,
mechanical, photocopying, recording, or otherwise, without the prior written
permission of the publisher.

Publisher: William A. Tony
Acquisitions Editor: Annemieke Hytinen
Project Editor: Paul O'Mara
Production Administrator: Randall Benson
Special Marketing Representative: David Luth

ASQ Mission: The American Society for Quality advances individual,
organizational, and community excellence worldwide through learning, quality
improvement, and knowledge exchange.

Attention Bookstores, Wholesalers, Schools, and Corporations: ASQ Quality Press
books, videotapes, audiotapes, and software are available at quantity discounts
with bulk purchases for business, educational, or instructional use. For
information, please contact ASQ Quality Press at 800-248-1946, or write to ASQ
Quality Press, P.O. Box 3005, Milwaukee, WI 53201-3005.

To place orders or to request a free copy of the ASQ Quality Press Publications
Catalog, including ASQ membership information, call 800-248-1946. Visit our Web
site at www.asq.org or http://qualitypress.asq.org.

♾ Printed on acid-free paper

Quality Press
600 N. Plankinton Avenue
Milwaukee, Wisconsin 53203
Call toll free 800-248-1946
Fax 414-272-1734
www.asq.org
http://qualitypress.asq.org
http://standardsgroup.asq.org
E-mail: authors@asq.org

This book is dedicated to all those in the quality profession worldwide, whether in the manufacturing or service industries, who are searching for a greater understanding of the broad field of quality and are willing to learn and teach others.

Contents

Preface

Webster's New World Dictionary (1988) defines a glossary as "a list of difficult, technical, or foreign terms with definitions or translations, as for some particular author, field of knowledge, etc., often included in alphabetical listing at the end of a textbook." Over the last 30-plus years working in the quality profession, I have consistently come across a myriad of difficult or technical terms and concepts. Many of these were either new to me, or the product of the ever-expanding field of quality and more recently the environmental field.

As I started to expand my vocabulary, I understood the only way for me to keep up was to compile a list of the various terms, concepts, acronyms, and the individuals who proposed them. This glossary comes from those personal notes and various other published sources compiled over the years (see Acknowledgments). Where various terms deal with a certain aspect of the quality profession and definitions previously published by ASQ are available, I have used them. Where terms come from fields outside the quality arena, I have defined them as closely as possible to generally accepted applications.

As such, the intent of *The Quality Improvement Glossary* is not to provide you with an all-inclusive description of the concept, word, or phrase, but rather to provide a brief explanation in an easily accessible format. For those of you interested in gaining an in-depth understanding of various topics or quality management principles, I encourage you to read the comprehensive publications available from ASQ Quality Press, such as *The Certified Quality Manager Handbook* or *Juran's Quality Handbook*. Books like *Principles of Quality Costs* will help you gain an indepth understanding of quality cost. For more on statistical quality control formulas and tables, consult the *Glossary and Tables for Statistical Quality Control*. In-depth and up-to-date information is readily available from ASQ Quality Press for any of the related quality fields, such as auditing, benchmarking, customer service, environmental issues, inspection, metrology, reliability, or other specialty subjects.

The Quality Improvement Glossary provides the novice as well as the seasoned quality professional with a brief explanation of the main concepts, terms, and acronyms used in the field. Anyone preparing to take an ASQ certification exam should find the text an invaluable aid. Note: For the official definitions of any word or phrase, refer to the appropriate standard(s) or regulation(s).

Acknowledgments

I want to thank the many people who have provided the quality profession with the knowledge we all currently enjoy—from the gurus who have identified concepts and proposed new methods to the inspectors who work every day to assure quality. They have all had a hand in providing and improving the quality of the products and processes we have grown to rely on. Several people have contributed greatly to the content of this glossary but may never receive due credit. Many of the terms dealing with statistical quality control were previously written by the ASQ Statistics Division and published in the book *Glossary and Tables for Statistical Quality Control*. Others were written by the ASQ Quality Cost Committee in *Principles of Quality Costs,* 3rd ed., edited by Jack Campanella, or in *The Certified Quality Manager Handbook,* 2nd ed., edited by Duke Okes and Russell T. Westcott. Many terms were published by ASQ in the journal *Quality Progress* (July 2002). These terms, concepts, and programs described in this glossary all belong to them. I merely compiled them.

I want to thank the many people who have influenced me over the years, both in my professional career and in my personal life. The support of my wife, Judy, and my family are foremost among these. I would like to acknowledge my parents, who always stressed the importance of doing things right the first time. I would also like to thank the staff at ASQ Quality Press for their tireless efforts and patience with me, and the countless people whose ideas are included in this glossary but whose ties to the contribution and application may have been lost over the years.

Introduction

I have arranged definitions of terms, concepts, persons, or acronyms alphabetically. Each entry provides enough detail to shed light on the concept or phrase as applied within the quality profession.

"See also" references provide titles of books or other published materials where the term or concept appears. "See" references are to other terms or phrases in the glossary that will supply additional or comparative information. When terms have more than one meaning or application, the definitions are divided into numbered sections. The ASQ Code of Ethics is reprinted in front of the glossary so it is always available for easy reference.

Noted influential persons in the quality field are referenced in Appendix A. Acronyms are included in the glossary but listed separately for convenience in Appendix B. SPC symbols and basic formulas are detailed in Appendix C. A matrix on what SPC charts to use in which application is included in Appendix D. Geometric dimensioning and tolerancing symbols and blueprint data are included in Appendix E. Various quality-related standards are listed in Appendix F. Finally, quality awards are listed in Appendix G.

The task of creating a glossary for our profession with such varied applications and audiences was challenging. The language we use is constantly changing, with new words and concepts being added and others becoming obsolete. As such, our vocabulary continues to change as well. ASQ Quality Press will continue to lead the way in helping us add to the growing list of terms and definitions. As new terms are developed, please contact me to have these included in a subsequent edition of the glossary. Despite the best efforts of all involved in this project, there may be errors or omissions that become evident as this glossary is used. Please feel free to submit updated/corrected terminology. I hope you find this glossary a useful tool in your efforts toward a more thorough understanding of the quality field.

ASQ Code of Ethics

To uphold and advance the honor and dignity of the profession, and in keeping with high standards of ethical conduct I acknowledge that I:

Fundamental Principles

Will be honest and impartial, and will serve with devotion my employer, my clients, and the public.

Will strive to increase the competence and prestige of the profession.

Will use my knowledge and skill for the advancement of human welfare, and in promoting the safety and reliability of products for public use.

Will earnestly endeavor to aid the work of the society.

Relations with the Public

1.1. Will do whatever I can to promote the reliability and safety of all products that come within my jurisdiction.

1.2. Will endeavor to extend public knowledge of the work of the Society and its members that relates to the public welfare.

1.3. Will be dignified and modest in explaining my work and merit.

1.4. Will preface any public statements that I may issue by clearly indicating on whose behalf they are made.

Relations with Employers and Clients

2.1. Will act in professional matters as a faithful agent or trustee for each employer or client.

2.2. Will inform each client or employer of any business connections, interest, or affiliations which might influence my judgment or impair the equitable character of my services.

2.3. Will indicate to my employer or client the adverse consequences to be expected if my professional judgment is overruled.

2.4. Will not disclose information concerning the business affairs of technical processes of any present or former employer or client without his [or her] consent.

2.5. Will not accept compensation from more than one party for the same service without the consent of all parties. If employed, I will engage in supplementary employment of consulting practice only with the consent of my employer.

Relations with Peers

3.1. Will take care that credit for the work of others is given to those whom it is due.

3.2. Will endeavor to aid the professional development and advancement of those in my employ or under my supervision.

3.3. Will not compete unfairly with others; will extend my friendship and confidence to all associates and those with whom I have business relations.

AA (1) Abbreviation for arithmetical average (technically the arithmetic mean). (2) In machining, a measure of surface roughness, typically on the machined areas of the part. The AA is the mean of a series of values. *See* **RMS.**

A-bar chart Most basic graph of all the statistical process control (SPC) charts. Small samples are taken at regular intervals and plotted on the horizontal scale. The average is plotted on the vertical scale, and the points are then connected and plotted. More commonly known as an **X-bar chart** or **average chart.**

Abatement Reducing the degree or intensity of or eliminating an unplanned adverse incident.

Abba chart Graphical chart named after Wayne Abba composed of different representations showing trends from historical, present, and projected performance.

Abbe's law Principle put forth by Ernest Abbe, which states that for maximum reliability in measurement, the axis of the measuring instrument must lie along the axis line of the part being measured.

Aberrations Term used in optics to designate what we know as errors in linear measurement. The errors induced as a result of the measuring instrument at an angle, other than 90° to the surface being measured.

Ability test Assessment device that measures a person's capability to learn or acquire skills (also referred to as an "aptitude test").

Abscissa Coordinate representing the distance from the y-axis in a two-dimensional plot.

Absolute dimensioning system   Dimensioning system used in certain N/C (numerically controlled) machine programming. All points are dimensioned from a common reference point on the part. The part reference point should not be confused with the machine table reference point. All tool movements on N/C machines with absolute control systems must be measured and programmed from the machine table reference point.

Absorption   (1) Uptake of water or other fluids or chemicals by a cell and/or organism (tree roots absorb dissolved nutrients from the soil). (2) In an environmental sense, the removal of a pollutant from air or water by collecting the pollutant on the surface of a solid material such as treating wastewater with activated carbon to remove the organic matter.

Abuse   Subjection of a product to situations it was not designed to accept or to accomplish (e.g., extreme environments, excess vibration, overloading, stress). The results may or may not be catastrophic but will diminish the life of the product.

Accelerated testing   Testing of components, assemblies, and or equipment in a controlled environment under very high stress so the time will be shortened for failures to occur. For example, high temperature is often used to create failures in electronic components. *See* **reliability/design validation** and **burn-in.**

Acceptable process level (APL)   The process level that forms the outer boundary of the zone of acceptable processes. (A process located at the APL will have only a probability of rejection designated α when the plotted statistical measure is compared to the acceptance control limits.)

Acceptable quality level (AQL)   In a continuing series of lots, a quality level that, for the purpose of sampling inspection, is the limit of the satisfactory process average. For complete information and usage, see the older Military Standards 105E and Military Standard 414.

Acceptable reliability level (ARL)   Nominal figure-of-merit specified for acceptance of parts or equipment. It is a measure of reliability, which is given some preassigned percentage of the time by which a reliability test plan is given.

Acceptance   (1) Decision that the product or process is operating satisfactorily with respect to the measures being taken. (2) In statistical terms, a decision made that the process is operating satisfactorily with respect to the statistical measure being plotted.

Acceptance control chart Graphical method for the dual purposes of evaluating a process in terms of (1) whether or not it can be expected to satisfy product or service tolerances for the characteristic(s) being measured or (2) whether or not it is in a "state of statistical control" with respect to sample, subgroup, or variability. The determinations are made through comparisons of values of some statistical measure(s) for an ordered series of samples, or subgroups, with acceptance control limits.

Acceptance control limit (ACL) Control limits for an acceptance control chart, which permit some assignable shift in process level based on specified requirements, provided within subgroup variability is in a state of statistical control.

Acceptance criteria Requirements that a product or service must meet before the customer will accept delivery or before the completion of a project. In the quality audit field, acceptance criteria may also include the standard against which a comparison is made to judge conformance.

Acceptance inspection Inspection of goods prior to placing them in inventory for use or shipment.

Acceptance number Maximum number of defects or defectives allowable in a sample from the lot for the lot to be acceptable.

Acceptance region In hypothesis testing, the region of values of the test statistic for which the null hypothesis is not rejected.

Acceptance sampling Inspection of a sample from a lot to decide whether to accept that lot. There are two types: *attributes* sampling and *variables* sampling. In attributes sampling, the presence or absence of a characteristic is noted in each of the units inspected. In variables sampling, the numerical magnitude of a characteristic is measured and recorded for each inspected unit; this involves reference to a continuous scale of some kind.

Acceptance-sampling plan Specific plan that indicates the sampling sizes and associated acceptance or nonacceptance criteria to be used for a lot. In attributes sampling, for example, there are single, double, multiple, sequential, chain, and skip-lot sampling plans. In variables sampling, there are single, double, and sequential sampling plans. (For detailed descriptions of these plans, see also the standard ANSI/ISO/ASQ A35342, Statistics—Vocabulary and Symbols—Statistical Quality Control.)

Acceptance testing Applying performance and/or dimensional requirements to a product or service to assure they meet customers' requirements.

A

Acceptance test procedure Detailed instructions applied to a process or product for the preparation and operation of the acceptance test and the evaluation of the test results.

Accident rate Measure of the disabling accidents occurring in any specified exposure of workers to employment hazards. Composed of two measures: the *frequency rate,* which is the number of disabling or lost time accidents in an exposure of one million person-hours worked, and the *severity rate,* the total number of lost person-days charged to disabling accidents during an exposure of one million person-hours worked.

Accountability Total responsibility of an individual for the satisfactory completion of a specific job or assignment. Assuming liability for something of value, either through someone's actions, position, or status.

Accreditation Certification by a duly recognized body of the facilities, capability, objectivity, competence, and integrity of an agency, service, operational group, or individual to provide the specific service or operation needed.

Accreditation body Agency formally sanctioned to provide recognition that a company or organization is competent to carry out specified tasks. The body that approves organizations, which in turn provides certificates of registration to standards such as the quality standard ISO 9001 and the environmental standard ISO 14001.

Accumulation of errors Compounding of errors in a series of measurements. In engineering blueprints, a method used to dimension features, one after the other in a sequence, with each dimension having its own tolerances. This method has a tendency to compound tolerances as they stack up. Compare with baseline dimensioning, which only allows tolerances to a feature from the baseline, without compounding the tolerances. *See* **tolerance stack up** or **chain dimensioning.**

Accuracy Closeness of agreement between an observed value and accepted reference value. The term when applied to a set of observed values is a combination of random components and of a common systematic error or bias component. Because routine application and random components and bias components cannot be completely separated, the so-called reported accuracy must be interpreted as a combination of these two elements.

Accuracy ratio Ratio of the tolerance of the instrument being calibrated to the uncertainty of the test standard.

Acid test   The most rigorous and severe form of testing for reliability, maintainability, and other criteria. The term originated from the fact that gold resists acids that will corrode other metals; the "acid test" was used to identify metals substituted for gold.

Acquisition   Obtaining materials, supplies, or services for use by an organization.

Action limit   In statistical process control (SPC), the upper and/or lower control limits, usually used in conjunction with warning limits when they are also used on the control chart.

Action plan   Specific method or process to achieve the results called for by one or more objectives. May be a simpler version of a project plan.

Active experimentation   Experiments are conducted where variable levels are changed to assess their impact on a response(s).

Active listening   Process of closely listening to what a person is saying, not being preoccupied with other thoughts, or thinking up other questions to be asked, particularly important in auditing. It may include asking the other party to describe what is meant and requesting that ideas be repeated to clarify any ambiguity or uncertainty.

Activity   Any element of work that is required by a project, uses resources, and takes time to complete. Activities have expected durations, cost, and resource requirements and may then be subdivided into tasks.

Activity-based costing/ management (ABC)   Managing with an accounting system that allocates cost to products based on resources employed to produce the product. It assigns functional cost, direct and indirect, to the activities or service being provided. It shows how effectively resources are being used and how all relevant activities contribute to the cost of a product or service.

Activity network diagram   Arrow diagram used in planning and managing processes and projects. Used when tasks are difficult or lengthy, such as in construction projects, where two or more activities must be carried on at the same time. Also used to plan the most appropriate schedule for all the related task and events. Projects the likely completion of the task or event for adherence to a schedule in relation to the other scheduled task. One of the seven management and planning tools.

A

Act of God   Act of nature and not assignable to a product or service. May include catastrophic failures of a product or system that is of chance and/or a combination of unforeseen and unavoidable conditions. Used to explain the failure.

Acute exposure   Single exposure to a toxic substance that may result in severe harm or death. Acute exposures are usually characterized as lasting no longer than one day, compared to continuing exposure over a longer period of time.

Adaptive control chart   Control chart that provides information for controlling a process by evaluating predicted values based on current data for the process and quantifying the adjustment needed to avoid undesirable deviations from the specified standard level.

Additive tolerances   Tolerances that are combined by their sums. Note that they are combined algebraically with both plus and minus values. *See* **chain dimensioning.**

Adequacy audit   Audit carried out to establish that the quality system or environmental system documentation adequately addresses the requirements of a prescribed standard. Note: An adequacy audit may also be called a documentation audit.

Adequate   Suitable to accomplish its intended purpose.

Adhocracy   Type of organizational management style that is low in complexity and whose formalization is decentralized. An adhocracy is highly adaptive in structure, which allows it to adapt to change rapidly.

Adjustable gage   Any of various gages that can be adjusted and then set to a predetermined dimension. Used to measure thickness, width, diameter, length, and so on. Commonly used to sort parts or materials.

Administrative operations   Those activities required for an organization to complete its overall mission, such as finance, personnel, security, data processing, plant engineering, maintenance, legal department, and other activities. *See* **support activities.**

Adult learning principles   Key issues about how adults learn, which impact how education and training of adults should be designed and presented. In general, adults learn in a different way than children: (1) in whole or in part (how is it segmented); (2) spaced (time to absorb new materials); (3) active (involve the student); (4) feedback (how is student doing); (5) overlearning (learn more than is required as some is lost); (6) reinforcement (relate to what is known and how to use); (7) primacy and recency (student retains more from start and end of session); (8) meaningful (relate to use by student);

and (9) multiple senses (student takes in 80% by sight, 11% by hearing, and 9% from other sources). Students retain 10% of what is read, 20% of what is heard, 30% of what is seen, 50% of what is seen and heard, 70% of what is seen and spoken, and 90% of what is said while doing what is explained. See also *Evaluating Training Programs* (Westport, CT: Greenwood Press, 1987).

Advanced product quality planning (APQP) Segment of QS-9000, ISO/TS 16949 process that uses tools to offer the opportunity to get ahead of problems and solve them before the problems affect the customer. One of the seven pack quality tools and reference manuals issued by the Automotive Industry Action Group (AIAG) to support the implementation of QS-9000, ISO/TS 16949 Quality System Requirements.

Advisory Nonregulated document that communicates risk information to those who may have to make decisions based on the information provided.

Aerosol Finely divided material suspended in air or other gaseous environments, usually used as a propellant in compressed liquids.

Aesthetics Subjective assessment of the look, feel, or performance of a product. Usually reflects individual preferences.

Affected public In an environmental sense, the people who live and/or work near a site under consideration. The human population adversely impacted following the exposure to an unplanned adverse incident.

Affiliates Associated individuals, businesses, or organizations that can either directly or indirectly control the other, or a third party may control all of them.

Affinity diagram Management tool used to organize information (usually gathered during a brainstorming activity). Used to achieve order out of the chaos that can develop in a brainstorming session and to organize large amounts of data, concepts, and ideas into groupings based on their natural relationship to one another. It is more a creative versus a logical process. One of the seven management and planning tools.

Agile approach Developing the means within a company to change rapidly to meet the needs of customers or changing business directions. *See also* **lean approach.**

Agility Creating a capacity for rapid change and flexibility.

A

Agreement Actions taken between two or more parties, usually documented in writing.

Air gage Gage that uses pressure changes in a compressed air stream to amplify changes in part size or shape. *See* **pneumatic metrology**.

Air pollutant Any substance in air that could, in high enough concentrations, harm humans, animals, or vegetation. Pollutants may include almost any natural or artificial composition of airborne matter; they may be in the form of solid particles, liquid droplets, gases, or any combination.

Algorithm Method for deriving a solution to a problem by using the results from each cycle to refine the following cycle. The process is repeated until a satisfactory answer is obtained.

Algorithm design Methodology to choose experiment design trials when fitting a model.

Alias Combining indistinguishably the main effect of a factor or a differential effect between factors (interactions) with the effects of other factors, block factors, or interactions in a designed experiment. *See* **confounding.**

Aligned section On engineering blueprints, a sectional view in which the cutting plane is angled to pass through features that do not lie in a straight line.

Alignment Actions taken to ensure a process or activity supports the organization's strategy, goals, and objectives. Alignment refers to a consistency of plans, processes, information, resource allocation, results, analysis, and any associated learning.

Alkaline Condition of water or soil that contains a sufficient amount of alkali substances to raise the pH above 7.0.

Alliance *See* **partnership/alliances.** Implies that two parties are working together. An alliance is the starting point of a partnership.

Allocation Technique for partitioning the inputs and outputs of a system among various products.

Allowance (1) In engineering tolerancing, the intended dimensional difference between mating parts, whether it is clearance or interference. (2) The cost of concessions made to customers due to a substandard product or service.

A

Alloy	Two or more metals or metals and nonmetals combined for various reasons to form another, usually stronger, substance.
Alpha risk	(α) Type I error. The maximum probability of saying a process or lot is unacceptable when, in fact, it is acceptable. *See also* **producers risk.**
Alternate hypothesis	As part of a statistical hypothesis testing, an assumption that a relationship exists between two or more factors. Contrast with **null hypothesis.**
Alternative analysis	Process of breaking down a complex situation to generate different solutions and approaches and to evaluate the impact of trade-offs to attain stated objectives.
Alternatives	Different means that are available to meet the same objectives.
Altruistic person	Someone motivated to contribute to the well-being of others.
Ambient temperature	Surrounding room or area temperature; air temperature.
Ambient testing	Testing of machines or equipment under the conditions it will be subjected to in the natural surroundings and conditions of normal operations.
Ambiguity	Language or instructions that can be understood to have more than one reasonable meaning.
American Association for Laboratory Accreditation (A2LA)	Organization that formally recognizes another organization's competency to perform specific tests, types of tests, or calibrations.
American Customer Satisfaction Index (ACSI)	Released for the first time in October 1994, an economic indicator and cross-industry measure of the satisfaction of U.S. household customers with the quality of the goods and services available to them—both those goods and services produced within the United States and those provided as imports from foreign firms that have substantial market shares or dollar sales. The University of Michigan Business School and ASQ co-sponsor the ACSI.
American gage design standards (AGD)	Classification system used to define gage types and their associated tolerances.

American National Standards Institute (ANSI)   Private nonprofit organization that administers and coordinates the U.S. voluntary standardization and conformity assessment system. It is the U.S. member body in the International Organization for Standardization, known as "ISO."

American national screw thread standard   The first widely published U.S. screw thread standard released in 1924, it was revised in 1935 to include coarse and fine threads. Since 1960, screw thread sizes and profiles are governed by ANSI as the B1.1-1960 standards.

American Production and Inventory Control Society (APICS)   Not-for-profit international educational society for resource management, respected throughout the world for its education and professional certification programs. Its mission is "To be the global leader and premier provider of information and services in production and inventory management and related areas to enable members, enterprises, and individuals to add value to their business performance."

American Society for Nondestructive Testing (ASNT)   World's largest technical society for nondestructive testing (NDT) professionals.

American Society for Quality (ASQ)   Professional not-for-profit association that develops, promotes, and applies quality-related information and technology for the private sector, government, and academia. The society serves more than 108,000 individuals and 1,100 corporate members in the United States and 108 other countries.

American Society for Quality Control (ASQC)   Former name of the American Society for Quality, from its formation in 1946 through the middle of 1997, when the name was changed to ASQ.

American Society for Testing and Materials (ASTM)   Not-for-profit organization that provides a forum for the development and publication of voluntary consensus standards for materials, products, systems, and services.

American Society for Training and Development (ASTD)   Membership organization providing materials, education, and support related to workplace learning and performance.

American Society of Mechanical Engineers (ASME) Organization founded in 1880 that today serves over 125,000 members worldwide with educational and technical information and services. Its mission is "To promote and enhance the technical competency and professional well-being of our members, and through quality programs and activities in mechanical engineering, better enable its practitioners to contribute to the well-being of humankind."

American standard code for information interchange (ASCII) Basic computer characters accepted by American machine manufacturers and many foreign ones.

Amortization Accounting procedure that incrementally accounts for the cost or revenue value of a limited-life or intangible asset through periodic adjustments to income.

Ampere Base unit of measure for electrical current rate of flow. The SI definition is that current, if maintained in each of two long parallel wires separated by one meter in free space, would produce a force between the two wires (due to their magnetic fields) of 2×10^7 newton for each meter of length. The standard unit for measuring the strength of an electrical current in a conductor. *See* **SI base units** for a complete listing.

Amplification To make larger for the purpose of discriminating a measurement. Most dial indicators and electronic gages amplify the measurement so a person can discriminate between very small differences in measurements. With a dial indicator you can readily detect .001 of an inch, but without an indicator you could not detect this small difference with the unaided eye.

Analogies Technique used to generate new ideas by translating concepts from one application to another. The use of comparisons to add emphasis and clarity to a thought: "Faster than a speeding bullet" or "More powerful than a locomotive."

Analog instrument In an analog instrument, a moving member (usually a hand) moves in proportion to the change in measurement.

Analysis Examination of facts and data that provides the basis to identify gaps between actual and desired organizational performance. Analysis often involves the determination of cause-and-effect relationships.

A

Analysis of goodness	Ranking of fractional factorial experiment trials according to the level of a response. An attempt is then made to identify factors or combination of factors that potentially affect the response.

Analysis of means (ANOM)   Statistical procedure for troubleshooting industrial processes and analyzing the results of experimental designs with factors at fixed levels. It provides a graphical display of data. Ellis R. Ott developed the procedure in 1967 because he observed that nonstatisticians had difficulty understanding analysis of variance. Analysis of means is easier for quality practitioners to use because it is similar to the control chart. In 1973, Edward G. Schilling further extended the concept, enabling analysis of means to be used with non-normal distributions and attributes data where the normal approximation to the binomial distribution does not apply. This is referred to as "analysis of means for treatment effects."

Analysis of variance (ANOVA)   Basic statistical technique for analyzing experimental data. It subdivides the total variation of a data set into meaningful component parts associated with specific sources of variation in order to test a hypothesis on the parameters of the model or to estimate variance components. There are three models: fixed, random, and mixed. Typically would be shown on the "F" table in many indexes. See also *The Design of Experiments* (Edinburgh: Oliver & Boyd, 1942). *See also* **Sir Ronald Aylmer Fisher** in Appendix A.

Analytical approach   An approach to problem solving using proven facts and data, based on learning and evaluation of past experiences, to improve future activities. The process of breaking problems down into their separate parts to understand them better and, thereby, more easily solve them.

Analytical thinking   Breaking down a problem or situation into discrete parts to understand how each part contributes to the whole.

Ancillary material   Material input used by the unit or process producing the output but not used directly in the formation of the product.

Andon board   Visual device (usually lights) displaying status alerts that can easily be seen by those who should respond.

Anecdotal   Refers to process information that lacks specific methods, measures, deployment methods, evaluation and improvement details, or learning factors. Anecdotal information usually only describes individual activities or events rather than describing a systematic process.

Angle　Rotation necessary to bring one line into coincidence with (or parallel to) another line in the same plane. Complementary angles total 90°. Supplementary angles total 180°. *See* Appendix E.

Angularity　In engineering blueprints, angularity refers to a part surface, center plane, or axis at a specified angle other than 90° to the datum or axis. *See* Appendix E.

Anneal　Heating a metal and letting it gradually cool for softening, relieving stress, and making it less brittle.

Anodize　Corrosion protection on materials provided by electrolytically depositing aluminum or magnesium oxides on the surface of the part.

ANSI Y14.5　American National Standards Institute (ANSI) standard that controls the symbols and dimensioning rules used to draw and interpret blueprints.

Applicant　In quality auditing, an organization applying for registration that undertakes the examination for compliance of its operating systems to a specified standard and then submits itself for formal registration.

Appraisal audit　A quality system audit, usually conducted by a third party to determine the overall implementation and effectiveness of the system and report the results to top management.

Appraisal cost　Cost associated with measuring, evaluating, or auditing products to assure conformance to quality standards and performance requirements. Examples could include the cost of incoming and source inspections and testing of purchased materials or products, in-process and final inspection and testing. Product, process or service audits, the cost of calibration of measuring and test equipment, and any associated supplies and materials. For a complete explanation of the principles of quality cost, see also the American Society for Quality (ASQ) Quality Cost Committee's *Principles of Quality Costs,* 3rd ed. (ASQ Quality Press, 1999).

Approach　Overall method by which project objectives will be realized, including the methodologies, life cycles, responsibilities, strategies, practices, and procedures taken.

Approved　Confirmed as meeting requirements after being subjected to verification by an authorized agency or qualified individual.

Approved suppliers　In many quality plans, a list of approved suppliers who have demonstrated their ability to supply goods consistently in conformance with requirements.

A

Arbitration   Formal system used to deal with grievances and administer corrective justice, normally as part of a collective bargaining agreement, but may be between other parties. May be binding or nonbinding. In binding arbitration, the parties must accept the decision of the arbitrator.

Arbitrator   Impartial person who resolves a dispute between two or more parties.

Area of opportunity   Unit or portion of a material, process, product, or service in which designated event(s) may occur. It may represent an interval of time, a production item, or a final manufactured product composed of many parts. Usually used to represent an opportunity for failure.

Arrhenius equation   Common model used to describe the accelerated life testing of electronic components in a high-temperature environment.

Arrow diagram   Planning tool to diagram a sequence of events or activities (nodes) and the interconnectivity of such nodes. Used for scheduling and especially for determining the critical path through nodes. The critical path method (CPM) and the program evaluation review technique (PERT) make use of arrow diagrams.

AS9100   Also specified as ASE AS 9000 in some references. International quality management standard for the aerospace industry published by the Society of Automotive Engineers; also published by other organizations worldwide, as EN9100 in Europe and JIS Q 9100 in Japan. The standard is controlled by the International Aerospace Quality Group. *See also* **International Aerospace Quality Group.**

Asbestos   Mineral fiber that can pollute air or water and cause cancer or other fatal diseases. The Environmental Protection Agency has banned or severely restricted its use in manufacturing and construction.

ASCII   American standard code for information interchange. Basic computer characters accepted by American machine manufacturers and many foreign ones.

ASME Y14.5M-1994   Authoritative document issued by the American Society of Mechanical Engineers (ASME) that governs the practice of geometric dimensioning and tolerancing in the United States.

Asperities   Deviations from perfection in surfaces generally for machined parts. The four most common types are roughness, waviness, error of form, and flaws. The first three occur in any given part. Their spacings are expressed as wavelengths. Flaws, however, are random. The roughness is considered the primary texture.

Assembly drawing: Blueprint or engineering drawing that shows parts assembled into a final product or subassembly.

Assertiveness: In conflict resolution, the extent to which a party attempts to satisfy personal concerns by forcing viewpoint or beliefs on another.

Assessment: Systematic process of collecting and analyzing data to determine the current, historical, or projected status of an organization, process, or project.

Asset: Property, real estate, goods, intellectual property, equipment, and so on, owned by an individual or organization.

Assignable cause: Name for the source of variation in a process not due to chance that therefore can be identified and eliminated. Also called "special cause." *See also* **common cause.**

Association for Quality and Participation (AQP): International not-for-profit membership association dedicated to improving workplaces through quality and participation practices. An affiliate of the American Society for Quality (ASQ).

Association for the Advancement of Cost Engineers (ACCE): Professional association that helps its members enhance their professional development and network with other cost engineers.

Assumption: Factors considered true, real, or certain and often used as the basis for decision making.

Assure: To give confidence to oneself and to others.

Attribute: Characteristic or property that is appraised in terms of whether it does or does not exist (e.g., go or not go) with respect to a given requirement.

Attribute control charts: Charts such as the "P" chart = % or fraction defective, with various sample sizes. "NP" chart = number defective, uses a constant sample size; "C" chart

A

= number of defects, constant sample size; "U" chart = number of defects per unit, various sample sizes. *See* Appendix D.

Attribute data Data that shows an item or feature either exists or it does not exist. Pass/fail type information. *See* **go/no-go.**

Attribute gage Gage that measures on a go/no-go basis (e.g., a plug gage for a hole).

Attribute sampling Statistical technique used to determine the quality, and therefore acceptance, of an item by inspecting samples of a larger population.

Attributes, method of Measurement of quality by the method of attributes consists of noting the presence (or absence) of some characteristic (attribute) in each of the units under consideration and counting how many units do (or do not) possess it (e.g., go/no-go gaging of a dimension).

Audit In the quality system area, an audit is the inspection and examination of records or activities of a process to ensure compliance to requirements. An audit can apply to an entire organization or may be specific to a function, process, or production step. An audit is usually carried out by someone other than the person responsible for the activities.

Audit client In ISO terms, an organization or person who requested an audit.

Audit conclusion Professional judgment or opinion expressed by an auditor about the subject matter of the audit, based on evidence obtained in the audit and on the reasoning of the auditor.

Audit criteria Policies, practices, procedures, or requirements against which the auditor compares collected audit evidence about the subject matter.

Auditee Person or organization being audited.

Audit evidence Verifiable information, records, or statements of fact.

Audit findings Results of the evaluation of the collected audit evidence compared to the established audit criteria. A negative audit finding should generate a corrective action request (CAR).

A

Audit objectives   Desired or expected results to be achieved by the audit. Objectives may include (1) whether certain agreed to provisions if met will yield the required results; (2) whether the provisions have yielded results that are fit for their purpose and meet the needs of those who require them; and (3) whether some improvement is necessary before awarding a contract or certificate.

Audit observation   Item of objective evidence found during an audit, usually of lesser importance than a finding, but still in need of addressing; may or may not require a corrective action response.

Audit plan   Chart or outline showing the areas to be audited during a specific audit. It may include the timing required, the persons to be audited; procedures to be covered, names of auditors, and so on.

Audit program   Organized structure, commitment, times scheduled for the audits, and documented methods used to plan and perform audits.

Audit report   Factual account of the results of the audit, including the good points, extent of compliance, nonconformities, conclusions, recommendations, and required corrective actions provided to the person or organization requesting the audit by the lead auditor or audit team.

Audit scope   Range or extent of the audit including the standard or contract against which the audit is to be conducted and the products and services and processes to be included, such as design, development, manufacturing, installation, shipping, warehousing, servicing, and so on.

Audit standard   Authentic description of essential characteristics of audits that reflects current thoughts and practices.

Audit team   Group of individuals conducting an audit under the direction of a team leader, relevant to a particular product, process, service, contract, or project.

Audit trail   Path of inquiry and discovery that an auditor follows in search of objective evidence. It includes the recorded documentation describing the actions taken and decisions made during an audit. Should be documented to a sufficient degree so another auditor could examine the same evidence if needed and reach the same conclusions.

A

Auditing organization	Unit or function that carries out audits through its employees. This may also include a department of the auditee, client, or an independent third party.
Auditor	Person trained and assigned to conduct audits.
Audit types	Audits are described by a myriad of terms such as "internal" (an audit a company does on itself) and "external" (an audit conducted by a customer or registrar). They are also identified as "first party" (conducted by a company on itself); "second party" (conducted on a supplier, a customer, or a company); and "third party" (conducted by a registrar or contracted by another party). Audits are also named for their purpose: supplier audit, system audit, process audit, product audit, and so on.
Authoritarian management style	Management approach in which the manager tells team members what is expected of them, provides specific guidance on what should be done, makes his or her role understood, schedules the work, sets rules, and directs the activities of members.
Authority	Power or influence, either granted to or developed by individuals, that leads to others doing what the one in power directs.
Authorize	Give final approval; a person who can authorize something is vested with authority to give final approval, which does not require any other level of approval.
Autocratic management	Autocratic managers are concerned with developing an efficient workplace and have little concern for people (theory X assumptions about people). They typically make decisions without input from subordinates, relying on their positional power.
Automotive Industry Action Group (AIAG)	Publisher and distributor of various automotive quality system standards such as the QS-9000 ISO/TS 16949 series of standards. ASQ's Automotive Division maintains a liaison to this group.
Autonomation	Term coined in Japan to describe features and controls used in a production system to stop the system automatically if a defective part is produced. The use of specially equipped automated machines capable of detecting a defect in a single part, stopping the process, and signaling for assistance. *See* ***jidoka.***

Autonomous work team	Self-managed teams that have responsibility for the entire process. The group members provide their own supervision, scheduling, hiring, and firing. *See also* **self-managed teams.**
Auxiliary view	On engineering blueprints, a view that represents the true shape and size of an inclined surface.
Availability	Ability of a product, process, or equipment to be in a state to perform its designated function under stated conditions at a given time.
Average	Also called the "arithmetic mean," it is the sum of all the data set, divided by the number of observations.
Average chart	Control chart in which the subgroup average, X-bar, is used to evaluate the stability of the process level.
Average life	In product testing, the mean value for a normal distribution of failures, generally for products that fail in testing through those that fail due to wearing out.
Average outgoing quality (AOQ)	Expected average quality level of outgoing product for a given value of incoming product quality.
Average outgoing quality limit (AOQL)	Maximum average of outgoing quality over all possible levels of incoming quality for a given acceptance sampling plan and specification.
Average run lengths (ARL)	On a control chart, the number of subgroups expected to be inspected before a signal is given by the control chart.
Average sample number (ASN)	Average number of sample units inspected per lot in reaching decisions to accept or reject.
Average total inspection (ATI)	Average number of units inspected per lot, including all units in rejected lots (applicable when the procedure calls for 100% inspection of rejected lots). Sometimes called "average total inspected."

A

Avoidance   Risk response strategy that eliminates the threat of a specific risk event, usually by eliminating the potential cause.

Award   Something given in recognition of performance or quality.

Azimuth   In optical metrology, azimuth is a horizontal angle measured in a clockwise direction from the true north position.

B

Background levels   Concentration of a substance in an environment such as air, soil, or water that occurs naturally or is not the result of human activities.

Backlash   (1) In gear or belt drive equipment, the amount of free play or movement in the system caused by wear or design. (2) In a measurement or control system, the unintentional play between linked or adjacent moving parts. A primary cause for dial and variable control inaccuracy.

Baffle   Plate, deflector, guide, or similar device constructed or placed in the flow path of a heat exchanger (furnace), water stream, and so on, to cause a more uniform flow of the velocities, to absorb more energy, or to divert the stream flow.

Balanced design   Fractional factorial experiment design in which for each factor an equal number of trials is performed at each combination of factor levels.

Balanced matrix   In project management, the project manager has authority over the project resources, roughly equal to the organization's functional managers.

Balanced scorecard   Approach used to measure business performance. Developed by Robert Kaplan and David Norton, it includes not only financial performance but other elements such as customer value, internal business process, innovation, and employee performance. It is implemented by translating the organization's vision and strategy statements into a comprehensive and quantifiable set of objectives and performance measures, by creating appropriate reward systems, and by collecting and analyzing performance results as they relate to the measures. See also "The Balanced Scorecard" (*Harvard Business Review* 74 [1966]: 86).

Baldrige Award   *See* **Malcolm Baldrige National Quality Award.**

Band-Aid   Temporary repair on a field-installed piece of equipment. Usually installed in a hurry or under unfavorable conditions to get a piece of equipment back in operation or until a permanent repair can be done.

Bar   Line drawn over a letter to mean it represents the statistical average of the samples. Common usage is with X-bar and R-bar charts. A double bar represents the grand average.

Bar charts   Charts used to illustrate graphically the magnitude of multiple examples of an output. Generally horizontal or vertical bars illustrate the magnitude of multiple situations (problems or defects).

Barriers to empowerment   Things that hinder the application of empowerment in an organization, such as lack of a clear commitment; failure to define what is to be empowered; failure to implement appropriate incentives; lack of an implementation plan; and an inability to modify organizational culture.

Baseline measurement   The beginning point, based on an evaluation of the output over a period of time, used to determine the process parameters prior to any improvement effort; the basis against which change is measured.

Basic dimension   In engineering blueprints, a numerical value used to describe the theoretically exact size, profile, orientation, or location of a part feature or datum target. On a drawing, it appears inside a box. A basic dimension is the basis for tolerances on other dimensions. *See* Appendix E.

Basic failure rate   Failure rate of a product derived from the catastrophic failure rate of its parts before applying use and tolerance factors. Also called "base failure rate."

Basic requirements   In the content of quality award criteria, the term *basic requirements* refers to the most central theme of an item. The fundamental or essential requirements of that item.

Batch   A definite quantity of some product or material accumulated under conditions considered uniform, or accumulated from a common source. The term is sometimes synonymous with **lot.**

Batch processing   Running large batches of a single product through the process at one time, resulting in queues awaiting next steps in the process.

Bathtub curve   Also called "life history curve" or "Weibull curve." This probability chart is so named because of its shape. This model can be conveniently divided into three regions. The first region, the "infant mortality phase," covers the period just after product delivery and includes any defects not caught by final inspection and any early failures. The second phase, which looks like the floor of the bathtub, consists of a supposed "constant failure rate," characterized by the inherent failure rate of the product's composite parts. The third region is the "wear-out phase," in which failures dramatically increase due to the parts reaching their useful life. *See* Appendix C.

Bayesian sampling plans   Sampling plans based on prior knowledge of the quality of prior lots. This sampling technique usually requires smaller sample sizes than MIL-STD-105.

Bayes theorem   Mathematical formula used to estimate the probability that subject items came from a specified lot or origin, when the rate for the subject items is known.

Bell-shaped curve   Curve or distribution showing a central peak and tapering off smoothly and symmetrically to tails on ether side. A normal, or "Gaussian," curve is one example.

Bench inspectors   Parts inspectors who work in an assigned area, where parts are either brought to them or inspectors will collect sample parts for themselves and return to the assigned area and complete their inspection process and then make a judgment on the acceptability of the process or lot.

Benchmark   Standard against which something can be measured. A survey mark of previously determined position used as a reference point. In the quality sense, a benchmark should be an organization or process considered to be "best in class."

Benchmarking   Improvement process in which a company measures its performance against that of best in class companies, determines how those companies achieved their performance levels, and uses the information to improve its own performance. The subjects that can be benchmarked include strategies, operations, processes, and procedures. The process used may include (1) determine current practices, (2) identify best practices, (3) analyze best practices, (4) model best practices, and (5) repeat the cycle. A 10-step process would include (1) review and refine existing practices, (2) determine what to benchmark, (3) form a benchmarking team, (4) identify benchmarking partners, (5) collect and analyze benchmarking information, (6) evaluate your performance versus the benchmark partner,

(7) determine how to upgrade your process, (8) establish new strategic targets, (9) implement the improvements, and (10) continue the cycle from the start.

Benefit Gain to be obtained from the successful completion of a task or project.

Benefit-cost analysis Examination of the relationship between the monetary cost of implementing an improvement and the monetary value of the benefits achieved by the improvement, both within the same time period. Projects are reviewed and considered on the basis of prospective payback and the overall fit to the operations business needs.

Beryllium Metal hazardous to human health when inhaled as an airborne pollutant. It is discharged by machine shops, ceramic and propellant plants, and foundries.

Best available control measures (BACM) In an environmental sense, a term used to refer to the most effective measures (according to Environmental Protection Agency guidelines) for controlling small dispersed particulates and other emissions from such sources as roadway dust, soot and ash from woodstoves, and open burning of brush, timber, grasslands, or trash.

Best available control technology (BACT) In an environmental sense, the best currently available technology producing the greatest reduction of air pollutant emissions, taking into account energy, environmental, economic, and other costs.

Best estimate When estimating probability it would represent a value where there is a 50% chance the true reading is higher or lower than the estimate. An estimate based on past experience.

Best management practices (BMP) In an environmental sense, the methods that have been determined to be the most effective, practicable means of preventing or reducing pollution from non–point of origin sources.

Best practice Superior method or innovative practice that contributes to the improved performance of an organization, usually recognized as "best" by other peer organizations.

Beta risk (β) Maximum probability that a batch or lot will be accepted by a sampling plan when in fact it contains more defects than the sampling plan should accept. *See also* **consumer's risk** or **Type II error.**

Beta test Test of a new product in its intended environment with the results used to verify its usefulness in its intended application.

Bevel Angled edge other than at a right angle.

Bias Systematic error that contributes to the difference between a population mean of measurements or test results and an accepted reference value. Bias is a systematic error in contrast to random error. There may be one or more bias elements contributing to the systematic error. In general, a good estimate of bias requires averaging a large number of test results representative of the population involved.

Biased sample Sample that is either not truly representative of the lot or not random as a result of poor sampling procedures.

Bias in measurement Systematic error that leads to a difference between the average readings in a population of measurements and the true, accepted value of the dimension or characteristic being measured.

Big Q, little q Terms coined by Joseph M. Juran and used to contrast the difference between managing for quality in all business processes and products (big Q) and managing for quality in a limited capacity—traditionally only in factory processes (little q).

Bilateral profile tolerance Profile tolerance in which variation is allowed on both sides of the true profile. These may be divided equally or unequally by the true profile. *See* Appendix E.

Bilateral tolerance Tolerances expressed on both sides of a nominal dimension or on both sides of the ideal dimension.

Bill of lading Document used to show receipt of goods for shipment issued by an organization in the business of transporting or forwarding goods.

Bill of materials (BOM) Set listing of physical elements required to build a product. A listing of the set of parts, subassemblies, and other component expense items used to fabricate a product.

Bimodal distribution Frequency distribution with two peaks. Often an indication of samples taken from two processes or two machines.

Binomial distribution Applies to the number of "successes" out of "n" trials. Needs constant probability of success too. It is independent of the lot or population size and assumes two points: (1) Only two outcomes are possible for each trial. The only possible outcome from inspection is that the item either good or bad. (2) The test must be independent of one another. That is, one test has no influence on another test For example, in tossing a coin, each toss has only two possibilities, heads or tails. The next toss also has only two possibilities, heads or tails, and the first toss does not have any effect on the second toss. Each side (heads or tails) has a probability of 50% of being the result. *See* Appendix C.

Biodegradable   Capable of decomposing under natural conditions.

Biosphere   That portion of the earth and its surrounding atmosphere capable of supporting life.

Black Belt (BB)   Full-time team leader responsible for implementing Six Sigma process improvement projects using specified methodologies such as Define, Measure, Analyze, Improve, and Control (DMAIC) or Define, Measure, Analyze, Design, and Verify (DMADV) and various other statistical and Design of Experiments (DOE). The goal is to eliminate quality problems and to drive up customer satisfaction levels and business productivity.

Black box testing   Testing for acceptability of external output given specified external inputs and without concern for intermediate internal functions.

Blemish   Imperfection severe enough to be noticed but should not cause any real impairment with respect to intended normal or reasonably foreseeable use. *See* **defect, imperfection,** and **nonconformity.**

Block diagram   Diagram that shows the operation, interrelationships, and interdependencies of components in a system. Boxes, or blocks (hence the name), represent the components; connecting lines between the blocks represent interfaces. There are two types of block diagrams: (1) a functional block diagram, which shows a system's subsystems and lower level products and their interrelationships and that interfaces with other systems; and (2) a reliability block diagram, which is similar to the functional block diagram except it is modified to emphasize those aspects influencing reliability.

Blocking   In a designed experiment, the process used to eliminate the effect of inhomogeneity in experimental material.

Blueprint   Engineering drawings designed to describe clearly the information necessary to meet the requirements a product has to meet to be a functional and a quality product.

Blue ribbon committee In project management, a group of experts who examine evidence, documents, and testimony to certify that a high-risk project has been properly planned, the risk have been addressed, and the probability of success is justifiable for the project to be funded.

Board of Standards Review (BSR) American National Standards Institute board responsible for the approval and withdrawal of American National Standards.

Body language Nonverbal communication, often unintended, from one person to another. It consists of facial expressions, physical stance, gestures, and any other physical expression that either complements or contradicts the spoken word. It often helps persons to better understand the real meaning of the spoken word.

Body of knowledge (BOK) The prescribed aggregation of knowledge in a particular field of study an individual is expected to have mastered to be considered or certified as a practitioner.

Bogey test A single-step go/no-go mechanical part test to a predetermined number of cycles run and stress that is calculated to equal some given life expectancy in the worst case for the user.

Boldness Term used to describe the choosing of the magnitude of the variable levels used within a response surface design. This concept suggests the magnitude of variables should be large enough to capture the minimum and maximum responses under examination.

Bolt circle (pattern) Collection of holes on a circular pattern, related to a common center.

Bootstrapping Resampling technique that provides a simple but effective methodology to describe the uncertainty associated with a summary statement without concern about the details of the chosen summary or exact distribution from which data are calculated. A procedure developed to estimate the uncertainty in a stable process, the procedure simulates resampling, with the resulting distribution of estimates called a bootstrap distribution. This is used to provide a close approximation of what would happen if the process were to be resampled numerous times. It is a process that approximately estimates the behavior of a stable process based on the parameters of a model of the data.

B

Bore Making a hole using a lathe, boring bar, drill press, or other means. Also the hole made by such a means.

Boss In metalworking or casting, a projection, usually on a casting or forging.

Bottleneck Process constraint that determines the capacity or capability of a system and restricts the rate, volume, or flow of a process.

Bottom line The essential or salient point; the primary or most important consideration. Also, the line at the bottom of a financial report that shows the net profit or loss.

Bottom-up management Style of management that solicits participation of employees starting from the bottom up through the top of the organization.

Boundaries of freedom Conceptual management tool used to define and communicate predetermined levels of authority for the use of time, funds, and resources.

Boundary spanners Individuals who have positions that link them with others outside of their work units. They exist to exchange information between groups.

Boundaryless organization Also known as a "network organization," a "modular corporation," or a "virtual corporation." An organization without internal or external boundaries limiting the traditional structures.

Box and whisker From a box plot, displays minimum and maximum observations within 1.5 IQR (75th to 25th percentile span) from either 25th or 75th percentile. Outliers are those that fall outside of the 1.5 range.

Brainstorming Technique that teams use to generate ideas on a particular subject. Each person in the team is asked to think creatively and write down as many ideas as possible. The ideas are not discussed or reviewed until after the brainstorming session. A brainstorming session typically follows these rules: Generate a large number of ideas. Freewheel to provoke ideas from others. Don't criticize any ideas put forth. Encourage everyone to participate. Record all the ideas. Let the ideas incubate to encourage other thoughts. Have a meeting place where everyone feels comfortable. Group size should range from 4 to 10 individuals.

Brass Alloy essentially made of copper and zinc.

Breakdown In project management, the identification of the smallest activity or task in a project for estimating, monitoring, or controlling purposes.

Break line On blueprints, a line that indicates where a view has been broken off or shortened.

Breakthrough improvement Improvement process proposed by Joseph Juran to include dynamic, decisive movement to a new, higher level of performance.

Bridging Process of finding an unknown dimension by the testing of measurements spanning the unknown dimension and successively closing the distance between them until the unknown dimension is approximated.

Brightfield Illumination technique that provides flat, even lighting of the field of view.

Brinell (1) A hardness testing method for metals. (2) The process of metals being hardened and made brittle by use, specifically bearings. *See also* **Brinelling.**

Brinelling Usually associated with bearing failures, where the failure mode is associated with impact loading or excess vibration.

Brink of chaos Don J. Wheeler defined the brink of chaos as an operation making products that conform to specifications but the process itself is out of control. See also *Understanding Variation: The Key to Managing Chaos* (Knoxville, TN: SPC Press, 1993).

British Standards Institute (BSI) An organization with headquarters in London, founded in 1901. It provides professional services to organizations worldwide.

British thermal unit (BTU) Unit of heat energy equal to the amount of heat required to raise the temperature of one pound of water by one degree Fahrenheit at sea level.

Broach Cutting tool for removing material to shape an outside or inside surface or hole. Also the process of using such a tool. Wrench openings are commonly broached to hold close tolerances.

Broken-out section On blueprints a sectional view in which a small portion of the part is broken away to expose the interior section.

Bronze Alloy made mostly of copper and some tin.

Brown fields In an environmental sense, abandoned, idled, or underused industrial and commercial facilities or sites where expansion or redevelopment is complicated by real or perceived environmental contamination.

BS 7799   British commerce standard. Government and industry stakeholders wrote BS 7799 to address information security management issues, including fraud, industrial espionage, and physical disasters. May become an ISO standard.

Budget   Quantitative management plan for the execution of a project, expressed in monetary terms. Used to express management's intentions and objectives to all levels in the organization, to monitor the implementation of those plans, and to provide a basis for evaluating and measuring the performance of the organization and individuals.

Buff   Polishing, sometimes with a wheel made of fabric that has abrasives added to it. The process of polishing a material with an abrasive wheel to provide a polished surface.

Bugs   Slang term used to describe problems that may occur in a process or in the use of a product. These may be the result of errors in design or in manufacturing.

Bulk material   Material bought in lots; generally, no one item is distinguishable from another item in the lot. Many times they are catalog-type items, to be used as needed.

Burden cost   Varying operating cost to the user to support maintenance, excluding labor and material, and including only cost chargeable through maintenance person-hours used to repair pertinent items.

Bureaucracy   As organizations become successful, they tend to add employees with more duties, more rules, a more formalized structure with specialized departments, and more levels of management. Bureaucracies tend to treat people as interchangeable tools, both management and hourly. Max Weber thought bureaucracy was the ideal organizational structure. Everyone would know their roles and responsibilities, lines of authority would be clearly defined, and the structure would produce more predictable and efficient output.

Bureaucratic authority   Influence obtained from an individual's position, knowledge of an organization's rules, regulations, and procedures, and the way to use them to obtain the desired results in an expedient manner.

B

Bureau of Alcohol, Tobacco, and Firearms (ATF)	Department of the U.S. government charged with regulation and control of alcohol, tobacco, firearms, explosives, and arson investigation.
Burn-in	Stress testing of electronic equipment, typically at high temperature or elevated voltages, for the purpose of capturing early failures before they get to the customer. *See also* **accelerated testing.**
Burnish	To rub a material with a tool for compacting or smoothing surfaces or for turning an edge.
Burr	Rough edge on a part produced by machining, drilling, shearing, stamping, and so on.
Business partnering	Creation of cooperative alliances between departments within an organization or between an organization and its customers or suppliers. Partnering occurs through a pooling of resources in a trusting atmosphere focused on continuous, mutual improvement. *See* **customer-supplier partnership.**
Business processes	Processes that focus on what the organization does as a business and how it goes about doing it. A business has functional processes (generating output within a single department) and cross-functional processes (generating output across several functions or departments).
Business Process Reengineering (BPR)	The fundamental rethinking and redesign of operating processes and organizational structure, focused on the organization's core competencies to achieve dramatic improvements in organizational performance. The results should show dramatic changes and improvements in the process, such as cost, quality, service, and speed. *See* **reengineering.**

C

C chart *See* **count chart.** For attribute data: A control chart of the number of defects found in a subgroup of fixed size. The C chart is used where each unit typically can have a number of defects.

Calibration Comparison of two instruments or measuring devices, one of which is a standard of known accuracy traceable to national standards, to detect, correlate, report, or to eliminate by adjustment any inaccuracy of the instrument or measuring device, as compared to the standard.

Calibration interval Specified amount of time or usage between calibrations where the accuracy of gages (or test equipment) is considered valid.

Calibration precision Concept of a measuring device obtaining accurate readings repeatable over a period of time, measuring the same characteristics. *See also* **accuracy** and **repeatability.**

Calibration ratio Traceable accuracy in a calibration system where the calibration instrument must be a specified ratio more accurate than the instrument being calibrated. In dimensional measurement this is usually 10 to 1, meaning the calibration instrument must be 10 times more accurate than the instrument being calibrated. For electronic/electrical instruments that ratio may be 4 to 1. The ratio should be defined within the calibration system.

Calibration standards Standards divided into five categories, depending on the precision and how they are used. (1) The most basic and most widely used are the working levels standards, those used by workers at their workstations. (2) The next level are the calibration standards, used to calibrate the working standards. (3) Functional standards are used in the plant calibration lab and to calibrate other standards and for very precise work. (4) Reference standards are directly traceable to national standards and used in place of the national standards. (5) The top level and most precise are the national and international standards. These are the final standards (grand standard) for the nation, to which all other standards are traceable.

Calibration system Management system of resources and responsibilities for the calibration of measuring instruments and measuring equipment.

Caliper Device for measuring length. Calipers come in wide variety of configurations, from vernier calipers, dial calipers, digital calipers, and in lengths from 2 inches and up to those in excess of 150 inches with metric reading equivalents.

Cam Rotating or sliding member that imparts motion to a roller or pin moving against its edge.

Camp-Meidell conditions For frequency distribution and histograms: a distribution is said to meet Camp-Meidell conditions if its mean and mode are equal and the frequency declines continuously on either side of the mode.

Canadian Standards Association (CSA) Performs similar safety-related standards writing and performance testing as Underwriters Laboratories (UL) performs in the United States.

Candela Base unit of measure for light. The SI definition is the luminous intensity, in a given direction, of a source that emits monochromatic radiation of frequency 540X10 to the 12th power (Hz) and has a radiant intensity in that direction of 1/683 watt per steradian. *See* **SI base units** for a complete listing of all SI base units.

Capability Ability to perform designated activities and to achieve results that fulfill specified requirements.

Capability audit Audit performed to verify that a process or organization has the capability to consistently yield products or services to meet specified requirements.

Capability maturity model (CMM) Framework that describes the key elements of an effective software process. An evolutionary improvement path from an immature process to a mature, disciplined process. The capability maturity model covers practices for planning, engineering, and managing software development and maintenance. When followed, these key practices improve the ability of organizations to meet goals for cost, schedule, functionality, and product quality.

Capability ratio (CP)   Simple expression of the relationship between the output of the process and the engineering specifications (the width of the spread of data). The result is usually expressed as a number or percentage. It is usually computed by subtracting the lower specification limit from the upper specification limit and dividing that by the Six Sigma of the process. *See* **C_{pk} ratio.**

Capability ratio (CR)   For process capability studies, the inverse of CP. CR can range from zero to infinity in value, with a smaller value indicating a more capable process.

Capillary action   Movement of liquids through very small spaces due to the forces called capillary forces. A type of capillary action is exhibited when a cloth absorbs water when only a small corner of the cloth is placed in the water.

Capital   In a corporate sense, capital means total enterprise assets. The money and any other property an organization uses in conducting and transacting business.

Capital assets   Physical property of an organization that generally has long, useful life such as equipment, vehicles, and buildings.

Capital expenditure   Money paid out for improvements that will have a useful life of more than a year.

Capitalization   Treatment of expenditures as assets rather than current expenses. Under general accounting practices companies are required to capitalize the cost of tangible assets when they exceed predetermined limits. Capitalized assets are depreciated or expensed out over time.

Career path planning   Process of integrating a person's career planning and development into the goals of the organization, with the objective of satisfying the organization's requirements and the individual's career goals.

Cartesian coordinate system   Basic machine programming geometry system.

Cascading   Continuing flow of the quality message down to, not through, the next level of supervision until it reaches all workers. Same concept as deploying.

C

Cascading training	Training implemented in an organization from the top down, where each level acts as trainers to those below.
Case harden	Hardening the outer surface of steel by heating then quenching. *See* **quench.**
Case study	Prepared scenario (story), which when studied and discussed serves to illuminate the learning points of a course of study.
Casting	Part produced by pouring molten material into a mold. The process of producing a part by this method.
Catalyst	Substance that changes the speed or yield of a chemical reaction without being consumed or chemically changed by the chemical reaction.
Catapult	Simple machine using weights and levers to propel an object. Small versions are used as a teaching aid used to show students how variations in the setup of the catapult can influence the end output, with repeatable results. There are usually various adjustments that can be made to the catapult that will affect the distance it will throw an object.
Catastrophic failure	Quick, unanticipated failure in a part or system that may cause severe physical harm to anyone depending on the part or system or excessive financial loss to a company.
Catchball	Term used to describe the interactive process of developing and deploying policies and plans with "hoshin planning."
Cause	Identified reason for the presence of a defect or problem.
Cause-and-effect diagram or analysis (C & E)	Tool for analyzing process inputs that relate to a problem. It is also referred to as the "Ishikawa diagram" because Kaoru Ishikawa developed it, and the "fishbone diagram," because the completed diagram resembles a fish skeleton. The diagram illustrates the main causes and subclasses leading to an effect (symptom). The cause-and-effect diagram is one of the **seven tools of quality.**
Caveat emptor	Latin term for "buyer beware," it implies buyers should use caution and have an understanding of any risk associated with their purchases.
Cell	(1) Grouping within specified boundaries of the values of individual observations along the divisions of a histogram. (2) Layout of workstations

and/or various machines for different operations (usually shaped in a U shape) in which multitasking operators proceed, with a part, from machine to machine, to perform a series of sequential steps to produce a whole product or a major subassembly.

Cellular processing   Technique used to design, group, and manage production operations as self-contained flexible cells capable of start-to-finish production.

Censored datum   In quality management, it means that the sample did not fail in testing, with use or at a specified stress level.

Center-drill   To drill holes in the ends of a part that is to be mounted on centers.

Centers for Disease Control and Prevention (CDC)   U.S. government agency charged with protecting the health and safety of people in the United States. Its activities are designed to improve the health and safety for all the people.

Centerline (CL)   (1) Line on a graph that represents the overall average (mean) operating level of the process. (2) On blueprints, a series of long and short fine dashed lines used to show the geometrical center of an object. *See* Appendix E.

Centralize   Movement of a measuring instrument, such as a micrometer or caliper, by feel of contact, so its axes are oriented parallel to the line of measurement. Sometimes called "rocking."

Central limit theorem   Mathematical estimate that all items taken from one population of random variables have the same distribution. Using the central limit theorem, you can make rather precise statements about the probabilities of the mean of the population. This theorem allows you to assume normal distribution when dealing with X-bar. The averages of different-sized subgroups will follow the normal distribution curve when a reasonably large sample size is used. The thrust of the central limit theorem is that "If a population has a finite variance s2 and mean mu, then the distribution of sample means from samples of N independent observations approaches a normal distribution with variance s2/N and mean mu as sample N increases. When N is very large, the sample distribution of M is approximately normal." The CLT is crucial for many applications in statistics because it says the distribution of sample means can be normal even if the distribution the sample came from is not normally distributed.

Central line   On a control chart, a line representing the long-term average or a standard value of the statistical measure being plotted.

Central tendency	Extent to which data gathered from a process tends to cluster toward a middle value somewhere between the high and low values of measurement.
Certificate of analysis (C of A)	Written statement supplied to a customer certifying that supplies or services conform to specified requirements. This may include such things as chemical analysis and so on.
Certification	Result of meeting the established criteria set by an accrediting or certificate-granting organization. The authoritative act of documenting compliance with agreed upon requirements.
Certification audit	Audit performed by an authorized agency or individual for the purpose of certifying a product, process, person, or organization.
Certification body	Impartial organization possessing the necessary competence to operate a certification program.
Certified Calibration Technician	This ASQ certification is presented to individuals in the field of gage calibration after they have met specified criteria and their proficiency has been tested and verified.
Certified Mechanical Inspector (CMI)	This ASQ certification is presented to individuals in the field of mechanical inspection after they have met specified criteria and their proficiency has been tested and verified.
Certified Quality Auditor (CQA)	This ASQ certification is presented to the individuals in the field of quality system auditing after they have met specified criteria and their proficiency has been tested and verified.
Certified Quality Auditor (CQA)— Biomedical	This ASQ certification is presented to individuals in the field of medical quality system comformance after they have met specified criteria and their proficiency has been tested and verified.
Certified Quality Auditor—Hazard Analysis and Critical Control Point (HACCP)	This ASQ certification is presented to individuals in the field of medical quality system and hazardous material control procedures after they have met specified criteria and their proficiency has been tested and verified.

Certified Quality Engineer (CQE) This ASQ certification is presented to individuals in inspection techniques, problem-solving techniques, statistical analysis, and various other aspects of advanced quality procedures after they have met specified criteria and their proficiency has been tested and verified.

Certified Quality Improvement Associate (CQIA) This ASQ certification is presented to individuals in quality improvement techniques and processes after they have met specified criteria and their proficiency has been tested and verified.

Certified Quality Manager (CQMgr) This ASQ certification is presented to individuals in project completion techniques, quality system functions, and advanced quality management practices after they have met specified criteria and their proficiency has been tested and verified.

Certified Quality Technician (CQT) This ASQ certification is presented to individuals in inspection techniques, problem solving, and basic quality system functions after they have met specified criteria and their proficiency has been tested and verified.

Certified reference material Per ISO Guide 25: 1990 (E) now replaced with ANSI/ISO 17025-1999. Reference material, one or more of whose property values are certified by a technically valid procedure, accompanied by or traceable to a certificate or other documentation issued by a certifying body.

Certified Reliability Engineer (CRE) This ASQ certification is presented to individuals in advanced quality system problem solving and reliability testing after they have met specified criteria and their proficiency has been tested and verified.

Certified Six Sigma Black Belt (CSSBB) This ASQ certification is presented to individuals in advanced problem-solving techniques, project system completion, advanced statistical analysis of information and data, and presentation skills after they have met specified criteria and their proficiency has been tested and verified.

Certified Software Quality Engineer (CSQE) This ASQ certification is presented to the individuals in the field of software data-gathering techniques and analysis of programs to assure their accuracy and integrity after they have met specified criteria and their proficiency has been tested and verified.

Chain dimensioning In engineering blueprints, a method used to dimension features, one after the other in a sequence, with each dimension having its own tolerances. This method has a tendency to compound tolerances as they stack up. Compare with baseline dimensioning, which only allows tolerances to a feature from the baseline, without compounding the tolerances.

Chain reaction In a Quality sense, the chain of events described by W. Edwards Deming as a business improvement process: improve quality, decrease costs, improve productivity, increase market with better quality and lower price, stay in business, provide jobs, and provide more jobs.

Chain sampling Sampling inspection in which the criteria for acceptance and nonacceptance of the lot depend in part on the results of immediately preceding lots meeting stated criteria. Sample sizes and frequency may vary depending on the sampling plan selected.

Chain sampling plan In acceptance sampling, a plan in which the criteria for acceptance and rejection apply to the cumulative sampling results for the current lot and one or more immediately preceding lots.

Chaku-chaku (Japanese) meaning "load-load" in a cell layout where a part is taken from one machine and loaded into the next.

Chamfer Beveled edge usually used to eliminate sharp edges left by machining, shearing, stamping, or forming operations.

Champion Business leader or senior manager who ensures that resources are available for training and projects and is involved in project stage and completion reviews. An executive who supports and addresses Six Sigma organizational issues and programs.

Chance cause Also called "common cause." A random and uncontrollable cause of variation.

Change In an organization, the process of improvement. Kurt Lewin proposed three steps that must take place: (1) unfreezing, getting people to understand a change is needed and accept it; (2) moving, actually trying the desired changes along with the behaviors and attitudes; and (3) refreezing, implementing the change establishing it as the normal methods and procedures.

Change agent Individual from within or outside an organization who facilitates change within the organization. May or may not be the initiator of the change effort.

Change control system Collection of formal documented procedures that defines the steps by which official documents may be changed.

Changeover Changing a machine or process from one type of product or service to another.

Change process For larger scale changes that may take three to five years. Steps may include awakening (recognizing the need for a change); envisioning (creating a vision and mobilizing commitment); and rearchitecturing (removing obstacles that inhibit the process).

Characteristic Factors, elements, or measures that define and differentiate a process, function, product, service, or other entity. A property that helps differentiate between items of a given sample or population. May be either quantitative (by variables) or qualitative (by attributes).

Charismatic leaders Leaders who derive influence over others through the use of their personality. People do what is asked of them because they like the person doing the asking.

Chart Tool for organizing, summarizing, and depicting data in graphic form.

Charter Written commitment approved by management stating the scope of authority for an improvement project or team.

Checklist Tool used to ensure all important steps or actions in an operation have been taken. Checklists contain items important or relevant to an issue or situation. Checklists are often confused with check sheets (*see* **check sheet**). A pilot uses a checklist to verify operational functions of a plane prior to a flight.

Check sheet Simple data-recording device. The check sheet is usually custom designed by the user, which allows him or her to readily interpret the results. May also be called a "tally sheet." The check sheet is one of the **seven tools of quality.** Check sheets are often confused with checklists. *See* **checklist.**

Check standard Stable well-characterized in-house standard measured periodically to ensure the calibration process remains intact. Traceable to the **National Institute of Standards and Technology (NIST)** standards.

Chi-square (χ^2) As used for goodness-of-fit test, a measurement of how well a set of data fits a proposed distribution, such as the normal distribution.

Chronic problem Long-standing adverse situation that can be remedied by changing the status quo. For example, actions such as revising an unrealistic manufacturing process or addressing customer defections can change the status quo and remedy the situation.

Circularity Circularity tolerance specifies how much a cross-section of a cylindrical, cone-shaped, or spherical feature is allowed to vary from the perfect circularity implied by the blueprint. The tolerance zone is bounded by two concentric circles a specified distance apart. *See* Appendix E.

Circular runout Runout is the deviation of a part surface from the desired form and orientation as it rotates 360° around a datum axis. A circular runout tolerance controls the relationship of individual circular elements of a part feature to the datum axis. *See* Appendix E.

Clarification Communication with another party for the purpose of eliminating minor irregularities, informalities, or apparent clerical mistakes in orders or other transmitted information.

Class One of several groupings of data, material, or observations to be analyzed.

Classification of defects Listing of possible defects of a unit, classified according to their seriousness. Note: Commonly used classifications are class A, class B, class C, class D; or critical, major, minor, and incidental; or critical, major, and minor. Definitions of these classifications require careful preparation and tailoring to the product(s) being sampled to enable accurate assignment of a defect to the proper classification. A separate acceptance-sampling plan is generally applied to each class of defects.

Class standards In gage calibration systems, the standards used to calibrate gages and test equipment. These range from class A standards, very close tolerance standards maintained in a clean controlled environment (usually traceable to National Institute of Standards and Technology [NIST] standards); class B standards used to calibrate or measure the accuracy of other measuring and test equipment; and class C standards commonly used in the shop environment.

Class variables Factors that have discrete levels.

Clause of a standard Numbered paragraph or subsection of a standard containing one or more related requirements.

Clean room Workspace environment or manufacturing process location within which the air is filtered to specified levels. The purpose is to prevent failures due to contamination in products or processes.

Clearance fit Type of fit that results when the specified size limits of mating part features always results in clearance at assembly.

Clearance number As associated with a continuous sampling plan, the number of successively inspected units or product that must be found acceptable during a 100% inspection sequence before action to change the amount of inspection is taken.

Client Person or organization requesting an audit. Depending on circumstances, the client may be a customer, the auditing organization, the auditee, or a third party.

Clinometer Very precise level used to level equipment that requires precise operating conditions.

Closed-loop corrective action (CLCA) Sophisticated system designed to document, verify and diagnose failures, recommend and initiate corrective action, provide follow-up activities, and maintain comprehensive records.

Closeout phase In project management, the fourth and final phase of the project. The outstanding issues are documented in preparation for turning the project over to the end user.

Closing meeting In quality auditing, a meeting between the auditor(s) and representatives of the organization audited convened to report and agree on the results of the audit. Also covered should be to agree on corrective actions if required or to notify the organization of acceptable results.

Cluster For control charts, a group of points with similar properties. Usually an indication of short duration, assignable causes.

Coaching Continuous improvement technique by which people receive one-to-one learning through demonstration and practice. Characterized by immediate feedback and correction.

Coaxiality Positional tolerance used to control the alignment of two or more holes shown on a common axis when rotation is not involved.

Code of conduct   Expectations of behavior mutually agreed on by a team or an organization.

Code of ethics   Written statement of principles addressing the behavior of the individuals employed in an organization. ASQ has a formal code of ethics for its members. *See* front of this book.

Code of Federal Regulations (CFR)   Documents that specifies all rules of the executive department and agencies of the federal government. It is divided into 50 volumes, known as "titles." Title 40 of the CFR lists all environmental regulations.

Coercive authority   Influence over others, predicated on fear. People do what is asked because they fear the consequences if they do not do what is expected of them.

Coin   In metalworking, forming a part, or surface of a part, by stamping using a mold or die.

Cold rolled steel (CRS)   Steel rolled to dimension while it is cold, producing smooth, dimensionally accurate material.

Collar   Used on shafts to prevent axial movement or to hold something in place.

Collective bargaining agreement   Contractual agreement with unions or other employee groups.

Combative management style   Management approach in which the manager displays an eagerness to fight or be disagreeable over any situation.

Command failure   Failure of a system because of incorrect commands or signals from the operator or from other components.

Comment cards   Printed cards or slips of paper to solicit and collect comments from users of a service or product.

Commercial/ industrial market   Business market customers who are described by variables such as location, NAICS codes, buyer industry, technological sophistication, purchasing process, size, ownership, and financial strength.

Commitment   State of being personally bound to something because of a delegation process or the assignment and acceptance of a task or project.

Commodity Any tangible goods or products.

Common causes Causes of variation inherent in a process over time. They affect every outcome of the process and everyone working in the process. Factors, generally numerous and individually of relatively small importance, that contribute to variation but are not feasible to detect or identify. *See* **special causes.**

Communication Effective transfer of information from one person to another; exchanging information between individuals through a common system of symbols, signs, or behavior. Communication is composed of four elements: (1) the sender, (2) the message, (3) the medium or how the message is sent, and (4) the receiver of the message.

Communication barrier Any impediment to effective communication. Barriers may be physical, environmental, cultural, psychological, emotional, language, or from many other sources that hinder or block the transmission and the receipt of messages.

Communication model The communication process defined in four parts: (1) sender (the originator of the message); (2) message (thoughts, ideas, and feelings being conveyed); (3) medium (how the message is being sent: verbal, electronic, written); and (4) recipient (the person to whom the message is sent).

Company Term used to refer to a business whose purpose is to supply a product or service.

Company culture System of values, beliefs, and behaviors inherent in a company. To optimize business performance, top management must define and create the necessary culture.

Companywide quality control (CWQC) Term coined by Kaoru Ishikawa, similar to total quality management (TQM). See also *What is Total Quality Control? The Japanese Way*, trans. D. J. Lu (Englewood Cliffs, NJ: Prentice Hall, 1985).

Comparator Sensing instrument that measures by comparison. It may be either mechanical or electronic. There are various types of comparators. Optical comparators measure by comparing the outline of an object to a grid on a screen or a contour screen. A dimensional comparator uses a standard to compare to another instrument.

Compatibility Ability of entities to be used together under specific conditions to fulfill relevant requirements.

Competence   Refers to a person's ability to learn and perform a particular activity. Competence generally consists of skill, knowledge, experience, and attitude components.

Competency-based training   Training methodology that focuses on building mastery of a predetermined segment or module before moving on to the next segment or module.

Competition   Other prospective suppliers of products or services that can independently secure the business a company or individual is engaged in. They do this by providing more attractive terms or offering higher quality products or services for the same relative cost.

Competitive advantage   Advantage one person or organization has over another.

Competitive analysis   Gathering of intelligence relative to competitors in order to identify opportunities or potential threats to current and future strategy.

Competitive benchmarking   Process of measuring products, services, and business practices against those of other organizations engaged in the same business.

Complaint   Information received from a customer indicating problems associated with a product or service. Usually associated with a request for corrective actions, replacement, repair, and so on.

Complaint tracking   Collecting and disseminating data to appropriate persons for resolution, monitoring complaint resolution progress, and communicating results. Each customer who is unhappy will tell 9 to 10 others about the experience and yet may not lodge a complaint.

Compliance   State of an organization that meets prescribed specifications, contract terms, and regulations or standards.

Compliance audit   Audit performed to determine compliance with specified requirements. Term is sometimes limited to the part of an audit that verifies whether documented practices are being followed.

Component   Device that is one piece or unit of many parts or units of a system. The brakes are a component of an automobile; the brake pedal is a component of the brake system.

Composite position tolerance   Position tolerance that provides for a composite application of positional tolerancing for the location of feature patterns as well as the interrelation (position and orientation) of features within these patterns. *See* Appendix E.

Computer-aided design (CAD)	Software used by architects, engineers, draftspeople, and artists to create precision drawings or technical illustrations. CAD software can be used to create two-dimensional (2-D) drawings or three-dimensional (3-D) models.
Computer-aided engineering (CAE)	Broad term used by the electronic design automation industry for the use of computers to design, analyze, and manufacture products and processes. CAE includes CAD (see entry) and computer-aided manufacturing (CAM), which is the use of computers for managing manufacturing processes.
Computer-aided software engineering (CASE)	Set of computer programs designed to help improve and automate the development of computer software.
Computer-based training (CBT)	Training delivered using computer software.
Computer program	Series of instructions or statements, in a format usable to the computer, which in turn is designed to cause the computer to execute an operation.
Concentricity	In engineering blueprints, concentricity describes the relationship between the axes of two or more cylindrical features. Perfect concentricity exists when the axes coincide. Concentricity tolerances are typically verified with a dial indicator while the part is rotated on its datum axis. The true analysis concentricity is not the same as total indicator reading (TIR) or full indicator movement (FIM). *See* Appendix E.
Concept	Imaginative gathering and arrangement of a set of new ideas.
Concern	(1) Problem expressed due to the lack of information about the skills, resources, equipment, time, and facilities that may turn into a risk if neglected. (2) A business organized for profit.
Concession	Permission granted by an acceptance authority to supply product of service that does not meet the prescribed requirements. *See also* **waiver** and **deviation.**
Conciliatory management style	Management approach in which the manager is friendly and agreeable and attempts to unite all people involved in order to provide a compatible working team.

Concurrent engineering (CE) Way to reduce cost, improve quality, and shrink cycle time by simplifying a product's system of life cycle tasks during the early concept stages. A process to get all departments from engineering, purchasing, marketing, manufacturing, and finance all working on a new design at once to speed development. May also be called simultaneous engineering.

Conductivity Measure of the ability of a conductor to carry an electrical current. Usually considered as a measure for metal conductors; however, other substances can carry electrical current (e.g., water).

Confidence coefficient Probability that an interval about a sample statistic actually includes the population parameter.

Confidence interval Range within which a parameter of a population (e.g., mean, standard deviation, and so on.) may be expected to fall, on the basis of measurement, with some specified confidence level.

Confidence level (1) The probability that the confidence interval described by a set of confidence limits actually includes the population parameter. (2) The probability that an interval about a sample statistic actually includes the population parameter.

Confidence limits The end points of the interval about the sample statistic that is believed, with a specified confidence level, to include the population parameter.

Configuration management Management approach used to apply administrative and technical direction to the documented functions of a management system. Used to maintain control over any changes to the characteristics, documentation, direction, status, or purpose of an organization.

Conflict Opposition or disagreement resulting from incompatible expectations.

Conflict management Process by which an individual uses managerial techniques to deal with disagreements, both technical and personal, that tend to develop among persons working together as a work group or a team or on a project.

Conflict recovery Once a problem has developed, the following six-step recovery process can help correct the problem: (1) Apologize. (2) Listen and empathize. (3) Fix the problem quickly. (4) Offer atonement. (5) Deliver on your promises. (6) Follow up to see if the problem was resolved satisfactorily.

Conflict resolution Management of a conflict situation in order to arrive at a resolution satisfactory to all parties. One model proposed is based on the two dimensions of assertiveness and cooperation. These are then defined as competing, collaborating, compromising, avoiding, and accommodating. See also *The Goal,* 2nd ed. (Great Barrington, MA: North River Press, 1992).

Conflict resolution diagram Described by Eliyahu Goldratt as an "evaporating cloud," in conflict resolution this concept identifies a potential conflict but is eliminated as the project advances.

Confocal microscope Visual inspection microscope that uses white light or lasers to construct a highly detailed map of a 3-D sample, optically sectioning a given sample point by point and layer by layer.

Conformance Affirmative indication or judgment that a product or service has met the requirements of a relevant specification, contract, or regulation.

Conformance audit Audit performed to determine compliance with specified requirements. *See also* **compliance audit.**

Conformity Fulfillment of specified requirements. Same as **compliance** or **conformance.**

Conformité Europeënne Mark (CE Mark) Conformity European Union mark. The European Union (EU) created the CE Mark to regulate the goods sold within its borders. The mark represents a manufacturer's declaration that its products comply with the EU's New Approach Directives. These directives apply to any country that sells products within the EU.

Confounding Combining indistinguishably the main effect of a factor or a differential effect between factors (interactions), with the effects of other factors, block factors, or interactions in a designed experiment. *See* **alias.**

Consensual management style Management approach in which the manager presents problems to the team members for discussion or input and encourages them to make decisions. This approach may result in an increase in team member commitment to the group but may also increase the time required to make a decision.

Consensus State in which all the members of a group support an action or decision, even if some of them do not fully agree with it. Although the decision may not be the first choice of all members of the group, it is acceptable to all because no one feels his or her vital interest has been ignored.

Consequential damages	Losses, injuries, or damages that are not the direct result of the acts of an organization or individual but the result of the consequences of those actions. The losses suffered from the breach of a warranty or lack of the fulfillment of contractual requirements.
Conservation	Preserving and renewing, whenever possible, the human and natural resources so they will yield the highest economic or social benefits.
Constancy of purpose	The first of 14 steps in Deming's management transformation process. Occurs when goals and objectives are properly aligned to the organizational vision and mission.
Constant cause system	Process or system where the variations are random and constant across time.
Constraint	A constraint may range from the intangible (e.g., beliefs and culture) to the tangible (e.g., posted rules prohibiting smoking, the buildup of work in process awaiting the availability of a machine or operator). Anything that constrains or holds back some performance or activity.
Constraint management	Pertains to identifying a constraint and working to remove or diminish the constraint while dealing with resistance to change. See also Eliyahu Goldratt's *Theory of Constraints,* Great Barrington, MA: North River Press, 1990.
Consultant	Individual who has experience and expertise in applying tools and techniques to resolve process problems and who can advise and facilitate an organization's improvement efforts.
Consultative	Decision-making approach in which a person talks to others and considers their input before making a decision.
Consultative-autocratic management style	Management approach in which extensive information input is solicited from team members, but the manager often makes all the substantive decisions.
Consumer	External customer to whom a product or service is ultimately delivered. Also called "end user."
Consumer market customers	End users of a product or service.

Consumer's risk (also called beta risk and type II error)	For a given sampling plan, the probability of acceptance of a lot, the quality of which has a designated numerical value representing a level that is seldom desirable to accept. Usually the designated value will be the limiting quality level (LQL). *See* **beta risk (β).**
Containment	Act of removing material from the production stream or from the possibility of shipment to the customer of product or material that is either defective or suspected of being defective. May also, by extension, include the management philosophy, which would have product-inspected or sorted to remove defective materials rather than fixing the problems that create them.
Contaminant	Any physical, chemical, biological, or radiological substance or matter that has an adverse effect on the air, water, or soil.
Contingency	Provisions taken for any risk associated with a project. Possible future actions that may stem from presently known causes but cannot be precisely or accurately determined in advance.
Contingency management	Flexible approach to management that may change with circumstances and over time.
Contingency plan	Documented plan prepared by an organization that sets out the coordinated course of action to be followed in case of fire, explosion, natural disasters, or other unforeseen incidents. The plans may include plans to meet new or changing markets, accidents, or forces of nature over which the organization cannot control.
Continual assessment	Assessment (audit) in which selected parts of the Quality/EMS system are assessed on each visit and which over a given period subject the entire system to reassessment.
Continual improvement	In ISO terms, the recurring activities to increase the ability to fulfill requirements.
Continuous data	Data for a continuous variable. The resolution of the value is only dependent on the measurement system used.
Continuous distribution	Distribution used in modeling the observed values of a response when the output is continuous.
Continuous flow production	Items are produced and moved from one processing step to the next one piece at a time. Each process makes only the one piece that the next process needs, and the transfer batch size is one.

Continuous improvement (CI)	Sometimes called continual improvement. The ongoing improvement of products services or processes through incremental and breakthrough improvements. *See **kaizen.***
Continuous probability distribution	Graph or formula representing the probability of a particular numeric value of continuous (variable) data based on a particular type of process that produces the data.
Continuous process improvement (CPI)	Includes the actions taken throughout an organization to increase the effectiveness and efficiency of activities and processes in order to provide added benefits to the customer and organization. Considered a subset of total quality management and operates according to the premise that organizations can always make improvements. Continuous improvements can also be equated with reducing process variation.
Continuous quality improvement (CQI)	Philosophy and attitude for analyzing capabilities and processes and improving them repeatedly to achieve the objective of customer satisfaction.
Continuous sampling plan	In acceptance sampling, a plan intended for application to a continuous flow of individual units of product. It involves acceptance and rejection on a unit by unit basis and employs alternate periods of 100% inspection and sampling, the relative amount of 100% inspection depending on the quality of submitted product. Continuous sampling plans usually require that each period "t" of 100% inspection be continued until a specified number, "I," of consecutively inspected units are found clear of defects. Note: For single-level continuous sampling plans, a single "d" sampling rate (for example, inspect 1 unit in 5 or 1 unit in 10) is used during sampling. For multilevel continuous sampling plans, two or more sampling rates may be used. The rate at any time depends on the quality of submitted product.
Continuous variable	Variable that can assume any value in a range of values on the number line; an example would be the measured size of a part.
Contour	The outside outline of any shape. In practice it is the irregular outlines that cannot be easily defined by combinations of straight lines and curved arcs of regular radii.
Contract	Agreement formally executed by both the customer and the supplier (enforceable by law) that requires performance of services or delivery of

products at a cost to the customer in accordance with stated terms and conditions.

Contract review Systematic activities carried out before signing a contract to ensure requirements are adequately defined, free of ambiguity, documented, and realized by the supplier. The contract review is the responsibility of the supplier but can also be carried out jointly with a customer.

Contractor Person or organization undertaking responsibility for the performance of a contract. A supplier, vendor, subcontractor, and so on.

Control The actions or ability to direct, measure, and improve performance and output of a process or system. The feedback loop of a process through which actual performance is measured.

Control chart Shows graphically the characteristic of a process by illustrating plotted values of that characteristic. It is usually shown on a chart with upper and lower control limits on which values of some statistical measure for a series of samples or subgroups are plotted. The chart frequently shows a central line to help detect a trend of plotted values toward either control limit. They are used to monitor variation in a process and to indicate when a process is tending toward unfavorable conditions or showing improving trends. Control charts are one of the **seven tools of quality.**

Control gate In project management, the specific points in time during the project life cycle at which key stakeholders convene to assess the project performance to date. May also be called phase exit, stage gate, kill point, or phase end review.

Control group Experimental group that is not given treatment under study. The experimental group given the treatment is compared to the control group to measure any changes due to the treatment applied.

Controlled conditions Arrangements that provide control over all factors that may influence the results.

Control limits (1) The calculated boundaries of a process within specified confidence levels, expressed as the upper control limit (UCL) and the lower control limit (LCL). (2) The limits on a control chart used as criteria for signaling the need for action or for judging whether a set of data does or does not indicate a "state of statistical control."

Control methods Particular ways of providing control that do not constrain the sequence of steps in which the methods are carried out.

Control plan (CP) Document that describes the required characteristics for the quality of a company, its product, or service, including measures and control methods.

Control procedure Procedure that controls product or information as it passes through an organization.

Convention Customary practice, rule, or method of doing something.

Conversion Process of moving data, information, or materials from the current state to a new state within an established method or process. ·

Cooperativeness In conflict management, the extent to which one party attempts to satisfy the concerns of the other.

Coordinate measuring machine (CMM) Device that dimensionally measures 3-D products, tools, and components with accuracy approaching 0.0001 inches. A CMM has three axes of travel to measure complex parts and shapes. The CMM will measure parts in the x-axes (side to side), the y-axes (front to back), and the z-axes (up and down) from the base plate.

Coordinate method of positioning features Older method of defining where a feature must be in relation to datum plane or reference surfaces. Still in limited use in some industries.

Cope In casting, the top part of a casting mold. (The **drag** is the bottom part.)

Core Using sand to form a shape that will produce an opening inside a casting when it is poured.

Core competency In a management sense, it pertains to the unique features and characteristics of an organization's overall capability, what it does best.

Corporate culture Although the word *corporate* typically appears, the culture referred to may be that of any type of organization, large or small, and relates to the collective beliefs, values, attitudes, manners, customs, behaviors, and artifacts unique to an organization.

Correction In ISO terms, actions taken to eliminate a detected nonconformity, for example rework, regrade, repair, and so on.

Corrective action (CA)	Implementation of solutions resulting in the reduction or elimination of an identified problem.
Corrective action request/ report (CAR)	Corrective action tool that offers ease and simplicity for employee involvement in the corrective action process and allows for documenting the process. When properly used, a full-cycle corrective action tool that offers ease and simplicity for employee involvement in the corrective action/ process improvement cycle.
Corrective action team (CAT)	Team from various functions within an organization assigned the responsibility to determine and initiate corrective action on an assigned problem.
Correlation chart	Scatter diagram that measures the strength of the relationship between two or more variables on a chart.
Correlation coefficient	Calculated for the purpose of measuring the strength of the linear relationship between two variables.
Correlation (statistical)	Measure of the strength of the linear relationship between two data sets of variables.
Corrosion	Gradual deterioration of a metal due to its contact with an environment that causes a chemical reaction to the material, such as rust on iron parts.
Cosmetic defect	Varying of a product from the norm that is visually noticeable, it may be a variation in color, texture, and so on, that does not affect a product's usefulness but may cause the customer to notice it and complain about it.
Cost	The cash value of a project or activity; the value associated with materials, resources, labor, and so on, of a product or operation. The sum that is expended, paid, or charged for something.
Cost-benefit analysis	Compares the cost and the potential benefits of two or more potential problem solutions that are identified or being considered.
Cost center	Division of an activity for which the identification of cost is desired and through which cost can be controlled through one overall manager.
Cost of capital	Rate of return a company could earn if it invested its money in another investment, venture, or property with equal risk.

Cost of poor quality (COPQ)   Costs associated with providing poor quality products or services. *See* **cost of quality.**

Cost of quality (COQ)   As defined by ASQ's Quality Cost Committee and published in *Principles of Quality Costs* (Milwaukee: ASQ Quality Press, 1999), quality costs are a measure of the cost specifically associated with the achievement or nonachievement of product or service quality, including all product or service requirements established by the company and its contracts with customers and society. More specifically, quality costs are the total of the cost incurred by (1) investing in the prevention of nonconformances to requirements; (2) appraising a product or service for conformance to requirements; and (3) failure to meet requirements. These can then be categorized as prevention, appraisal, and failure. (1) **Prevention cost:** the cost of all activities specifically designed to prevent poor quality in products or services. Examples are the cost of new product review, quality planning, supplier capability surveys, process capability evaluations, quality improvement team meetings, quality improvement projects, quality education, and training. (2) **Appraisal cost:** the cost associated with measuring, evaluation, or auditing products or services to assure conformance to quality standards and performance requirements. These include the cost of incoming and source inspection/test of purchased material, in process and final inspection/test, product, process, or service audits, calibration of measuring and test equipment, and the cost of associated supplies and materials. (3) **Failure cost:** the cost resulting from product or services not conforming to requirements or customer/user needs. Failure costs are further divided into internal and external failure cost categories. *Internal failure cost:* failure cost occurring prior to delivery or shipment of the product, or the furnishing of a service, to the customer. Examples are the cost of scrap, rework, reinspection, retesting, material review, and downgrading. *External failure cost:* failure cost occurring after delivery or shipment of the product, and during or after furnishing of a service, to the customer. Examples are the cost of processing customer complaints, customer returns, warranty claims, and product recalls. For a complete explanation of the principles of quality cost, see also *Principles of Quality Costs.*

Coulomb   Meter-kilogram-second unit of electrical charge equal in magnitude to the charge of 6.28 times 10 to the 18th power of electron flow. As calculated through a conductor by a current of one ampere flowing for one second.

Count chart   Control chart for evaluating the stability of a process in terms of the count of events of a given classification occurring in a sample.

Counterbore Larger diameter drilled hole on the same centerline of an existing hole to provide clearance.

Countersink Bit or drill for making a funnel-shaped enlargement at the outer edge of a drilled hole. Generally it is used to seat the head of a screw or to make it easier to start a bolt.

Count per unit chart Control chart (U-chart) for evaluating the stability of a process in terms of the average count of events of a given classification per unit occurring in a sample.

Covariance Measure of the relationship between pairs of observations from two variables such as X and Y to determine if they are related (correlated).

C_{pk} ratio Defines the process centering relative to the specifications. It equals the lesser of the USL (upper specification limit) minus the mean, divided by three sigma. Or the mean, minus the LSL (lower specification limit), divided by three sigma. The greater the C_{pk} value, the better the process capability. A C_{pk} greater than 1.33 is usually preferred and indicates a capable process. C_{pk} is used to define where the distribution falls within the control limits. Contrast with C_p, which indicates how wide the distribution is.

Cradle to grave Term used for a documented system used to identify and track materials as they are obtained, produced, treated, transported, used, and disposed of.

Crashing In project management, a term used to indicate the process of adding more resources to the project in order to shorten the project's duration. The object of crashing is to shorten a project with the least cost.

Crawford slip method Refers to a method of gathering and presenting anonymous data from a group. Often used in brainstorming sessions.

Creativity Ability to comprehend new concepts, develop the concept, and put it to use.

Creativity, stages of (1) Generate, (2) percolate, (3) illuminate, and (4) verify. Also defined as (1) visualization, (2) exploration, (3) combination, and (4) modification.

Creep (1) The gradual progressive increase in a gage reading because of wear or other factors, usually unnoticed by the user until unacceptable parts are detected. (2) A similar slow change in a project scope or job function, due to external influences.

Criteria   Stated objectives, guidelines, procedures, and/or standards to be used on a project, in a process, or on a part or assembly.

Criterion   Standard, rule, or test on which a judgment can be based.

Critical activity   Activity on a critical path commonly identified by using the critical path method of process mapping.

Critical chain   Term used to describe the main constraints affecting any project. The critical path and the scarce resources that need to be managed effectively to assure a successful project.

Critical defect   This classification of a defect is one that experience or judgment indicates is likely to cause unsafe conditions for those who use, maintain, or depend on the product; or a defect that is likely to prevent acceptable performance of the function of a major end item.

Critical incident   Event that has greater than normal significance, often used as a learning or feedback opportunity.

Critical path   Refers to the sequence of tasks that takes the longest time and determines a project's completion date.

Critical path method (CPM)   *Activity-oriented* project management technique that uses arrow-diagramming techniques to demonstrate both the time and cost required to complete a project. It provides one time estimate—normal time. Similar to **PERT chart.**

Critical path network (CPN)   Flow charting technique to show the activity flow, step by step, and the time required (usually a number in a small circle) for each step or phase. Parallel paths are used to indicate where the start and completion of each activity takes place or overlaps. *See* **PERT chart.**

Critical processes   Processes that present serious potential dangers to human life, health, and the environment or that risk the loss of very large sums of money or customers.

Cross-functional   Term used to describe a process or an activity that crosses the boundary between functions. A cross-functional team consists of individuals from more than one organizational unit or function.

Cross-functional management Management strategy supported by top management requiring interdepartmental coordination. The main focus is setting objectives for cross-functional teams, with an intensive focus on follow-through to achieve success in the concentrated efforts extended.

Cross plot *See* **scatter diagram.**

Cultural resistance Form of resistance based on opposition to the possible social and organizational consequences associated with change.

Culture System of values, beliefs, and behaviors inherent in an organization. *See also* **corporate culture.**

Culture change Major shift in the attitudes, norms, sentiments, beliefs, values, operating principles, and behavior of an organization.

Culture, organizational Common set of values, beliefs, attitudes, perceptions, and accepted behaviors shared by individuals within an organization.

Cumulative sum control chart (CUSUM) Control chart on which the plotted value is the cumulative sum of deviations of successive samples from a target value. The ordinate of each plotted point represents the algebraic sum of the previous ordinate and the most recent deviation from the target.

Current carrying capacity In electrical terms the maximum continuous electrical flow, in amperes, allowed for a specified conductor under specified conditions.

Current good manufacturing practices (CGMP) Regulations enforced by the U.S. Food and Drug Administration for food and chemical manufacturers and packagers.

Current rating The maximum continuous electrical flow, in amperes of current, allowed for a given conductor under specified conditions.

Current reality tree Technique used in applying Eliyahu Goldratt's theory of constraints to identify undesirable effects as in root cause analysis.

Customer Someone for whom work or a service is performed. The ultimate consumer, user, client, beneficiary, or recipient of a product or service. *See* **external customer** and **internal customer.** This concept is not limited to the final customer who pays for the product or service, but rather includes anyone to whom a product or service or information is provided.

Customer complaints   Feedback received from a customer who was not satisfied with the product or service provided. Only about 10% of complaint cards are turned in. An unhappy customer will tell 9 to 10 people, a happy customer may only tell 5 people about a good experience.

Customer council   Group usually composed of representatives from an organization's largest customers who meet to discuss common issues.

Customer defection   Customer moves to another supplier. This may occur because of price, delivery, quality, or a number of other reasons.

Customer delight   Result of delivering a product or service that exceeds customer expectations.

Customer dissatisfaction   Frustration that customers experience because of the inconvenience, economic loss, delays, and so on, when they encounter unexpected problems with products or services.

Customer dissatisfaction (recovery)   The five steps to recover from an unhappy customer are apologize, restate the reason, empathize, make restitution, and follow up.

Customer driven   Company that focuses more on care of existing customers and less on trying to get additional customers, until it can provide adequately for the increased business.

Customer expectations   As defined by Karl Albrecht, customer expectations can be explained in four stages: (1) basic (you get what you pay for); (2) expected (some features provided as part of the purchase); (3) desired (a few extra attributes that are worthwhile to the purchase); and (4) unanticipated (some surprises that go beyond what you expected from your purchase). See also *At America's Service* (New York: Warner Books, 1988).

Customer (external)   Any customer that is not part of the organization. They could be governmental agencies, end users, wholesale dealers, and so on. *See* **customer (internal).**

Customer focused   Company that focuses more on attracting new customers and less on maintaining good service for existing customers. They may at times neglect older customers and concentrate on attracting new customers in order to broaden their customer base or expand into new markets.

Customer (internal) Internal customers can be anyone within the company, next person on the assembly line, support personnel, mangers, board of directors, and so on. *See* **customer (external).**

Customer life cycle In business the five stages of a customer life cycle are acquisition, retention, attrition, defection, and reacquisition.

Customer loyalty/ retention The result of an organization's plans, processes, practices, and efforts designed to deliver their services or products in ways which create customer satisfaction so customers are retained and committed to remain loyal.

Customer needs Joseph Juran lists customer needs as follows: (1) stated needs, (2) real needs, (3) perceived needs, (4) cultural needs, and (5) unintended needs. Needs as related to the use of a product are defined as (1) convenience, (2) safety needs, (3) product simplification features, (4) communications, (5) service for product failures, and (6) customer service.

Customer relationship management (CRM) Strategy used to learn more about customers, their needs and behaviors, in order to develop stronger relationships with them. It brings together information about customers, sales, marketing effectiveness, responsiveness, and market trends. It helps businesses use technology and human resources to gain insight into the behavior of customers and the value of relationships with those customers.

Customer retention Measures to retain even satisfied customers include reward usage (volume discounts), reward loyalty (frequent flyer programs), unpaid services (free lessons on how to use products), and personal relationships (honoring clients, golf outings).

Customer satisfaction (CS) Result of delivering a product or service that meets customer requirements.

Customer segmentation Process of differentiating customers based on one or more dimensions for the purpose of developing a marketing strategy to address specific segments such as by volume of business, geographical location, product line, and so on.

Customer service Activities of dealing with customers' questions; also sometimes the department that takes customer orders or provides postdelivery services.

Customer service recovery   Five-step program to handle and recover from customer problems and complaints: (1) Apologize (fast and honest). (2) Restate (restate the problem as the customer relates it). (3) Empathize (make sure you communicate your concern for the customer). (4) Make restitution (take immediate action to resolve the problem; offer a concession if possible). (5) Follow up (see if the actions taken have satisfied the customer). This last step is where most programs fail.

Customer service representative (CSR)   Person who has direct interface with the customer and usually handles issues requiring more than just sales.

Customer-supplied product   Any hardware, software, documentation, or information owned by the customer that is provided to a supplier for use in connection with a contract and returned to the customer either incorporated in the product or at the end of the contract.

Customer-supplier model (CSM)   Model depicting inputs flowing into a work process that, in turn, add value and produce outputs delivered to a customer. Also called "customer-supplier methodology."

Customer-supplier partnership   Long-term relationship between a customer and supplier characterized by teamwork and mutual confidence. The supplier is considered an extension of the buyer's organization. The partnership is based on several commitments. The buyer provides long-term contracts and uses fewer suppliers. The supplier implements quality assurance processes so incoming inspection can be minimized. The supplier also helps the buyer reduce costs and improve product and process designs.

Customer value   The market-perceived quality adjusted for the relative price of a product or service.

Customer value package   Made up of these five factors: price, product quality, innovation, service quality, and company image relative to competition.

Cutover   Process of moving from one system to another. Generally this means changing without the benefit of running the two systems in parallel. There may be a high risk if the target system should fail.

Cutting plane   In engineering blueprints, a thick broken or dashed line to show a sectioned view of a part or where a part is to be cut or reviewed by the inspection process. *See* Appendix E.

Cybernetic control system   Automated control system with a feedback loop.

Cycle time   Elapsed time between the start and completion of a task or an entire process; for example, in order processing it can be the time between receipt and delivery of an order.

Cycle time reduction   To reduce the time it takes, from start to finish, to complete a particular process, and to eliminate bottlenecks and areas that slow down production. A major principle in lean manufacturing.

Cyclical   Process affected by factors that cause the process to shift and then return to its original level and then repeat the process in a regular fashion. Similar to seasonal cycles of summer to fall, fall to winter, winter to spring, spring to summer, in a continuing sequence.

Cylindricity   Cylindricity tolerance specifies how much the surface of a pin, shaft, or other cylindrical feature is allowed to vary from the perfect cylinder implied by the blueprint. The tolerance zone consists of two concentric cylinders a specified distance apart. *See* Appendix E.

C=Zero   Sampling plan similar to MIL-STD-105, proposed by Nicholas Squeglia, allowing for no defects in the sample taken. See also *Zero Acceptance Number Sampling Plans,* 4th ed. (Milwaukee: ASQ Quality Press, 1994).

Damages Monetary or other compensation that may be recovered by a party who has suffered loss through a breach of contract, an act of omission, negligence, or other causes of another party.

Damping In measurement the reduction in amplitude of an oscillation to make the observation of the measured quantity more readable.

Darkfield Illumination technique that lights the specimen surface from an oblique angle to highlight surface problems.

Data Set of collected facts. There are two basic kinds of numerical data: measured or variable data (e.g., 16 ounces, 4 miles, 0.75 inches) and counted or attribute data (e.g., 162 defects).

Datum In engineering blueprints, a theoretically exact point, axis, or plane derived from the true geometric counterpart of a specified datum feature. A datum is the origin from which the location or geometric characteristics of features of a part are established. *See* Appendix E.

Datum feature Actual physical part feature used to establish a datum.

Datum line In engineering blueprints, a datum line is a theoretically exact point, axis, or plane from which a location or geometric characteristic of a part feature are established. It is established by a datum feature, an actual physical part feature that has an important relationship to the part feature being controlled. It is identified as a letter in a square box attached to a datum feature. *See* Appendix E.

Datum reference frame   In engineering blueprints, a theoretical set of three mutually perpendicular planes used to establish the geometric characteristics of part features. Duplicates the X-Y-Z axes of many machines and inspection equipment. Usually specified in a rectangular box. *See* Appendix E.

Datum target   In engineering blueprints, a specified point, line, or area of contact between a part and the machine tooling or inspection equipment. Used to establish datums on castings, forgings, sheet metal, and other irregularly shaped parts. Usually specified in the top of a datum target symbol (a split circle with the top half indicating the size and the bottom half indicating the reference point). *See* Appendix E.

D chart   *See* **demerit chart.**

Deadly diseases   In management, according to Deming, there are seven deadly diseases that management must control: (1) lack of constancy of purpose and plan, (2) emphasis on short-term profits, (3) personal employee evaluations, (4) managers mobility (job hopping), (5) use of visible figures for management, with little or no consideration for unknown data, (6) excessive medical cost, and (7) excessive warranty and failure cost. See also *Out of the Crisis* (Cambridge: Massachusetts Institute of Technology, Center for Advanced Engineering Study, 1986).

Dead on arrival (DOA)   Product that does not work the first time it is used or tested.

Decimal-inch system   The customary inch-pound system used in the United States, in which the inch has been divided into decimals in order to avoid fractions that are awkward in calculations.

Decision-making position   In ASQ certification requirements, defined as the authority to define, execute, or control projects/processes and to be responsible for the outcome. This may or may not include management or supervisory positions.

Decision matrix   Matrix used by teams to evaluate problems and possible solutions. After a matrix is drawn to evaluate possible solutions, for example, the team lists them in the far-left vertical column. Next, the team selects criteria to rate the possible solutions, writing them across the top row. Third, each possible solution is rated on a scale of 1 to 5 for each criterion, and the rating is recorded in the corresponding grid. Finally, the ratings of all the criteria for each possible solution are added to determine its total score. The total score is then used to help decide which solution deserves the most attention.

Decision sampling — Audit technique used to validate the ability of people to make valid quality decisions. Basically, inspection, test, and other inspection type personnel are used to make quality related decisions based on their techniques and or experience.

Decision table — Table of all contingencies that are to be considered in a problem along with the actions to be taken. It can be in either a matrix or in a tabular form.

Decision tree — Graphical decision-making tool that integrates for a defined problem both uncertainties and its estimated cost with alternatives to decide on the "best" alternative.

Deductive reasoning — Testing based on facts and figures, real information, rather than on assumptions.

De facto authority — Influence exercised regardless of formal authority and often derived as a result of charisma, knowledge, or position. May be exercised by the project manager or by certain team members.

Defect — Product or service's nonfulfillment of an intended requirement or reasonable expectation for use, including safety considerations. There are four classes of defects: class 1, very serious, leads directly to severe injury or catastrophic economic loss; class 2, serious, leads directly to significant injury or significant economic loss; class 3, major, is related to major problems with respect to intended normal or reasonably foreseeable use; and class 4, minor, is related to minor problems with respect to intended normal or reasonably foreseeable use. *See* **blemish, imperfection,** and **nonconformity.**

Defective — Defective unit; a unit of product that contains one or more defects with respect to the quality characteristic(s) under consideration.

Define — To make clear, to make distinct, to fix the limits of. To give the distinguishing characteristics of, to trace the precise boundaries of an object or practice.

Deformation — Bending or distorting of an object due to the forces applied to it. Deformation can contribute to errors in measurement if the measuring instrument applies enough force.

Degradation — (1) Gradual deterioration in performance as a function of time and/or stress. (2) Gradual impairment in ability to perform a specified task or mission. Decreasing mechanical or electrical strength.

Degree (circular)   The circle is divided into 360 parts or one degree. This is further divided having each degree divided by 60, making each graduation one second. Thus a full circle has 1,296,000 seconds. 90 deg. is equal to 100 grads. *See* **grad, mil,** and **radian.**

Degree of demonstration   Extent to which evidence is produced to provide confidence that specified requirements are fulfilled. The extent depends on criteria such as economics, complexity, innovation, safety, and environmental considerations.

Degrees of freedom   Parameter that, in general, is the number of independent comparisons available to estimate a specific parameter and serves as a means of entering certain statistical tables. The number of unconstrained parameters in a statistical determination.

Delay time   (1) Time to recognize a problem or start a corrective action. (2) Downtime due to supply or administrative delay during which there are no maintenance activities scheduled.

Delegation   In the management concept, a decision-making approach in which a manager, supervisor, facilitator, or someone with responsibility for an activity shifts the responsibility for making a decision to someone else, usually to a lower level or subordinate person.

Delighter   Feature of a product or service that a customer does not expect to receive but gives pleasure to the customer when received.

Deliverable   Any measurable, tangible, verifiable outcome, result, or item that must be produced to complete a project or task. Often used more narrowly in reference to an external deliverable, such as a deliverable (product or service) that is subject to approval by the customer.

Delphi technique   Form of participative expert judgment; an anonymous, interactive technique using survey methods to derive consensus on work estimates, approaches, and issues.

Delta (δ)   Greek symbol delta, fourth letter of the Greek alphabet. The minimum acceptable.

Demassification   Concept where customer markets split up and each market segment develops its own special needs, proposed by Alvin and Heidi Toffler in their book *The Third Wave. See also* **mass customization.** See also *Powershift* (New York: Free Press, 1983).

Demerit chart Control chart for evaluating a process in terms of a demerit (or quality score); in other words, a weighted sum of counts of various classified non-conformities.

Deming cycle Sometimes called the Shewhart cycle. *See also* **plan-do-check-act cycle.**

Deming Prize Award given annually to organizations that, according to the award guidelines, have successfully applied companywide quality control based on statistical quality control and will keep up with it in the future. Although the award is named in honor of W. Edwards Deming, its criteria are not specifically related to Deming's teachings. There are three separate divisions for the award: the Deming Application Prize, the Deming Prize for Individuals, and the Deming Prize for Overseas Companies. The award process is overseen by the Deming Prize Committee of the Union of Japanese Scientists and Engineers in Tokyo.

Demographics Variables among buyers in the consumer market, which include geographic location, age, sex, marital status, family size, social class, education, nationality, occupation, and income.

Demonstration Verifying compliance with specifications by witnessing how something operates. To provide assurance by reasoning, objective evidence, experiment, or practical application.

Density Measure of how heavy a specific volume of a solid, liquid, or gas is in comparison to water.

Dependability Degree to which a product is operable and capable of performing its required function at any randomly chosen time during its specified operating time, provided that the product is available at the start of that period. (Nonoperation-related influences are not included.) Dependability can be expressed by the ratio time available divided by (time available + time required). The term used to describe the availability for performance, reliability performance, and maintainability performance of a piece or equipment or system. Dependability is a time-related aspect of quality.

Dependent samples Samples chosen from one or more populations in a way that they are not independent of each other.

Dependent tasks Tasks that are related such that the beginning or end of one task is contingent on the beginning or end of another.

Deployment (1) Dispersion, dissemination, broadcasting, or spreading of a communication throughout an organization, downward and laterally. (2) How well a management system (quality, environmental, and so on.) is implemented and used throughout the entire organization.

Depreciation Changes in value to current operations or equipment that systematically and logically distributes the cost of tangible capital assets value over the asset's estimated useful life.

Design Creation of a product or service in the form of specifications, drawings, data flow diagrams, or any other specified methods to provide detailed information on how to build the product or perform the service.

Design failure mode and effects analysis (DFMEA) The design failure mode and effects analysis process is used to identify and evaluate the relative risk associated with a particular design.

Design for assembly (DFA) The purpose of using the design for assembly techniques is to make a product easier to manufacture and assemble.

Design for manufacturability (DFM) The purpose of using the design for manufacturability techniques is to design a product in a way that makes it easier to manufacture.

Design for Six Sigma (DFSS) Robust design that is consistent with the applicable manufacturing processes to assure a fully capable process that will deliver quality products. *See* **DMADV.**

Designing in quality versus inspecting in quality *See* **prevention versus detection.**

Design margin The self-imposed restriction on a design that is more severe than either what is specified or what is required for the expected operational use.

Design of experiments (DOE) Branch of applied statistics dealing with planning, conducting, analyzing, and interpreting controlled tests to evaluate the factors that affect the value of a response variable. *See also* **Ronald Aylmer Fisher.** See also *The Design of Experiments* (Edinburgh: Oliver & Boyd, 1942).

Design review Formal, documented, comprehensive, and systematic examination of a design to evaluate the capability of the design to meet the requirements for functionality, manufacturability, and quality, conducted to identify possible problems. A design review is normally held before production starts, but it may be held at any stage of the design process.

Desired quality Refers to the additional features and benefits a customer discovers when using a product or service that leads to increased customer satisfaction. If missing, a customer may become dissatisfied.

Desktop audit Documentation audit performed at a desk using the audited organization's Quality/EMS system documentation.

Destructive testing (DT) Testing and inspection of product or material that damages or destroys the product or materials so they are not usable. Contrast with nondestructive testing.

Detail drawing An engineering blueprint that contains all the information needed to manufacture a part.

Detection Ability or probability of finding an object or defect.

Detection rating In a failure mode and effects analysis (FMEA), the rating scale of from 1 to 10. The easier it is to detect a failure, the better. The detection rating defines the relative ease of finding a failure that has or might occur. A low rating of 1–2 would indicate the probability of finding the defect is high; a high rating of 9–10 would indicate the probability of detecting a defect would be low.

Development methodology Prescribed set of supportive and integrated processes and procedures organized into a series of phases making up the development cycle of a product or service.

Development phase In a project life cycle, the second of four phases, where the planning activities normally occur. *See* **project life cycle.**

Deviation (1) In numerical data sets, the difference or distance of an individual observation or data value from the center point (often the mean) of the set distribution. (2) The departure from established requirements. *See* **waiver** and **concession.**

Diagnosis Activity of discovering the cause(s) of quality deficiencies; the process of investigating symptoms, collecting and analyzing data, and conducting experiments to test theories to determine the root cause(s) of deficiencies.

Diagnostic journey and remedial journey Two-phase investigation used by teams to solve chronic quality problems. In the first phase, the diagnostic journey, the team journeys from the symptom of a chronic problem to its cause. In the second phase, the remedial journey, the team journeys from the cause to its remedy.

Diagram Simple line drawing containing explanatory data or information to describe a process, relationship, or a condition.

Dial indicator Any of various gages using a dial to provide for amplified visual variations in the dimensions being measured.

Diameter Distance across a round or cylindrical object when measured through its center.

Die Tool made of hard metal used to cut or form a required shape in metal, forgings, and so forth.

Die casting Metal poured under pressure into a metal die to make a very accurate casting.

Dielectric test Test conducted at elevated voltages for a specified time, used to determine how well insulated and prone to an electrical breakdown (short circuit) an electrical component is.

Differential measurement Use of a device that transforms actual movement into a known value A dial-indicating gage is an example.

Differentiation in organization Principle of a bureaucratic organization that states an organization should be structured around the environment in which it operates. A manufacturing organization that produces durable consumer goods would also set up repair facilities or complementary services.

Diffusion Movement of suspended or dissolved particles from a highly concentrated area to a less concentrated area. The process tends to distribute the particles more uniformly.

Digital instruments Digital instruments display the measurement in numerals.

Dimension   Expression of length, depth, or width, in relation to a measurement.

Dimension line   On blueprints these are light solid arrows used to dimension the part or to show the distance between the extension lines. They will usually have the stated dimension within the line. *See* Appendix E.

Dimensions of quality   Refers to different ways in which quality may be viewed, for example, meaning of quality, characteristics of quality, drivers of quality, and so on.

Dioxin   Any of a family of compounds known chemically as dibenzo-p-dioxins. Concern about them comes from their potential toxicity as contaminants in commercial products.

Direct cost   Cost identified with a specific final product or service, such as materials and labor. *See* **indirect cost.**

Directive   Written communication to indicate a set course of action, conduct, or procedure.

Direct labor   Labor identified with a specific final product or service. In manufacturing it would include: fabrication, inspection, and assembly. Direct labor is incurred for the exclusive benefit of the product or service versus indirect labor, which would include such activities as moving materials, maintenance activities, and so on.

Direct measurement   Where the standard is directly applied to the part and a reading can be taken. A steel rule used to measure a length is an example of a direct measurement.

Discipline   Area of technical expertise or specialty.

Discovery audit   Audit with the purpose of finding something that may be or may cause a problem.

Discovery sampling   Sampling or auditing within certain preestablished guidelines or areas to determine if problems are present.

Discrepancy   Failure to meet specified requirements supported by evidence. Often used interchangeably with nonconformance, deficiency, or finding.

Discrete distribution   Requires that the characteristic being evaluated have only a countable number of outcomes. In most quality applications this would be either good or bad, pass or fail, acceptable or not acceptable, and so on. A distribution function that describes the probability for random discrete variables. *See* Appendix C.

Discrete probability distribution   The measured process variable takes a finite or limited number of values; no other possible values exist.

Discrete variable   Variable that can take on only a countable number of values; for example, the number of people in a room is a discrete variable.

Discrimination (of a measurement system)   Discrimination or resolution of a measurement system is its capability to detect and indicate even small changes in the measured characteristic. The main concern when selecting or analyzing a measurement system.

Discrimination rule   Never attempt to "read between the lines." Always use an instrument that has the proper discrimination for the measurement being taken.

Dispersion analysis diagram   Cause-and-effect diagram for analysis of the various contributions to variability of a process or product. The main factors contributing to the process are first listed, and then the specific causes of variability from each factor are enumerated. A systematic study of each cause can then be performed.

Dispersion (of a statistical sample)   Tendency of the values of the elements in a sample to differ from each other.

Disposition   Act or manner of disposing of something.

Disposition of nonconformity   Action taken to deal with an existing nonconformity; actions may include repair, rework, regrade, scrap, obtain a concession/deviation/waiver.

Disruptive management style   Management approach in which the manager tends to destroy the unity of the work teams, be an agitator, and causes disorder within the organization.

Dissatisfiers   Features or functions a customer expects that either are not present or are present but not adequate; also pertains to employees' expectations.

Distance learning   Learning where student(s) and instructor(s) are not at the same location, often carried out through electronic means.

Distillation Process of purifying liquids through boiling, so the steam or gaseous vapors condense to a pure liquid. Any pollutants or contaminants may then remain in the residue in a concentrated form.

Distribution (statistical) Amount of potential variation in the outputs of a process, typically expressed by its shape and average or standard deviation. Common continuous distributions are shown as normal, exponential, or Weibull. Common discrete distributions are listed as Poisson, binomial, or hypergeometric. *See* Appendix C.

Division of labor Specifically assigning persons to various activities within a work cell by categories of skill, labor, or expertise.

DMADV Acronym for a data-driven quality strategy for designing products and processes, it is an integral part of a Six Sigma quality initiative. It consists of five interconnected phases: define, measure, analyze, design, and verify.

DMAIC Acronym for a data-driven quality strategy for improving processes and an integral part of a Six Sigma quality initiative. It stands for define, measure, analyze, improve, and control.

Dobson unit (DU) Measurement system developed to measure ozone levels. If, for example, 100 Dobson units of ozone were to develop on the earth's surface, they would form a layer one millimeter thick. In nature the ozone levels vary geographically, even with the absence of any ozone depletion.

Document Something written, printed, and so on, that gives information or proof of some fact. Any procedure, form, record, and so on, used as evidence to prove or support a finding or observation.

Document control Formal system used to control and distribute documents in an orderly fashion so persons who need them have them at the proper time, and obsolete documents are removed.

Documentation Use of documentary evidence; the documents used.

Documentation audit Audit carried out to determine whether an organization's documented Quality/EMS system makes adequate provision for meeting the requirements of a given standard. *See also* **adequacy audit** or **desktop audit.**

Documentation tier In the ISO format, documentation is structured so it covers all levels of the management system being described. Typically the levels are tier 1, quality system manual (this may include a corporate manual as well as divisional or unit manuals); tier 2, quality procedures, quality plans, training manuals, operational procedures, and so on; tier 3, work instructions; tier 4, the forms, specification sheets, drawings, and other documents required by your system. Records may be applicable to any level in the documentation structure; they show something was accomplished.

Dodge-Romig sampling plans   Plans for acceptance sampling developed by Harold F. Dodge and Harry G. Romig. Four sets of tables were published in 1940: single sampling lot tolerance tables, double sampling lot tolerance tables, single sampling average outgoing quality limit tables, and double sampling average outgoing quality limit tables.

Dot plot   Form of graph that starts out as a line marked off in units corresponding to data measurements. A dot is placed above each value, each time that value appears in the data set.

Double-sided test   Statistical consideration where, for example, the mean of a population is to be equal to a criterion, as stated in a null hypothesis.

Downgrading   Process of setting the difference between the normal value or use of a product to a lower value, due to some imperfection in the product.

Downsizing   Planned reduction in workforce due to economics, competition, mergers, sale, restructuring, or reengineering.

DPMO   Defects per million opportunities; same as **PPM.**

Draft   Tapered shapes in parts to allow them to be easily taken out of a mold or die.

Drag   Lower part of a flask used in casting. *See also* **cope,** the upper part of a mold.

Draw   In metal forming, to deform or stretch metal, usually through dies. Wire is drawn using this method.

Drawing   Shortened term for engineering drawing or blueprint.

Drift   Tendency of a process or machine to move from making acceptable parts or material to unacceptable parts or material over time; may be from tool wear or other sources.

Drivers of quality — Factors that are crucial to quality. If the quality drivers are controlled, the quality of the product or service will also be controlled. These may include processes, customers, products, services, employee satisfaction, and a total organizational focus.

Driving forces — Forces that tend to change a situation in desirable ways.

Ductile — Capable of plastic deformation without being fractured. Examples may include rolling, forming, stretching, and drawing materials.

Due diligence — In legal terms, taking reasonable care, which is required of any person involved to prevent an accident or reduce the probability of hazard to persons or the environment.

Dummy activity — Activity with no time involved; it merely shows the relationship of activities in an arrow diagram. It is used when the logical relationships cannot be correctly defined by the normal graphical methods. It is usually shown as an arrow with dashed lines.

Duplication — In a designed experiment, the execution of a treatment more than once under similar conditions.

Durability — Measure of reliability used to measure the useful life of a product, it is equal to the probability that the product will survive its intended service life, without failure.

Durometer — Test instrument used to obtain accurate measures of hardness on relatively soft materials such as rubber, plastics, leather, wood, and fruits.

Dye penetrant test — Inspection type of test used mainly on nonferrous materials to detect cracks, porosity, and other surface defects. The inspector applies the dye penetrant to the surface, allows it to soak in, wipes off the excess, applies a developer, and then the dye shows up any defects on the contrasting background. A nondestructive test procedure.

Dynamic measurement — Dynamic measurement is performed on a changing quality; by contrast most linear measurement is "static," in that it is performed on something that is stable and unchanging at least over a short period of time.

Dynamic test — Test of one or more of the characteristics of the equipment or of any component part that is performed while the equipment is energized.

E

e-business   (Electronic business) Refers to conducting all facets of business on the Internet. The term is used by many organizations in advertising to describe a range of product and service offerings over the Internet.

Ecology   Relationships of living things to one another and their environment, or the study of such relationships.

e-commerce   (Electronic commerce) Conducting business transactions between businesses over the Internet.

Education   Process undertaken to learn required additional knowledge. *See also* **training.**

Educational objectives   As presented by Benjamin S. Bloom in his *Taxonomy* (1956), these are defined in three domains: (1) cognitive (mental skills), (2) affective (growth, emotion, and feelings), and (3) psychomotor (manual and physical skills). The cognitive subset is further divided into six "behaviors": knowledge, comprehension, application, analysis, synthesis, and evaluation. The affective subset is further divided into five "behaviors": receiving, responding, valuing, organization, and characterization. See also *Taxonomy of Educational Objectives: The Classification of Educational Goals* (New York: Longman Group, 1999).

Effect   What results after an action has been taken; the expected or predicted impact when an action is to be taken or is proposed. The impact of a failure should the failure occur.

Effectiveness   State of having produced a decided upon or desired effect or result.

Efficiency	Ratio of the output to the total input in a process. The goal is to use less resources, time, and so on.
Efficiency factor	Ratio of standard performance time to actual performance. Usually expressed as a percentage.
Efficient	Term describing a process that operates effectively while consuming the minimum amount of resources (such as labor and time).
Effluent	In an environmental aspect, an effluent is wastewater, whether treated or not, that flows out of an industrial outlet, sewer, or a treatment facility.
Egoless team	Team structure where there is no obvious leader and the decisions of the team are reached through consensus. Works well with small short duration teams, a high-priority project, and skilled team members.
Eighty–twenty (80–20)	Term referring to the Pareto principle, which was first coined by Joseph Juran in 1950. The principle suggests most effects come from relatively few causes; that is, 80% of the effects come from 20% of the possible causes.
Eighty-five–fifteen (85–15)	Term used by Joseph Juran to indicate that 85% of problems are management controlled and only 15% are operator controlled.
e-learning	(Electronic learning) Form of distance learning that is Internet based.
Electronic data interchange (EDI)	Electronic exchange of data between customers and suppliers and vice versa. Usually it is considered the exchange of data over the Internet.
Element	*See* **unit.**
Empirical	Any conclusion based on hard evidence and past experience, rather than on theory.
Employee involvement (EI)	Practice within an organization whereby employees regularly participate in making decisions on how their work areas operate, including making suggestions for improvement, planning, goal setting, and monitoring performance.
Employee satisfaction	Those factors that contribute to employee satisfaction, what employees want. One theory gives these factors: (1) interesting work, (2) apprecia-

tion, (3) involvement, (4) job security, (5) good pay, (6) promotion and growth, (7) good working conditions, (8) loyalty to employees, (9) help with personal problems, and (10) tactful discipline. See also Abraham Maslow and Frederick Herzberg's *The Motivation to Work,* 2nd ed. (New York: John Wiley & Sons, 1959).

Employee stock ownership plan (ESOP)   Under an ESOP, employees take over, or participate in, the management of the organization that employs them by becoming shareholders of company stock.

Empowerment   Condition whereby employees have the authority to make decisions and take action in their work areas without prior approval. For example, an operator can stop a production process if he or she detects a problem, or a customer service representative can send out a replacement product if a customer calls with a problem. Management gives up some of the power traditionally held by management.

Enabler   For empowerment to be successfully implemented, the leader's role must shift from that of a traditional manager to that of an enabler and allow others to act on their own.

EN 46000   Medical device quality management systems standard. EN 46000 is technically equivalent to ISO 13485:1996, an international medical device standard. So few differences exist between the two that if an organization is prepared to comply with one, it may easily comply with the other as well.

EN 9100   International quality management standard for the aerospace industry (*see* **AS9100**).

End standard   Special gage blocks used on the ends of stacks of gage blocks to convert to other measurements. Also known as "wear gage blocks" and used to minimize wear on the majority of gage blocks in a set.

End users   External customers who purchase products/services for their own use.

Engineering change notice (ECN)   Formal means an engineering department has to notify the purchasing, manufacturing, and quality departments that a change has been made to materials, process requirements or to specifications. The formal release of an engineering change to the departments that must make the change happen.

Engineering change order (ECO) Directive to incorporate project improvements that have been designed after release of the initial product design.

Engineering drawing Blueprint that contains the information needed to manufacture or assemble a final product or subassembly. *See* Appendix E.

Engineering specifications Documents prepared in advance or in addition to drawings typically to provide information relating to function, durability, performance, and so on, of materials or a product. They may contain test methods and procedures as well as minimum performance requirements.

Engineering standards Additional specifications describing what materials, process requirements, reliability requirements, quality standards, and so on, a part or a family of parts or materials must meet.

Enlarged view On blueprints, a portion of a view to a larger scale than the rest of the drawing in order to clarify a part feature or to allow more room for dimensioning.

Entity *(Per ISO A8402)* Item that can be individually described and considered. May be an activity or process, a product, system, an organization, a person, or any combination thereof.

Entropy Tendency of a process (or system) to run down and collapse on itself.

Environment Surroundings in which an organization operates, including air, water, land, natural resources, flora, fauna, humans, and their interrelation.

Environmental analysis/ scanning Relates to monitoring factors from both inside and outside the organization that may impact the long-term viability of the organization.

Environmental aspect Any element of an organization or its activities or products that has the potential to interact positively or negatively with the environment.

Environmental audit Systematic, documented periodic and objective review by regulated entities of facility operations and practices related to meeting environmental requirements.

Environmental Auditors Registration Association (EARA)	Merged with the Institute of Environmental Management and the Institute of Environmental Assessment to form the Institute of Environmental Management and Assessment (IEMA).
Environmental claim	Any environmental declaration that describes or implies by whatever means the effects that the raw material extraction, production, distribution, use, or disposal of a product or service has on the environment. This applies to effects that are local, regional, or global, and the environment that an individual lives in, affects, or is affected by.
Environmental impact	Any change to the environment, whether adverse or beneficial, wholly or partially resulting from an organization's activities, products, or services.
Environmental impact statement	Document required of federal agencies by the National Environmental Policy Act for major projects of legislative proposals significantly affecting the environment. It describes the positive and negative effects of the undertaking and cites alternative actions.
Environmental indicator	Expression used to provide information about environmental performance or the condition of the environment.
Environmental management system (EMS)	Management system for addressing the environmental policies, objectives, procedures, principles, authority, responsibility, accountability, and implementation of an organization's means for managing its environmental affairs.
Environmental objective	Overall environmental goal arising from the environmental policy that an organization sets for itself to achieve and that is quantified where practicable.
Environmental performance	Measurable results of the environmental management system, related to an organization's control of its environmental aspects, based on its environmental policy, objectives, and targets.
Environmental policy	Organization's statement of environmental principles that serves as the basis for setting performance goals and environmental targets and objectives.

Environmental Protection Agency (EPA)	The federal agency of the U.S. government used to protect human health and to safeguard the natural environment.
Environmental sustainability	Long-term maintenance of the ecosystem and its components and functions for future generations.
Environmental target	Detailed performance requirement, quantified where practicable, applicable to the organization, that arises from the environmental objectives and needs to be set and met in order to achieve those objectives.
Environmental test	Test in which conditions are controlled and altered to assure the product or assembly being tested; will function when used in the environment for which it was designed.
Equivalent method	Any method of sampling, inspection, or analyzing for compliance that has been demonstrated to the satisfaction of the relevant authority as an acceptable alternative to the normally used methods and provides the same level of assurance.
Equity theory	Theory that states job motivation depends on how equitable the individual believes the rewards or punishment to be.
Equipment	Machines, tools, data processing systems, office furnishings, and other hardware items required to complete a task or to operate a business.
Ergonomics	Evaluation of the design of a product or system to ensure compatibility with the capabilities of humans, including the interaction between humans and the product or system.
Error	Discrepancy between an observed or measured value or condition and the theoretically correct value or condition.
Error proofing	Efforts extended to eliminate the possibility of operators or processes being able to make errors. *See* **poka-yoke.**
e-signature	Electronic symbol, typed name, digitized image or a signature, and so on, associated with a special algorithm to verify the authenticity of an electronic document.
Establish and maintain	In the context of Quality/EMS system audits, to set up on a permanent basis and retain or restore procedures in a state in which they can fulfill their intended purpose.

Ethical management style Management approach in which top management is honest, sincere, and able to motivate and press for the best and most fair solution to most situations.

Ethics Practice of applying a code of conduct based on moral principles to day-to-day actions to balance what is fair to individuals or organizations and what is right for society. Three questions posed by Ken Blanchard are (1) Is it legal? (2) Is it balanced? (fair to all involved) (3) How will it make me feel about myself? See also *The Power of Ethical Management* (New York: Ballantine Press, 1988). *See* the ASQ Code of Ethics at the front of this book.

European Organization (Agency) for Conformity Assessment (EOCA) Unit organized within the European Community to provide oversight of conformity assessment for products produced and or imported in the European Community.

European Union (EU) Group of European nations who collectively have banded together to promote economic, political, and social cooperation.

Evaporating cloud Concept described by Eliyahu Goldratt, in conflict resolution, as an identified potential conflict that disappears as the project progresses. See *The Goal*, 2nd ed. (Great Barrington, MA: North River Press, 1992).

Event Starting or ending point for a task or group of tasks. An occurrence of some attribute.

Event-on-node Network diagramming technique in which events are represented by boxes (nodes) connected by arrows to show the sequence in which events are to occur. Uses the program evaluation and review technique (**PERT**).

Evidence Information, material, or observations based on verifiable facts to support a finding.

Evolutionary Operations (EVOP) Developed by G. E. P. Box, this technique adjusts variables in a process in small increments, in a planned pattern of changes, in the search for a more optimum point on the response scale. Although this approach may be slower than a DOE, the changes are small enough to prevent nonconformances, but large enough to establish changes. This process is accomplished in a production environment.

Examination   Element of inspection consisting of investigation of supplies and services to determine conformance to specified requirements without using special equipment or procedures.

Exception reporting   Process of documenting those situations in which significant variances from specifications or from expected results have occurred.

Excited quality   Additional benefit a customer receives when a product or service goes beyond basic expectations. Excited quality wows the customer and distinguishes the provider from the competition. If missing, the customer will still be satisfied.

Exciter   *See* **delighter.**

Executive responsibility   Responsibility vested in those personnel who are responsible for the whole organization's performance. Often referred to as "top management."

Expectancy theory   Motivational theory that says what people do is based on what they expect to gain from the activity.

Expectations   Customer perceptions about how an organization's products and services will meet their specific needs and requirements.

Expected quality   Also known as "basic quality." The minimum benefit a customer expects to receive from a product or service.

Experiment   Process undertaken, usually empirically, to determine something that is not already known.

Experimental design   Formal plan that details the specifics for conducting an experiment, such as which responses, factors, levels, blocks, treatments, and tools are to be used.

Experimental error   Variations in the experimental response under identical test conditions. Also called "residual error

Expert   Someone who has the training skills and knowledge in a specific field, who is generally recognized as being able to understand and operate skillfully in that field.

Explicit knowledge	Represented by the captured and recorded tools of the day, for example, procedures, processes, standards, and other like documents.
Exponent	Symbol used in an algebraic equation to show how many times the number is to be multiplied by itself. For example, $10^3 = 10 \times 10 \times 10$.
Exponential cause	Characteristics of products that are likely to exhibit a random failure rate.
Exponential distribution	Continuous distribution where data are more likely to occur below the average than above it. Typically used to describe the break-in portion of equipment. *See also* **bathtub curve.** *See* Appendix C.
Exponentially weighted moving average chart (EWMA)	This chart uses the moving average value of a set number of recent plots adding the latest and dropping one previous plot. This gives the most weight to the most recent observations. This detects small shifts in the process and highlights trends in data from processes that take a long time to produce.
Express warranty	Promise actually written or spoken in an agreement or contract.
Extension line	On blueprints, light solid lines used to extend a feature or surface from the view so it can be dimensioned. *See* Appendix E.
External audit	Audit performed by anyone outside the organization being audited. *See also* **second-party audit** or **third-party audit.**
External customer	Person or organization that receives a product, service, or information but is not part of the organization supplying it. See also **internal customer.**
External failure	Nonconformance found during or after delivery of the product or service by the external customers.
External failure cost	*See* **external quality cost.**
External quality cost	Cost involved after production, such as warranty, repairs, customer ill will, lost sales, returned goods, recalls, and penalties.
External risks	Risks beyond the control or influence of the company or organizational unit.

Extrapolate   Usually used in the context of using statistics to obtain an estimate or to infer a value beyond the known range. An educated guess based on known values or past practice.

Extrinsic   From outside the organization, an extrinsic audit would be conducted by an external party (auditor).

F

Face   (1) A surface at right angles to the centerline of rotation, on any of the plane surfaces that bound a geometric solid. (2) In machining, to remove material from an unfinished surface to provide a flat surface, so additional work may be continued.

Facilitating management style   Management approach in which top management makes themselves available to answer questions and to provide guidance when needed but does not interfere with day-to-day activities.

Facilitator   Specifically trained person who functions as a teacher, coach, and moderator for a group, team, or organization. Initially a facilitator provides guidance and direction while the team concentrates on the problem or task at hand.

Facilitator roles   Focuses on progress, monitors change within group, coaches the group, shows by example, asks questions, provides direction, helps with content of meetings, and provides feedback.

Factor   Variables that are changed to different levels within a factorial designed experiment or response surface experiment. A variable that may affect the responses (test results) and of which different versions (levels) are included in the experiment.

Factor analysis   Statistical technique that examines the relationships between a single dependent variable and multiple independent variables. For example, it is used to determine which questions on a questionnaire are related to a specific question such as "Would you buy this product again?"

Factorial experiment   In a designed experiment, where all possible treatment combinations are formed from two or more factors, each being studied at two or more versions (levels) are run.

**Factor of
ten rule**   Estimated multiplier used to project cost associated with potential failures
as a product advances through production to the end user. For instance, a
1 cent part at design may increase in cost to $10 at final inspection, and it
can cause $100 in expense for the customer.

Failure   The inability, because of defect(s), of an item, product, or service to perform its required functions as needed.

Failure analysis   Process of breaking down a failure to determine what caused the failure
and to put measures in place to prevent any future problems.

Failure cost   Cost resulting from products or services not conforming to requirements
or customer/user needs. Failure cost can be further divided into **internal
failure cost** (those that occur prior to delivery or shipment of a product
or service to the customer) and **external failure cost** (cost that occurs
after delivery or shipment of the product or service to the customer).
Examples of internal failure cost could include scrap, rework, reinspection, retesting, material review, downgrading material, the cost associated
with maintaining rework departments, and so on. Examples of external
failure cost could include the cost of processing customer complaints, customer returns, warranty claims, product recalls, service calls, rework at a
customer's site, and so on. See also individual entries.

**Failure
mechanism**   The physical, chemical, or mechanical process that caused the failure or
defect to occur.

Failure mode   The type of defect contributing to a failure. Examples are an open or short
circuit condition, a gain change, leakage, fracture, and so on.

**Failure mode
analysis
(FMA)**   Procedure to determine which malfunction symptoms appear immediately
before or after a failure of a critical parameter in a system. After all the possible causes are listed for each symptom, the product is designed to eliminate the problems.

**Failure mode
and effects
analysis
(FMEA)**   Procedure in which each potential failure mode in every subitem of an
item is analyzed to determine its effect on other subitems and on the
required function of the item. May be further divided into process failure
modes and effects analysis (PFMEA) and design failure modes and effects
analysis (DFMEA).

Failure mode effects and criticality analysis (FMECA)	Procedure performed after a failure mode effects analysis to classify each potential failure effect according to its severity and probability of occurrence.
Failure rate	Average number of failures per unit of time. Used for assessing reliability of a product or service.
Fast-tracking	Compressing a project schedule by overlapping activities that would normally be performed in sequence, such as design and assembly. May be confused with concurrent engineering.
Faraday shield	Mesh network of conductors enclosing a component that is tied to a grounding system to provide for electrostatic shielding.
Fatigue failure	Breaking failure of a metal or rigid part due to stress, or flexing and spreading that starts in a weak point and spreads to a point of failure.
Fault	Accidental condition that causes a functional unit to fail to perform its required function.
Fault tree analysis (FTA)	Technique for evaluating the possible causes that might lead to the failure of a product. For each possible failure, the possible causes are determined, then the situations leading to the failure are determined, and so forth, until all possible causes have been determined. The result is a flow chart for the failure process. Plans are then made to deal with each cause.
F distribution	Distribution of "F"=, the ratios of variances for pairs of samples. Used to determine whether the populations from which two samples were taken have the same standard deviation. The "F" distribution is usually expressed as a table of the upper limit below which "F" can be expected to lie with some confidence level for samples of a specified number of degrees of freedom.
Feasibility	Assessment of the capability for successful implementation; the possibility, probability, and suitability of accomplishment.
Feasibility study	Examination of technical and cost data to determine the economic potential and practicality of a project or application of equipment. It involves

the use of techniques such as the time value of money so competing projects may be evaluated and compared on an equal basis.

Feature   (1) Definable portion or section of a workpiece. A product characteristic such as a radius, dimension, hardness, and so on, or a process characteristic such as torque, melting temperature, and so on. (2) Definable portion or application of a service. A service characteristic such as greeting at a customer interface, prompt refund on defective products, explanations of reports, and so on.

Feature control frame   On engineering blueprints, a feature control frame identifies, from left to right, the geometric characteristic, the geometric tolerance zone, and the datum reference. These are listed in a rectangular box. Provides a consistent format, which makes interpretation easier. *See* Appendix E.

Federal Supply Code for Manufacturers (FSCM)   Five-digit number assigned to drawings drafted for the federal government.

Feedback   Process in which the factors that produce a result are themselves modified, corrected, strengthened, and so on, by that result. The return of information in interpersonal communication; it may be based on fact or feeling and helps the party who is receiving the information judge how well he or she is being understood by the other party. More generally, information about a process that is used to make decisions about its performance and to adjust the process when necessary.

Feedback from customer   Communication from customers about how delivered products or services compare with customer expectations. Internal communications that indicate how a process is performing.

Feedback loops   Pertains to open-loop and closed-loop information feedback systems.

Feel   In measurements, the perception of distortion that results from physical contact between a measuring instrument and the part or standard being measured, such as using a micrometer on a workpiece.

Femto   One-quadrillionth. Expressed as 10 to the minus 15th power.

FIFO In inventory management, a term meaning "first in first out." Where inventory is rotated so the inventory placed in stock first is used first. An example is at the grocery store where milk is placed on the shelf by date so the oldest date is at the front of the shelf and first available to the customer and the newer stock is at the back.

Fillet In casting or machining, an internal radius.

Filtering Relative to human communication, those perceptions (based on culture, language, demographics, experience, etc.) that affect how the sender transmits a message and how the receiver interprets a message. Anything that helps clarify the message.

Fin In metalworking or casting, thin blades of metal cut or squeezed out between dies or molds.

Final inspection/ testing Last inspection or test carried out by the supplier before ownership passes to the customer.

Financial statement Written record listing the financial status of an individual or an organization, showing its assets and liabilities.

Financing Raising of funds required for a project.

Finding Conclusion of importance based on observation(s) usually in an audit.

Fingernail test Method used to compare a surface finish to a known roughness standard. A comparison is made by rubbing the fingernail over the surface and comparing that to the standard.

Finite element analysis (FEA) Mathematical model used to compare a complex structure to varying loads to examine the displacement of the various components. The results are used to predict the capability of the structure.

Fire fighting Expression used to describe the process of performing emergency fixes to problems.

FIRO-B awareness scale Personality test used to determine how people fit into a group according to three dimensions: inclusion, control, and affection.

First-angle projection System of orthographic projection commonly used on blueprints in Europe and Asia.

First article testing/ inspection Evaluation of the first items produced before or in the initial stages of production to see whether they conform to specifications.

First-party audit Audits of a company or parts thereof by personnel employed by the company. These audits are also called "internal audits."

First time yield (FTY) Amount of product produced through a system that is fully acceptable to the customer, without any rework or additional unscheduled steps. Also called "rolled throughput yield."

Fishbone diagram *See* **cause-and-effect diagram or analysis.**

Fit In machining or assembly, the degree of tightness (or looseness) between mating parts. Fit may be classified three ways, as "clearance," "interference," or "transition."

Fitness for use Term used to indicate that a product or service fits the customer's defined purpose for that product or service.

Five M's Commonly used in a cause-and-effect diagram, it includes the original four M's of man, material, machine, method, but also has a fifth: mother nature. (Other examples would include or substitute measure or measurement for one of the original terms.)

Five S's Five terms beginning with S utilized to create a workplace suited for visual control and lean production. *Seiri* means to separate needed tools, parts, and instructions from unneeded materials and to remove the latter. *Seiton* means to neatly arrange and identify parts and tools for ease of use. *Seiso* means to conduct a cleanup campaign. *Seiketsu* means to conduct *seiri, seiton,* and *seiso* at frequent, indeed daily, intervals to maintain a workplace in perfect condition. *Shitsuke* means to form the habit of always following the first four S's.

Five whys Technique for discovering the root causes of a problem and showing the relationship of causes by repeatedly asking the question, "Why?"

Five W's and H   In problem solving, who, what, when, where, why and how. The how can be either how did this happen or how can we fix it?

Fixed assets   Property or equipment, such as machines, buildings, and land, used by the organization.

Fixed-effects model   Factorial experiment where the levels of the factors are specifically chosen by the experimenter (as opposed to a random effects model).

Fixture   Device for holding a workpiece.

Flammable   Any material that can ignite easily and will burn rapidly.

Flange   In casting or machining, a rim or rib used for strength, for guiding, or for attachment to another object.

Flask   In casting, a box made of two or more parts for holding sand in a mold.

Flatness   Degree to which the reference plane corresponds to the theoretically perfect plane. See Appendix E.

Flat organization   Horizontal organizations are known as "flat," meaning they have a minimum number of layers in the management structure. Also known as "wide" organizations.

Flaw   In machining, flaws are unintentional irregularities that occur at one place or at relative infrequent or widely varying intervals on surfaces. Flaws may include such defects as cracks, blowholes, checks, ridges, scratches, and so on. Where flaws should be controlled or restricted, a special note should be included on the engineering blueprint.

Float   In project planning, the amount of time an activity may be delayed from its early start without delaying the project and completion date. Also referred to as "slack time."

Floating task   In project management, a task that can be performed either earlier or later in the schedule of events, without affecting the overall project time frame, or critical path.

Flowchart   Graphical representation of the steps in a process. Flowcharts are drawn to better understand processes. The flowchart is one of the **seven tools of quality.**

F

Flow diagram   Graphic representation of work flow and the sequence of the work elements without regard to a time scale. Used to show the logic associated with a process rather than duration for the work completed.

Flowmeter   Gage indicating the velocity of a liquid through a process.

Fluorescent dye penetrant test   Test used to locate flaws, cracks, pores, and other surface defects in materials. The part is sprayed with the dye and allowed to dry, and the part is cleaned and subjected to a fluorescent lamp to show if any surface flaws are present. A nondestructive test.

Flute   Groove on twist drills and taps that allows for the removal of displaced material.

Focus group   Group, usually of 8 to 10 persons, that is invited to discuss an existing or planned product, services, or process.

Fog index   Method developed to measure the readability of a written work (in the English language) based on a combination of two criteria: (1) the average number of words per sentence and (2) the percentage of words containing three or more syllables.

Follow-up audit   Audit whose purpose and scope are limited to verifying that corrective action taken as a result of a previous audit finding has been accomplished and is effective.

Food and Drug Administration (FDA)   A U.S. government agency that administers quality guidelines such as CGMP (current good manufacturing practice) and GMP (good manufacturing practice) for food and drug suppliers, manufacturers, and providers.

Food chain   Sequence of organisms, each of which uses the next, lower member of the sequence as a food source.

Foolproofing   *See* **error proofing** and **poka-yoke.**

Force field analysis   Technique for analyzing the forces that aid or hinder an organization in reaching an objective. An arrow pointing to an objective is drawn down the middle of a piece of paper. The factors that will aid the objective's achievement, called the driving forces, are listed on the left side of the arrow. The factors that will hinder its achievement, called the restraining forces, are listed on the right side of the arrow.

Forecast Estimate or prediction of future conditions and events based on information and knowledge available at the time of the estimate.

Forge Heating, then hammering or pressing metals into a desired shape.

Formal authority Influence that is based on an individual's position in the organization and granted to that person by the organization. May also be known as "legitimate authority."

Formal communication Officially sanctioned data within an organization that includes publications, memoranda, training materials, recorded events, public relations information, and company meetings.

Form tolerances In engineering blueprints, form tolerances are used to control the geometric shape of a part feature when conventional size tolerances alone are not sufficient. They place tighter limits on the amount of variation allowed. Form tolerances are not referenced to a datum. Instead they specify how much the part feature is allowed to vary from the perfect geometric shape implied by the blueprint. Form characteristics would include flatness, straightness, circularity, and cylindricy. *See* Appendix E.

Fourteen Points W. Edwards Deming's 14 management practices to help companies increase their quality and productivity: (1) create constancy of purpose for improving products and services, (2) adopt the new philosophy, (3) cease dependence on inspection to achieve quality, (4) end the practice of awarding business on price alone; instead, minimize total cost by working with a single supplier, (5) improve constantly and forever every process for planning, production, and service, (6) institute training on the job, (7) adopt and institute leadership, (8) drive out fear, (9) break down barriers between staff areas, (10) eliminate slogans, exhortations, and targets for the workforce, (11) eliminate numerical quotas for the workforce and numerical goals for management, (12) remove barriers that rob people of pride of workmanship, and eliminate the annual rating or merit system, (13) institute a vigorous program of education and self-improvement for everyone, and (14) put everybody in the company to work to accomplish the transformation.

Fractional factorial experiment Designed experiment strategy that assesses several factors/variables simultaneously in one test, where only a partial set of all possible combinations of factor levels are tested to more efficiently identify important factors. This type of test is more efficient than a traditional one-at-a-time testing strategy.

Fraction defective chart (p chart)	Attribute control chart used to track the proportion of defective units.
Freak distribution	Set of substandard products that are produced by random occurrences in a manufacturing process.
Free float	Amount of time that an activity may be delayed without delaying any of the immediately succeeding activities. Also called "secondary float." *See also* **float.**
Freedom (degrees of)	There are many possible degrees of freedom. However there are three traditional that are transitional and involve movement in the X, Y, and Z axes. The other three are rotational about these axes. If movement in any of these is prevented, it is said to be constrained.
Free on board (FOB)	Pricing scheme in which the seller agrees to pay for the shipment of goods to a specific point and no farther. Or terms of sale that identify where title passes to the buyer.
Frequency diagram	*See* **histogram.**
Frequency distribution	Set of all the various values that individual observations may have and the frequency of their occurrence in the sample population.
Frequency distribution (statistical)	Table that graphically presents a large volume of data so the central tendency (such as the average or mean) and distribution are clearly displayed. *See* Appendix C.
Fretting corrosion	Any of a type of damage caused by the movement by parts not properly lubricated. The wearing out of such parts by motion, vibration, expansion/contraction, and so on.
Friable	Capable of being crumbled, pulverized, or reduced to powder with relative ease.
Friable asbestos	Any material containing more than 1% asbestos and that can be easily reduced to powder. May contain nonfriable asbestos if any mechanical force can damage it.
F test	Test whether two samples are drawn from populations with the same standard deviation, with some specified confidence level. The test is per-

F

formed by determining whether "F," as defined here, falls below the upper limit, as given by an "F" distribution table.

Full cycle corrective action (FCCA) Management process that provides for the evaluation of the causes of a defect and puts into place corrective actions and then provides for follow-up to see if the corrective action was effective. This process leads to continual improvements.

Full factorial experiment Factorial experiment where all combinations of factor levels are tested.

Full indicator movement (FIM) On a dial indicator, the swing of the needle between its lowest and its highest reading. Also known as total indicator reading (TIR) or runout. *See* Appendix E.

Full section On blueprints, the sectional view that results when the cutting plane passes straight through the part.

Function Group of related actions contributing to a larger action.

Functional department Specialized department in a company that performs a particular function, such as engineering, manufacturing, human resources, or marketing.

Functional organization Organization organized by discrete functions, for example, marketing and sales, engineering, production, finance, or human resources.

Functional requirements Characteristics of the product or service described in ordinary terms that are understandable to both the supplier and the customer.

Function-quality integration Process of ensuring that quality plans and programs are integrated, consistent, necessary, and sufficient, across all departments, to achieve defined product quality.

Function test Test performed to validate product features operate as designed and as expected by the customer.

Funnel experiment Experiment that demonstrates the effects of tampering. Marbles are dropped through a funnel in an attempt to hit a flat surfaced target below. The experiment shows that adjusting a stable process to compensate for an undesirable result will produce an output that is worse than if the process had been left alone.

Future reality tree   Technique used in the application of Eliyahu Goldratt's theory of constraints used to show what to change and to identify any new unfavorable aspects to be addressed before implementing the change. *See also* **Eliyahu Goldratt** and **constraints.** See also *The Goal,* 2nd ed. (Great Barrington, MA: North River Press, 1992).

Fuzzy boundary   Concept of areas of control that are not well defined. This comes into play with joint ventures, partnerships, and so on, where all the details of the process have not been identified and documented.

Gage   Any device used to obtain measurements.

Gage accuracy   Difference between the observed average of measurements and the true average of the same parts using precision instruments (a gage).

Gage blocks   Standards of precise dimensions, used in combination to form usable length combinations. They are traceable to the national standards in the country of use.

Gage calibration   *See* **calibration.**

Gage linearity   Accuracy of the gage expressed throughout its entire operating range.

Gage repeatability & reproducibility (gage R & R)   Evaluation of a measuring instrument's accuracy by determining whether the measurements taken with it are repeatable (there is close agreement among a number of consecutive measurements of the output for the same value of the input under the same operating conditions) and reproducible (there is close agreement among repeated measurements of the output for the same value of input made under the same operating conditions over a period of time).

Gage stability   Difference between the average of a minimum of two sets of measurements taken with one gage on the same parts as measurements are taken over a long period of time.

Gain sharing   Reward system that shares the monetary results of productivity gains among owners and employees. Typically handled through such mechanisms as suggestion programs, profit sharing, or employee stock ownership plans.

Galling Failure mode in bearing surfaces that have overheated and caused material from adjacent nonbearing surfaces to fuse onto the part of the surface of the bearing that does not support the load. Also called "adhesive wear."

Gang answering Usually used in the context of a survey or questionnaire, where the person completing the form will circle a whole series of similar answers or responses, in order to rapidly complete the form.

Gantt chart Type of bar chart introduced by Henry Gantt, used in process planning and control to display planned work and finished work in relation to time. Shows "milestones" and timelines in the project completion process. Also known as a "milestone chart." See also *Industrial Engineering Handbook,* 3rd ed. (New York: McGraw-Hill, 1971).

Gap analysis Comparison of a current condition to the desired state.

Gasket Thin piece of material put between mating parts generally to form a seal.

Gate In casting, an opening in a sand mold through which the molten metal enters the mold. The excess material left on the part as a result of removing the part from the mold.

Gatekeeper Often a person who because of job function comes in contact with many people and will often be at the crossroads of a great deal of information.

Gauge Mostly obsolete spelling of "gage" in the United States. *Gage* is the spelling in common usage in U.S. industry and by gage makers in their sales catalogs. *Gauge* is still used when referring to sheet metal thickness, wire size, and shotgun bore size.

Gauge repeatability and reproducibility (GR&R) *See* **gage repeatability and reproducibility.**

General linear modeling (GLM) Statistical procedure for univariate analysis of variance with balanced/ unbalanced designs, analysis of covariance, and regression.

General requirements Nontechnical specifications that define the product or service, procedures, methods, and final acceptance requirements of the product or service.

Geographic organization

This type of organization is based on its location and designed to provide rapid support of its customer needs by being in close proximity to the customer base.

Geometric characteristic

Characteristic that affects the fit and function of mating part features, such as straightness, perpendicularly, concentricity, and so on.

Geometric dimensioning and tolerancing (GD&T)

Method to minimize production costs by showing the dimensioning and tolerancing on a drawing while considering the functions or relationships of part features. *See* Appendix E.

Geometric tolerance

Amount by which a part feature may vary from the theoretically perfect geometric characteristic represented on a part print. *See* Appendix E.

George M. Low Trophy

Trophy presented by NASA to those NASA aerospace industry contractors, subcontractors, and suppliers who consistently maintain and improve the quality of their products and services. The award, formerly called the NASA Excellence Award for Quality and Productivity, is given in two categories, small business and large business. George M. Low was the NASA administrator for nearly three decades.

GIGO

In computer terminology, "garbage in garbage out," meaning you cannot get good information from bad data.

Goal

Broad statement describing a desired future condition or achievement without being specific about how much and when. Goals should be acceptable, precise, attainable, and congruent (not in conflict with other organizational values).

Gold plating

Providing more than the customer specifies or reasonably expects, and thus spending more time and resources than is necessary to achieve quality and/or customer satisfaction.

Gon

Equivalent of "grad," it is *pi* divided by 200 radians. Or is equal to 337.747 minutes, or 206,264.8 seconds. Or 63.662 grads. *See also* **grad, radian,** and **degree.**

Go/no-go

State or attribute of a unit or product. Two parameters are possible: go (conforms to specifications) and no-go (does not conform to specifications).

Good laboratory practices (GLP) or 21 CFR, part 58   The 144 requirements that control the procedures and operations of toxicology laboratories.

Goodness-of-fit   Any measure of how well a set of data matches a proposed distribution. Chi-square is the most common measure for goodness-of-fit; a histogram may also be used but is less quantitative.

Good manufacturing practices (GMP) or 21 CFR, parts 808, 812, and 820   Requirements governing the quality procedures of medical device manufacturers. GMP can be applied to most products regulated by the government.

Gozinto chart   Representation of a product to show how the various elements required to build the product fit together.

Grad   In circular measurement, particularly for land surveying, the full circle is divided into 400 parts called grads, so 100 grads = 90°. This system has been further divided into 6400 parts called "mils." One mil is the distance extended out to 1000 units. For example, 1 mil is 1 yard displacement at 1000 yards. This has been compromised slightly to 6283 parts of a circle. This then makes 1000 mils equal to 1 "radian." *See* **radian, mil,** and **degree.**

Grade   An indicator of category or rank related to features or characteristics that cover different sets of needs for products or services intended for the same functional use. Grade reflects a planned difference in requirements or, if not planned, a recognized difference. The emphasis is on functional use and cost relationship.

Graduations   Small incremental divisions on a scale or face of a dial.

Grand average   Overall average of data represented on an X-bar chart as (X double bar) at the time the control limits were calculated. Also called "X Bar-Bar." *See also* **centerline (CL).**

Grapevine   Informal communication channels over which information flows within an organization, usually without a known origin of the information and without any confirmation of its accuracy or completeness (sometimes referred to as the "rumor mill").

Graph   Display or diagram that shows the relationship between activities or events; a pictorial representation of relative variables. Examples include trend graphs, histograms, control charts, frequency distributions, and scatter diagrams.

Graphical evaluation and review technique (GERT)   Network analysis technique that allows for conditional and probabilistic treatment of logical relationships (for example, some activities may not be performed).

Green Belt (GB)   Person who has been trained on the improvement methodology of Six Sigma and will lead a process improvement or quality improvement team as part of his or her full-time job. Many times a business team leader responsible for managing projects and implementing improvement in his or her organization.

Group dynamic   Interaction (behavior) of individuals within a team.

Group problems   Peter Scholtes in *The Team Handbook* defined 10 common problems that occur with groups: (1) floundering, (2) overbearing participants, (3) dominating participants, (4) reluctant participants, (5) unquestioned acceptance of opinions as facts, (6) rush to accomplishment, (7) attribution, (8) discounts and "plops," (9) wanderlust, digression, and tangents, and (10) feuding members. See also *The Team Handbook* (Madison: Oriel, Inc., 2003).

Group process   *See* **team process.**

Groupthink   Situation in which critical information is withheld from the team because individual members censor or restrain themselves, either because they believe their concerns are not worth discussing or because they are afraid of confrontation. See also *The Team Handbook* (Madison: Oriel, Inc., 2003).

Guide   (1) Person assigned during an audit to escort an auditor during an audit. (2) Instructions that provide for general good practices but are not mandatory for compliance.

Guideline   Generally a suggested practice, whose use and application is discretionary, even in the context of complying with a standard.

H

Habitat Places where a population (such as humans, animal, plants, or other microorganisms) lives, and the surrounding areas.

Half-normal probability plot Normal probability plot where the absolute data measurements are plotted.

Half section view On blueprints, a sectional view that results when the cutting plane passes halfway through the part. Half the view is in section and the other half is left as drawn.

Halo effect In customer satisfaction surveys, the tendency to place general comments or categories that will receive favorable comments early in the survey. These then tend to lead the person being surveyed to provide favorable comments on the more specific questions of performance evaluation.

Harden Heating metal to a specified temperature and then quenching (rapidly cooling) it in water or oil to provide greater strength to the metal.

Hardness In metals, hardness in defined as the resistance to penetration. This property can be affected by heat-treating the metals.

Hardness test Nondestructive test to estimate the tensile strength of metals. The most common of these are the Brinell test, the Rockwell test, the Vickers test, and the Knoop test.

Hat (^) Symbol used to show "best guess" above a parameter. The hat symbol is usually placed above the 6 on most keyboards (^).

Hawthorne effect Concept that every change in workplace surroundings results (initially, at least) in increased productivity. Shows the importance of human factors in motivating employees.

Hawthorne studies	Conducted by Elton Mayo at the Western Electric Company in Chicago in 1924 to study the effect of employee fatigue on their efficiencies, by varying working conditions.
Hazard analysis	Process of risk evaluation that involves gathering and evaluating data on the types of health and safety risk that may be produced or have the potential for causing injuries or diseases, within a operating or proposed system.
Hazard analysis and critical control point (HACCP)	Quality management system for effectively and efficiently ensuring farm to table food safety in the United States. HACCP regulations for various sectors are established by the U.S. Department of Agriculture and the Food and Drug Administration.
Hazardous substance	Any material that poses a threat to human health and/or safety and the environment. Typical hazardous substances are toxic, corrosive, ignitable, explosive, or chemically reactive.
Hazard paper	Specialized graph paper that yields information about populations similar to that of probability paper.
Hazard rate	Rate at which a device will fail between specified times, after it has survived usage. At a given point in time, the hazard rate and the instantaneous failure rate are equal.
Hearsay evidence	Oral statements concerning a situation that has not been observed directly or verified.
Heat sink	(1) In metrology or parts measurement, a body with rapid heat transfer on which workpieces can be placed to arrive at the same temperature before measurement. This process is also known as "normalizing." (2) A body with rapid heat transfer built into equipment to dissipate heat and provide cooling for components within an assembly.
Heat-treating	Changing the properties of metals by heating, then cooling them.
Heavy metals	Metallic elements with high atomic weights, such as mercury, chromium, cadmium, arsenic, and lead. These can damage the living things at low concentrations and tend to accumulate in the food chain.

H

Heijunka Act of leveling the variety or volume of items produced at a process over a period of time. Used to avoid excessive batching of product types, volume fluctuations, and excess inventory.

Heuristic Problem-solving technique that results in an acceptable solution; often arrived at through trial and error.

Hexadecimal Numbering system in which the base used is 16. In that 1 = 16 and 10 would = 160.

Hidden agenda Personal goal or expectation affecting a member's behavior unknown to others within a group. This may be as simple as a strong desire for visibility or recognition.

Hidden factory Rework and wasted efforts within an organization that has no value and are often not considered within the metrics of a factory. Usually considered the cost of doing business without considering ways to reduce or eliminate them. A cost of quality reference for chronic waste.

Hidden line On blueprints, hidden lines are shown as short dashed lines that are used to show surfaces and features that exist but cannot be seen in that particular view. *See* Appendix E.

Hierarchical management Traditional functional or line management in which areas and departments are created and staffed with people with various levels of expertise, who report to a boss, who reports to a boss, and so on, until you eventually have one person in charge of the organization.

Hierarchy structure Describes an organization that is organized around functional departments, product lines, or around customers. Customers may be segmented and the organization is characterized by top-down management (also referred to as a "bureaucratic model" or "pyramid structure"). Traditional functional or line management.

High-low technique Used in problem-solving sessions, the team members are given a preset number of votes/dots. These are used to prioritize a list of options as important or less important.

Highly accelerated life test (HALT) Process developed to uncover design defects and weaknesses in electronic and mechanical assemblies using a vibration system combined with rapid high and low temperature changes. The purpose of HALT is to optimize product reliability by identifying the functional and destructive limits of a product. HALT addresses reliability issues at an early stage in product development.

Highly accelerated stress audits (HASA) Technique in which a sample of parts (as opposed to 100% of the production as in HASS, below) is taken and subjected to stresses similar to the levels and duration for HALT. In monitoring the production process, the intent of HASA is to detect slight shifts in the attributes of the product so corrective actions can be taken and implemented before the performance of outgoing product approaches the specifications.

Highly accelerated stress screening (HASS) Technique for production screening that rapidly exposes process or production flaws in products. Its purpose is to expose a product to optimized production screens without affecting product reliability. Unlike HALT, HASS uses nondestructive stresses of extreme temperatures and temperature change rates with vibration.

High-performance work Defined by the MBNQA criteria as work approaches that are systematically directed toward achieving ever higher levels of overall performance, including quality and productivity.

Hi-Pot Electrical test of short duration to determine the highest potential voltage that can be applied to an electrical component without causing a dielectric breakdown of the component's insulation.

Hiring steps/ procedure Usually defined as (1) justify the need to add employees, (2) define job description duties, (3) gain approval to hire, (4) interview applicants, and (5) select applicant.

Histogram Graphic summary of variation in a set of data. The pictorial nature of the histogram lets people see patterns that are difficult to detect in a simple table of numbers. The histogram is one of the **seven tools of quality.** May also at times be known as a "relative frequency diagram."

Historical organization Organizational types that have been in existence for most of humankind's existence. These would have an established chain of command; the military is an example.

Historic records Documents such as blueprints, project plans, quality procedures, inspection reports, and so on, that are outdated or obsolete but kept for legal or other reasons.

Hold point Point, defined in an appropriate document, beyond which an activity must not proceed without the approval of a designated individual or authority.

Holistic Oriented toward viewing the whole rather than considering each piece individually.

Homogeneous Poisson process (HPP) Model that considers the failure rate does not change with time.

Homogeneous preferences The preferences of customers with roughly the same needs and desires.

Horizontal Any line or plane at right angles to the vertical axis. For convenience, the x- and y-axis are said to be in the horizontal plane, and the z-axis is said to be in the vertical axis.

Horizontal organizational structure Describes an organization that is organized along a process or value-added chain, eliminating hierarchy and functional boundaries (also referred to as a "systems structure").

Hoshin planning Breakthrough planning (closed loop). A Japanese strategic planning process in which a company develops up to four vision statements that indicate where the company should be in the next five years. Company goals and work plans are developed based on the vision statements. Periodic audits are then conducted to monitor progress. Uses a wide variety of quality tools.

House of quality Product planning matrix, somewhat resembling a house that is developed during quality function deployment and shows the relationship of customer requirements to the means of achieving these requirements. Also called "quality function deployment."

Human relations theory Theory focusing on the importance of human factors in motivating employees. *See* **Hawthorne studies.**

Hydrology Science of dealing with the properties, distribution, and circulation of liquids, and the resulting influences and pressures.

Hygiene factors Term used by Frederick Herzberg to label "dissatisfiers": things in the working environment that make employees upset with their job. Hygiene

H

factors prevent dissatisfaction, whereas motivators create satisfaction. See also *The Motivation to Work,* 2nd ed. (New York: John Wiley & Sons, 1959).

Hypergeometric distribution   The hypergeometric distribution is the only discrete distribution where the lot or population size has a major impact. It is used when random sampling without replacement, with a quantity of defective units in the lot. *See* Appendix C.

Hypothesis testing   Consists of testing an unproved theory, it is used to test whether two outputs of a process are equal; a "null hypothesis," an alternative hypothesis, indicates there is a difference. In reality it is an assertion made about a population. Usually the assertion concerns the numerical value of some parameter of the population. For example, a hypothesis may state that the mean life of a projector lamp is 30 hours. This assertion may or may not be correct. A test of the hypothesis provides a test of the validity of the assertion. Careful evaluation of the sample results must be made for two reasons. First, the sampling process alone may induce errors, by not being completely random. Second, the values obtained from the samples may be compatible with other parameters. These two types of errors are recognized as a type I error or type II error. Type I error is to reject the hypothesis when it is true (alpha error). The second, or type II error, is to accept the hypothesis when it is false (beta error). *See* **alpha** or **beta risk.**

I

Identification   Act of segregating an entity, by giving it a set of characteristics by which it is recognized as a member of a group, department, or organization.

Idle time   In project management or time studies, the time interval during which the operator, equipment, or both do not perform useful work.

Imagineering   Creative process used to develop in the mind's eye a process without waste.

Impact   Estimate of the effect that a risk will have on a schedule, cost, quality, safety, performance, or the environment.

Impact strength   (1) Ability to withstand shock or loading. (2) Ability of a material to absorb impact energy without fracturing. (3) Minimum work energy required to fracture a test specimen in a specified manner under shock loading.

Imperfection   Quality characteristic's departure from its intended level or state without any association to conformance to specification requirements or to the usability of a product or service. *See* **blemish, defect,** and **nonconformity.**

Implement   To carry out a directive, to establish a plan so it is fully functional.

Implementation audit   Audit carried out to establish whether actual practices conform to the documented Quality/EMS system. *See* **conformance audit** or **compliance audit.**

Implementation phase   In project planning and management, the third phase in which the project is executed, monitored, and controlled. Also called "execution phase" or "operation phase."

Implied warranty Promise that is implicitly included in a transaction regardless of whether it is expressly written or not. For example, an implied warranty or merchantability states that a product must reasonably operate or comply with the ordinary purposes for which it is intended or used.

Improvement Positive effect of a process change effort. To make a product or situation better in the sense of usefulness or effectiveness.

Impulse strength Minimum voltage at which insulation breakdown occurs under microsecond surges.

Impulse test Short duration dielectric insulation test, in which the voltage applied to a unit under test is in an impulse voltage of a specified wave pattern.

Inch-pound system Conventional measurement system used in the United States. It is based on the foot, pound, second, degree Fahrenheit, ampere, and candela.

Incidental characteristic Any element that may add value to a product or service but is not required by the customer.

Incineration Treatment technology involving destruction of waste by controlled burning at high temperatures (e.g., burning sludge to remove the water and reduce the remaining residues to a state that can be disposed of safely).

In control Description of a process where variation is consistent over time and only normal variation (common cause variation) exist.

In-control process Process in which the statistical measure being evaluated is in a state of statistical control; in other words, the variations among the observed sampling results can be attributed to a constant system of chance causes. *See also* **out-of-control process.**

Incremental dimensioning In certain N/C machine tools, the incremental dimensioning system is used. With this method, the distance between points on a given part is given without reference to a fixed point. Programmed dimensions for each tool movement are measured from the position of the tool at the starting point of each move.

Incremental improvement Improvements implemented on a continual basis.

Indemnification Act of reimbursing a person for a loss already sustained. Two general types exist: common law and contractual.

Independence	Freedom of outside influences, bias, or pressures to do something.
Independent evaluation report (IER)	System to report system effectiveness results objectively by allowing a independent third party, who has no vested interest in the outcome of a test, to judge whether the outcome is favorable or lacks the expected favorable results.
Independent failure	Failure not caused by the failure of any other item or function.
Independent samples	Samples chosen at random that are not related to each other.
Indexing	As used in quality procedures, the means of enabling information to be easily located.
Indicators	(1) Established measures used to determine how well an organization is meeting its customers' needs as well as other operational and financial performance expectations. (2) Mechanical or electronic measuring devices used to measure length; dial indicators are the chief types.
Indices	Plural of index. In the context of reporting it is the mixture of various data indicating a trend that is monitored. *See* **balanced scorecard.**
Indifference quality level (IQL)	Quality level is somewhere between the acceptable quality level (AQL) and the rejectable quality level (RQL) in acceptance sampling.
Indifference (zone of)	Process levels located between the "zone of acceptance" and the "zone of rejection." These processes can be considered as borderline, it is a matter of "indifference" whether these processes are accepted or rejected, based on the current sample information. It can be reduced by increasing the sample size, reducing the inherent variability, or increasing the risk of defects.
Indirect cost	Cost not directly related to the finished product. Cost allocated to a product as a cost of doing business, such as maintenance, utilities, office staff, and so on. Also called "overhead" or "burden."
Indirect customers	Persons or groups that do not receive the output of a process but are affected by it.

Indirect labor   Labor needed to run a company but not expended directly in the product, such as maintenance, setup, office staff, shipping and receiving, and so on. *See* **indirect cost.**

Individual development   Process that may include education and training but also includes many additional interventions and experiences to enable an individual to grow and mature both intellectually as well as emotionally.

Individual chart with moving range   Control chart used when working with one sample per subgroup. The individual samples are plotted on the X-bar chart rather than the subgroup averages. The individual chart is always accompanied by a moving range chart, usually using two subgroups to calculate the moving range points.

Inductive reasoning   Reasoning from particulars to the general premise.

Inert ingredient   In an environmental context, an inert ingredient would be components in pesticides such as solvents, carriers, dispersants, and surfactants that are not active against the targeted pest. Note that not all inert ingredients are harmless; many may induce harmful effects in and of themselves.

Infant mortality rate   In product testing this is characterized by high failure rates that show up in early use. These are commonly the results of poor design or poor quality construction.

Inflation   Factors in cost evaluation that are controlled by external factors over which the organization has no control. Such factors are the cost of living index, interest rates, and so on.

Informal communication   Unofficial communication that takes place in an organization as people talk freely and easily; examples include impromptu meetings and personal conversations.

Information   Data transferred into an ordered format that makes it usable and allows one to draw conclusions.

Information overload   Exposure to such a quantity, type, and complexity of information that a person cannot comprehend and grasp the extent of or use all the information.

Information system   Technology-based systems used to support operations, aid in day-to-day decision making, and support strategic analysis. Other names often used include management information system, decision system, information technology (IT), or data processing.

Infrastructure In ISO terms, includes the system of facilities, equipment, and services required for the operation of an organization.

In-house Work performed by a company's own employees as opposed to having an outside contractor do the work.

Initial functional specification First formal record of what a product is expected to do and how it will be used. Generally this document is not complete or firm enough to be fully implemented, but does contain enough detail and scope so the product can be evaluated. Such specifications often start with a product description and state how the product is to perform.

Inner array In a Taguchi-style fractional factorial experiment, the structured factors that can be controlled in a process as opposed to the factors that cannot be controlled (an outer array).

Innovation In the context of quality award criteria, refers to making a meaningful change to improve products, services, or processes and create new value for stakeholders. Innovation involves the adoption of an idea, process, technology, or product that is either new or new to its proposed application.

Inputs Products, services, material, and so on, obtained from suppliers or that crosses internal process boundaries and is used to produce outputs to be delivered to customers.

Inside diameter Cross-sectional inside measurement of a diameter, hole, cavity, and so on.

In situ Unmoved, remaining in its original place, not being displaced by human intervention.

Inspection A conformity evaluation by observation and judgment accompanied, as appropriate, by measurement, testing, or gauging.

Inspection authority Person or organization who has been given the right to perform or authorize inspections.

Inspection by attributes Inspection to determine the presence or absence of one or more characteristic. This is often with go/no-go gages.

Inspection by variables   Inspection to determine qualitative or measurable characteristics. This is often to determine size, weight, finish, time, and so on, to determine if the characteristic meets dimensional requirements.

Inspection cost   Cost associated with inspecting a product to ensure it meets the internal or external customer's needs and requirements; an appraisal cost.

Inspection, curtailed   Sampling inspection in which inspection of the sample is stopped as soon as a decision is certain. Thus, as soon as the rejection number for defectives is reached, the decision is certain and no further inspection is necessary. In single sampling, however, the whole sample is usually inspected in order to have an unbiased record of quality history. This same practice usually is followed for the first sample in double or multiple sampling.

Inspection level   Frequency and quantity of samples required to be examined from an established lot of production as stated by a sampling plan.

Inspection lot   Collection of similar units or a specific quantity of similar material offered for inspection and acceptance at one time.

Inspection, normal   Inspection in accordance with a sampling plan that is used under ordinary circumstances.

Inspection, 100%   Inspection of all the units in the lot or batch. In reality it is estimated to be only about 85% effective in removing all defects.

Inspection, rectifying   Removal or replacement of variant units during inspection of all the units, or some specified number, in a lot or batch that was not accepted by acceptance sampling.

Inspection, reduced   Inspection in accordance with a sampling plan requiring smaller sample sizes than those used in normal inspection. Reduced inspection is used in some inspection systems as an economy measure when the level of submitted quality is sufficiently good and other stated conditions apply. Note: The criteria for determining when quality is "sufficiently good" must be defined in objective terms for any given inspection system.

Inspection, tightened   Inspection in accordance with a sampling plan that has stricter acceptance criteria than those used in normal inspection. Tightened inspection is used in some inspection systems as a protective measure when the level of submitted quality is sufficiently poor. It is expected the higher rate of rejections will lead suppliers to improve the quality of submitted product.

Note: The criteria for determining when quality is "sufficiently poor" must be defined in objective terms for any given inspection system.

Instability A process is said to show instability if it exhibits variation greater than its normal control limits or shows a pattern of systematic variation.

Instant pudding Term initially coined by James Bakken of Ford Motor Co. and used to illustrate an obstacle to achieving quality or the supposition that quality and productivity improvement are achieved quickly through an affirmation of faith rather than through sufficient effort and education. W. Edwards Deming used this term in his book. See also *Out of the Crisis* (Boston: MIT, 1986).

Institute of Electrical and Electronic Engineers (IEEE) Not-for-profit worldwide organization whose vision (according to their website) is "To advance global prosperity by fostering technological innovation, enabling members' careers and promoting community world-wide."

Institute of Environmental Management and Assessment (IEMA) Not-for-profit organization established to promote best practice standards in environmental management, auditing, and assessment. It was formed with the merger of the Institute of Environmental Management, the Institute of Environmental Assessment, and the Environmental Auditors Registration Association in 1999.

Institute of Quality Assurance (IQA) Organization with headquarters in London whose purpose (according to their website) is "To work with industry and government to educate people generally about the importance of quality and to bring about the better regulation of the process of assessing quality standards."

Instructions Detailed written or spoken directions given in regard to what is to be done.

Integrated logistics support (ILS) Combination of all materials, services, and supplies required to support a system over its operational life. Major components may include maintenance planning, supplies, data, personnel, training, equipment, packaging, handling, storage, and transportation.

Integration In quality award criteria, the term *integration* refers to the harmonization of plans, processes, information, resource allocation, actions, results, analysis, and learning required to support the organizationwide goals.

Integrity (1) Absolute truthfulness and honesty. (2) Preservation of data or programs for their intended purpose. (3) The certainty of accurate test conduct, analysis, and representation of test results, within stated bounds of confidence.

Intellectual property Concepts, ideas, thought, or process, including computer programs, that are definable, measurable, and proprietary in nature.

Intensity function Function used to describe a failure rate as a function of time.

Interaction In a designed experiment, a term that describes the measure of differential comparison for the responses for each version (level) of a factor at each of the several versions (levels) of one or more factors.

Interactive multimedia Term encompassing technology that allows the presentation of facts and images with interaction by the viewer (e.g., taking a simulated CQMgr exam on a computer), training embedded in transaction processing.

Interchangeable Parts made to dimensions so they will fit and function when interchanged among the same upper-level part number assemblies.

Inter-changeability Ability of a part or system component to be used in place of another, without modifications, to fulfill the same requirements.

Inter-dependence Shared dependence between two or more items.

Interested party Individual or group concerned with or affected by the activities of another organization. Specifically these need to be identified within the environmental concerns of ISO 14000.

Interfaces Interaction among individuals, departments, work units, companies, and so on, that allows the meaningful exchange of information, often not well defined.

Interference fit Type of fit that results when the specified size limits of mating part features always produces interference at assembly.

Interferometer Any instrument used for precise comparisons to master standards.

Interferometry Formation of visible bands of light by interacting wave fronts. Is used for precise comparisons using gage blocks and for surface evaluation.

Intermediate customers Organizations or individuals who operate as distributors, brokers, or dealers between the supplier and the consumer/end user.

Internal audit   Audit conducted within an organization by members of the organization to measure its strengths or weaknesses against its own procedures and/or external standards. Also called a "first-party audit."

Internal capability analysis   Detailed review of the internal workings of the organization (e.g., to determine how well the capabilities of the organization match its strategic needs).

Internal customer   Recipient (person or department) within an organization of another person's or department's output (product, service, or information). *See also* **external customer.**

Internal documentation   Written information associated with the organization, the quality system, its processes, projects, and so on. Retained for informational or other purposes but not part of the final product or service.

Internal failure   Product failure that occurs before the product is delivered to external customers.

Internal failure cost   Cost incurred before the delivery or shipment of a product. Examples would include scrap, rework, reinspection, retesting, and downgrading of materials.

Internal rate of return (IRR)   Discount rate that causes net present value to equal zero.

Internal risks   Risks under the direct control and influence of the organization. *See* **external risks.**

International Academy for Quality (IAQ)   An independent, self-supported, nonprofit organization run by academicians who have been chosen from the most respected, active, and experienced protagonists of quality in the world.

International Aerospace Quality Group   Cooperative organization of the global aerospace industry that is mainly involved in quality cost reduction and process improvement efforts. *See* AS9100.

International Organization for Standardization (ISO)   Network of national standards institutes from 148 countries working in partnership with international organizations, governments, industry, and business and consumer representatives to develop and publish international standards. Acts as a bridge between public and private sectors. The International Organization for Standardization, based in Geneva, Switzerland, is the worldwide controller of ISO standards.

International Register of Certified Auditors (IRCA)   Operationally independent organization within the Institute of Quality Assurance (IQA) in London. The UK's leading body for quality and quality-related matters.

Interpolation   Selection of the nearest graduation on a measuring instrument, when a measurement lies between two lines. The observational rounding off.

Inter-relationship digraph   Management tool that depicts the relationship among factors in a complex situation. Also called a "relations diagram." It is used to simplify a network or cycle of problem causes. It breaks down tasks into increasingly detailed levels and can effectively pinpoint the root causes that may initially appear only to be symptoms. One of the seven management and planning tools.

Intervention   Action of a team facilitator when interrupting a discussion to state observations about group dynamics or the team process.

Intervention intensity   Refers to the strength of the intervention by the intervening person; intensity is affected by words, voice inflection, and nonverbal behaviors.

Intimidating management style   Management approach in which the top managers frequently reprimands employees to uphold their image as a demanding manager, at the risk of lowering employee morale.

Intrinsic availability   Amount of time a system is available for use calculated on operational conditions and statistical assumptions. Internal operations based.

Inverted pyramid   Management philosophy put forth by Karl Albrect, encouraging managers to turn their organizations upside down in an effort to become more customer focused. See also *At America's Service* (New York: Warner Books, 1988).

Invoice   Written itemized statement addressed to the purchaser of merchandise, with the quantity, description, price, and other charges, along with terms of payment, provided with the goods or services performed under a contract.

Irradiation   Exposure to radiation of wavelengths shorter than those of visible light, for medical purposes, to sterilize milk or other foods.

Irrelevant failure   Classification of a failure that is excluded from consideration because it is verified to be either caused by a condition that would not be present in the user environment or else peculiar to an item's design and that will not enter the user operational environment.

Irritant   In an environmental sense, a substance that can cause irritation of the skin, eyes, or of the respiratory system. Effects may be acute from a single high level of exposure or chronic from repeated low-level exposures.

Ishikawa diagram   Fishbone diagram. *See* **cause-and-effect diagram or analysis.**

Is/Is-Not Matrix   Problem-solving process proposed by Peter Scholtes in *The Team Handbook* based on ideas originally developed by Charles Kepner and Benjamin Tregoe in which data is sorted out to identify patterns of time or sequence that may lead to the problem being analyzed.

ISO 9000 series of standards   Set of international standards on quality management and quality assurance developed to help companies effectively document the quality system elements to be implemented to maintain an efficient quality system. The standards, initially published in 1987, are not specific to any particular industry, product, or service. The standards were developed by the International Organization for Standardization (ISO), a specialized international agency for standardization composed of the national standards bodies of 148 countries. The standards underwent a major revision in 2000 and now include ISO 9000:2000 (definitions), ISO 9001:2000 (requirements), and ISO 9004:2000 (continuous improvement).

ISO 14000   Environmental management system standard related to what organizations do that affects their physical surroundings, including employees, customers, products, services, and applicable laws and regulations.

ISO/TS 16949   The International Organization for Standardization (ISO)'s international technical specification for quality management systems, with particular requirements for the application of ISO 9001:2000 for automotive production and relevant service part organization. Replaces QS-9000.

ISO 17025-1999   General requirements for the competence of testing and calibration laboratories.

Isolated lot   Lot separated from the sequence of lots in which it was produced or collected and not forming part of a current sequence of inspection lots.

Isomorphic team structure   Organizational structure of a project team so it closely resembles the finished product or deliverable; for example, if the project is to write a book, then each team member would write a portion. The team/project manager would be responsible for the overall project and results.

Isotope   Variation of an element that has the same atomic number of protons but a different weight because of the number of neutrons. Various isotopes of the same element may have different radioactive behaviors, some being highly unstable.

Issues of documents   On blueprints, the revision level. For quality/environmental management system documents or procedures, it is also the revision number or level. *See also* **revision block.**

Item   In an object sense, it would be an object or quantity of material on which a set of observations can be made. In a measurement sense, it would be the result of making an observation on an object or quantity of material. In any sense it would be a tangible or intangible object that can be individually described and considered. Can be considered the same as a unit or an individual.

J

Jidoka   Japanese method of autonomous control involving the adding of intelligent features to machines to start or stop operations as control parameters are reached and to signal operators when necessary. *See also* **autonomation.**

Jig   Fixture used to hold an object in a correct positional relationship, so it can be worked on.

JIS Q 9100   International quality management standard for the aerospace industry. *See* **AS9100.**

Job aid   Any device, document, or other media that can be provided to a worker to aid in correctly performing their task. For example, laminated setup instructions at the machine, photos of product at different stages of assembly, metric conversion charts, and so on.

Job description   Narrative explanation of the work, responsibilities, and basic requirements of the job.

Job enlargement   Increasing the variety of tasks to be performed by an employee.

Job enrichment   Making work more meaningful for the employee. This can be accomplished by increasing the worker's authority in the work to be done, providing more variety, and so on.

Job specification   List of the important functional and quality attributes, such as knowledge, skills, aptitudes, and personal characteristics needed to succeed in the job.

Joiner triangle   Identified in *The Team Handbook* as quality, scientific approach, and all one team (all employees working as one). See also *The Team Handbook* (Madison: Oriel, Inc., 2003).

Joint Committee for the Accreditation of Healthcare Organizations (JCAHO)   Organization that sets voluntary standards for, evaluates, and accredits healthcare organizations and programs in the United States.

Joint planning meeting   Meeting involving representatives of a key customer and the sales and service team for the specific account to determine how better to meet the customer's requirements and expectations.

Joint probability   Probability that two events occur together. For independent events, their joint probability is the product of their individual probabilities.

Joint venture   Contractual partnership between organizations for a particular transaction to achieve common goals for mutual profit.

Joule   Unit of work or energy. The amount of work or energy required to move one newton a distance of one meter.

Journal   That portion of a rotating shaft that turns in a bearing.

Judicial management style   Management style in which the manager tries to exercise sound judgment and to apply that approach to each task as required.

Juran trilogy   Three managerial processes identified by Joseph M. Juran for use in managing for quality: *quality planning, quality control,* and *quality improvement.*

JUSE   Union of Japanese Scientists and Engineers.

Just-in-time   Inventory control system designed to maintain a bare minimum of inventory necessary to keep a perfect system running.

Just-in-time (JIT) manufacturing   Optimal material requirement planning system for a manufacturing process in which there is little or no manufacturing material inventory on hand at the manufacturing site and little or no incoming inspection.

Just-in-time training   Provision of training only when it is needed to all but eliminate the loss of knowledge and skill caused by a lag between training and use.

K

Kaikaku Japanese term that means a breakthrough improvement in eliminating waste (*muda*).

Kaizen Japanese term (*kai,* "change," and *zen,* "good") that means gradual unending improvement by doing little things better and setting and achieving increasingly higher standards. Author Masaaki Imai made the term famous in his book *Kaizen: The Key to Japan's Competitive Success* (New York: McGraw-Hill, 1986).

***kaizen* blitz/ event** Intense short time frame, team approach event to employ the concepts of continuous improvement. For example, to reduce cycle time or to increase throughput.

Kanban Japanese term that simply means signboards, cards, or chits, used as one of the primary tools of a just-in-time inventory control system. It maintains an orderly and efficient flow of materials throughout the entire manufacturing process. It usually has a printed card that contains specific information such as part name, description, and quantity. A *kanban,* or signboard, is attached to specific parts in the production line signifying the delivery of a given quantity. When the parts have all been used, the same sign is returned to its origin, where it becomes an order for more of the same parts to replenish the supply to be used. Note: The Japanese spelling is *kamban,* but it is commonly known as *kanban* in the United States.

Kano model (Naritaki Kano) Representation of the four levels of customer satisfaction defined as satisfaction, must be, delighters, and dissatisfaction.

Kelvin Scale of thermodynamic temperature measured from absolute zero. On this scale one Kelvin equals one degree Celsius. The SI definition is the fraction 1/273.16 of the thermodynamic temperature of the triple point of

K

water. The temperature 0 Kelvin is called absolute zero. *See also* **SI base units** for a complete listing of all SI base units.

Kerf Wasted material removed by a saw.

Key In machine assembly, a small piece of metal seated in a slot in a shaft and a slot in a hub to prevent rotation between the two pieces.

Key performance indicator (KPI) Statistical measure of how well an organization is doing. A KPI may measure a company's financial performance or how it is holding up against customer requirements.

Key process Major system-level process that supports the mission of the organization and satisfies major consumer requirements.

Key results area Major category of customer requirements that is critical for the organization's success.

Keyway Slot on a shaft or on the inside of a hub that holds a key.

Kilo One thousand. Expressed as 10 to the 3rd power. A kilogram is equal to 1000 grams, a kilovolt is equal to 1000 volts, a kilometer is equal to 1000 meters, and so on.

Kilogram Base unit of measure for weight. The SI definition is a cylinder of platinum-iridium alloy kept by the International Bureau of Weights and Measures in Paris. A duplicate is kept in the U.S. National Institute of Standards and Technology in Boulder, Colorado. The only SI base unit that requires a comparison to the physical standard; all other SI base units can be duplicated in a suitably equipped laboratory. *See also* **SI base units** for a complete listing of all SI base units.

Kinetic energy That energy possessed by a moving object.

KISS model Pragmatic philosophy of conducting business in which the objective is to keep things, such as procedures, reports, and any aspect of the work, as simple as possible, and yet get the job done. The acronym is simply stated "Keep It Simple Stupid."

KJ method *See* **affinity diagram.**

Knoop hardness Hardness testing method and value system developed by the National Bureau of Standards.

Knowledge management Involves transforming data into information, the acquisition or creation of knowledge, as well as the process and technology employed in identifying, categorizing, storing, retrieving, disseminating, and using information and knowledge for the purposes of improving decisions and plans.

Knowledge transfer Flow of knowledge, skills, information, and competencies from one person to another. It can happen through any number of channels and methods including coaching, training, mentoring, and on-the-job experience.

Knurl Uniform pattern of small ridges or beads (usually in a diamond-shaped pattern) on a surface to aid in gripping. Usually used on the handle of many handheld tools.

Koalaty Kid An American Society for Quality initiative to advance the concept of providing quality in the classroom for grades kindergarten through high school.

Kruskal-Wallis test Nonparametric test to compare three or more samples. It tests the null hypothesis that all populations have identical distribution functions against the alternative hypothesis that at least two of the samples differ only with respect to location (median). It is the analogue to the F-test used in analysis of variance. Whereas analysis of variance tests depend on the assumption that all populations under comparison are normally distributed, the Kruskal-Wallis test places no such restriction on the comparison. It is a logical extension of the Wilcoxon Mann-Whitney Test (see entry).

Krypton 86 Krypton 86 is a gas that, when electrically excited, emits a wavelength of light. Because of its stability it is the basis for the international length standards.

Kurtosis Measure of the shape (flatness) of a curve. Used to describe curves that are symmetrical, but not normal. If the distribution has longer tails than a normal distribution with the same standard deviation, it is said to have positive kurtosis (platykurtosis); if it has shorter tails, then it is said to have negative kurtosis (leptokurtosis).

L

Labor Effort expended by people for wages or a salary. Generally labor is classified as either direct or indirect. Direct labor is applied to meeting product or service objectives and is one of the primary elements used in costing a product or service. Indirect labor is a component of indirect cost, such as overhead or general operating and administrative cost.

Laboratory Per ANSI/ISO 17025 (1999), a body that calibrates and/or tests. As used in calibration terminology it refers to a body that carries out calibration or testing. May be internal to the organization or an external party that performs calibration services.

Lack of fit Value determined by using one of many statistical techniques stating the probability that data can be shown not to fit a model. Lack of fit is used to assess the goodness of fit of a model to data.

Lack of objective evidence In auditing, the process of suspecting something is not being accomplished according to established procedures, but there is not sufficient evidence to prove the point or to establish the fact.

Laddering Term used where there is an assumption made that customers choose between suppliers by selecting the one that will more closely provide the most benefit in helping them achieve their desired goals. It uses a series of questions to obtain desired linkages among perceived benefits, values, and consequences of the various suppliers.

Ladder of inference Mental model that explains how individuals have different interpretations about what happens in an organization. The model explains how most people move beyond observable data and socially understood meanings by providing their own interpretations.

Lag   In management planning, the time delay in successor task. For example, in a finish-to-start dependent project with a five-day lag, the successor activity cannot start until five days after the predecessor activity has finished. The lag time in warranty claims, as such they may not start until three months after the first shipments have been made.

Laissez-fare management style   Management approach in which team members are not directed by management. Little information flows from the manager to the workers or vice versa. This type of management style is useful where there are highly skilled and knowledgeable employees.

Lambda (λ)   English pronunciation of the Greek letter often used as the variable name for "failure rate."

Lambda plot   Technique to determine a data transformation when analyzing data.

Landscape   Traits, patterns, and structure of a specific geographical region, including its flora, fauna, and living organisms. In an environmental sense this would include the entire ecosystem.

Lap   In machining, to produce a fine surface by sliding a lapping material (usually an abrasive powder) over the surface.

Large quantity generator   In an environmental sense, a person or organization generating more than 2200 pounds of hazardous waste per month. Such organizations produce about 90% of the hazardous waste produced in the United States and are subject to all environmental regulations.

Lateral communication   Communication across lines of an organization of equivalent authority.

Lateral thinking   Refers to the concept of creative thinking techniques and methods used to generate new ideas as proposed by Edward DeBono. See also *Lateral Thinking: Creativity Step by Step* (New York: Harper Colophon Books, Harper & Row, 1973). See also *Six Thinking Hats* (Boston: Little, Brown, 1985).

Lathe   Machine used to shape a diameter on a workpiece by rotating the piece and then moving a cutting tool against the piece while it is in motion.

Latin square design   In a design of experiments, this type of experiment requires only one test with each factor and combination, such that three variables used with three factors will only require nine tests. This design assumes there are no interactions with the variables.

Lay In surface finish measurement, the predominant surface pattern. Surface finish measurements should be made in a direction that is perpendicular to the lay of the surface pattern.

Layout Use of measurement instruments to mark features on a workpiece for subsequent machining. The documenting of dimensions to verify conformance to specifications.

Lead auditor Individual appointed by the audit authority to be responsible for the Quality/EMS audit. The audit team leader who supervises the other audit team members.

Leader Individual recognized by others as a person they will follow. This individual then encourages all to become team players.

Leader line On blueprints, medium solid line with an arrow used to point or lead the reader from a dimension or note to the feature or surface where the note or dimension applies. *See* Appendix E.

Leadership Organization leaders must establish a vision, communicate that vision to those in the organization, and provide the tools and knowledge necessary to accomplish the vision. An essential part of a quality improvement effort.

Leadership system In quality award criteria, the term *leadership system* refers to how top leadership is exercised, formally and informally, throughout the entire organization. It forms the basis for and the way key decisions are made, communicated, and carried out. It includes structures and the mechanisms for decision making, selection and development of leaders and managers, reinforcement of values, directions, and performance expectations.

Lead pull test Test of mechanical integrity in which tension is applied to the leads or connectors until degradation or separation in order to measure terminal or lead strength.

Lean approach/ thinking Focuses on reducing cycle time and waste using a number of different techniques and tools. For example, value stream mapping and identifying and eliminating "monuments" and non-value-added steps. Note: "Lean" and "agile" are at times incorrectly used interchangeably.

L

Lean manufacturing	Initiative focused on eliminating all waste in manufacturing processes. Principles of lean include zero waiting time, zero inventory, scheduling (internal customer pull instead of push system), batch to flow (cut batch sizes), line balancing, and cutting actual process times. An integrated quality approach developed and evolved as the Toyota Production System. See also *Toyota Production System—Beyond Large Scale Production* (Portland, OR: Productivity Press, 1988).
Learner-controlled instructions (LCI)	Learners work without an instructor, at their own pace, building mastery of a task. Computer-based training is a form of LCI. Also called "self-directed learning."
Learning curve	Time it takes to achieve mastery of a task or body of knowledge.
Learning effectiveness retention	*See* **training retention.**
Learning objectives	Objectives to be met upon completion of a course of study or the learning of a skill. Bloom categorizes three learning objectives as *cognitive* (mental skills), *affective* (growth in feelings and emotional areas), and *psychomotor* (manual and physical skills). Also called "terminal objectives."
Learning organization	Organization that has as a policy to continue to learn and to improve its products, services, processes, and outcomes; organization that is continually expanding its capacity to create its future (as defined by Peter Senge). See also *The Fifth Discipline* (New York: Doubleday, 1990)
Learning principles for adults	Six factors that affect adult learning are these: (1) Adults have a need to know why they should learn something. (2) Adults have a deep need to be self-directed. (3) Adults have a greater volume and different quality of experience. (4) Adults become ready to learn when they experience the need. (5) Adults enter into a learning experience task centered, with an orientation to learning. (6) Adults are motivated to learn by both external and internal forces. It is generally considered that adults learn differently than children.
Lease	Customer's legal agreement with a supplier to use specified items that the lessee owns or controls for a fee. The lessor in some cases may agree to service and maintain those products and will have some liability for product system effectiveness.

Least material condition (LMC)	When a feature of size contains the least amount of material within its specified size limits. An external feature in its LMC would be at its lowest size limit. An internal feature in its LMC would be at its upper size limit.
Least squares	Method used in regression analysis to estimate the equation coefficients and constants so the sum of squares on the differences between the individual responses and the fitted model is at a minimum. It minimizes the squared differences between observed values and the estimated values.
Leptokurtosis	For frequency distributions, it has shorter tails = negative kurtosis. *See also* **kurtosis.**
Level	Instrument for establishing a horizontal line. By means of two or more such lines intersecting, a horizontal plane may be established. The standard for a level is gravity.
Levels	(1) Settings of factors in a factorial experiment (e.g., high and low levels of temperature). (2) In quality award criteria, the term *levels* refers to numerical information that places or positions an organization's results and performance on a meaningful measurement scale. Performance levels permit evaluation relative to past performance, projections, goals, and appropriate comparisons.
License	Official grant of permission needed to do a particular thing, exercise a certain privilege, or engage in a particular business or occupation. Licenses may be granted by governments, businesses, or individuals.
Life cycle	Consecutive and interlinked stages of a product or system, from raw material acquisition or generation of natural resources to the final product disposition.
Life cycle of a customer	Acquisition, retention, attrition, defection, and reacquisition.
Life cycle of a product	Design, manufacturing, assembly, installation, operation. and shutdown.
Life cycle of a project	Concept, planning, design, implementation, and evaluation.
Life cycle of technology	Emergence, growth, and redesign/improvement. Very seldom will saturation play a part because technology becomes obsolete rapidly.

Life test   (1) Test performed on a group of parts, assemblies, or units that is continued until a specified percentage of the group fails or some predetermined minimum operating time or cycles have been completed. (2) Test to failure using age life units as the stress test.

LIFO   In inventory management a term meaning "last in first out." This process uses newer inventory before using older inventory.

Limiting constraints   Factors for determining control limits.

Limiting operation   Operation or function with the least capacity in a total system with no alternative routings. The worst-case system effectiveness can be predicted using the limiting operation. *See also* **bottleneck.**

Limiting quality   Maximum number of defects in a product quality (the worst product quality) that a customer is willing to accept, at a specified probability of occurrence.

Limiting quality level (LQL)   Percentage or proportion of lots submitted for acceptance inspection for which the use of switching rules in a sampling scheme would have essentially no effect on the quality of lots occurring later in the production sequence because of the small number of lots involved.

Linear distance   Straight-line distance between two planes.

Linearity   Extent to which a measuring instrument's bias varies along its full operating range with the measured quantity. In a gage R&R study, linearity is the difference in the bias values throughout the expected operating range of the gage.

Linear metrology   Measurements taken along a line. In general use, it includes measurements along curved lines as well as straight lines and angles. It applies to volumes because these can be reduced to their component lines. Often referred to as "dimensional metrology."

Linear regression   Mathematical application of the concept of a scatter diagram where the correlation is actually a cause-and-effect relationship.

Linear responsibility matrix   Matrix providing a three-dimensional view of project tasks, responsible person, and level of relationship.

Line function That part of an organization responsible for producing its goods or performing its services.

Line manager Lower level manager that makes a product or performs a service. Also called a "functional manager."

Line precedence On blueprints, a convention that is applied when one line lies directly over another. A visible line takes precedence over a hidden line or centerline. A hidden line takes precedence over a centerline. *See* Appendix E.

Linked activity Any activity that is tied to another activity, usually defined in diagramming techniques with the preceding or following step.

Listening post Individual who, by virtue of his or her position or job function, has the potential for having contact with customers. Usually designated to collect, document, and transmit pertinent feedback to a central collection authority within the organization.

Listening post data Customer data and information gathered from a designated listening post.

Little q, big Q Terms coined by Joseph M. Juran and used to contrast the difference between managing for quality in all business processes and products (big Q) and managing for quality in a limited capacity—traditionally only in factory products and processes (little q).

Loaded rates In cost accounting, the charges for human and material resources that incorporate both hourly or per-use charges and all additional general and administrative cost associated with the product's manufacture or service provided.

Lobing Deviation from true roundness, the term is usually associated with shafts. It is to a round surface what waviness is to a flat surface. The standard for roundness is found in ANSI Y14.5 and more completely in ANSI B89.31.

Location tolerances In engineering blueprints, the control variation in the specified location or a feature in relation to another feature or datum. Includes the geometric characteristics of position, concentricity, and symmetry.

Longevity Useful lifetime of a product until it finally wears out or at a point where it requires a complete overhaul. Generally used to define a maximum useful life for equipment under the conditions of storage and use to which it will be exposed during its lifetime.

Long term goals   Refers to goals that an organization hopes to achieve in the future, usually in three to five years. Commonly referred to as "strategic goals."

Loop test   Fault detection technique in which a signal is transmitted to equipment connected through a line or network and looped back, or returned to the unit to check it is receiving.

Lose-lose   Outcome of a conflict resolution that results in both parties being worse off than before the conflict. Based on the strategy that it is better for each party to get something rather than both getting nothing, even if the something does not accomplish either party's goals.

Loss function   Taguchi function that measures the cost implications of product variability. See also *Introduction to Quality Engineering* (Dearborn, MI: American Supplier Institute, 1986).

Lost customer analysis   Analysis conducted to determine why a customer or a class of customers was lost or defected to a competitor.

Lot   Definite quantity of product accumulated under conditions that are considered uniform for sampling purposes.

Lot, batch   Definite quantity of some product manufactured under conditions of production that are considered uniform.

Lot quality   Value of percentage defective or of defects per hundred units in a lot.

Lot size *(also referred to as N)*   Number of units in the lot.

Lot tolerance percentage defective (LTPD)   Expressed in percentage defective or proportion of nonconforming units in a batch or lot for which, for the purposes of acceptance sampling, the consumer wishes to be restricted to a specified low value. Used as a basis for some inspection systems and commonly associated with a small consumers' risk.

Low hanging fruit   Typically in process improvement activities, the easiest problems to tackle, ones that will provide early success and provide good benefits or payback.

Lower control limit (LCL) Control limit for points below the central line in a control chart.

Lower specification limit (LSL) Lowest value of a product dimension or measurement that is acceptable.

Lower tolerance limit On engineering blueprints, the lowest permissible limit allowed by the specifications.

Lug Projection of metal, not usually round like a boss, but some other shape, usually used to contain a tapped hole for a bolt.

LURD Convention for expressing measurement changes to minimize misunderstandings. It stands for left, up, right, down.

M

Machinability   In metalworking, the ease with which a metal or material may be machined.

Machine   Device that transmits energy into motion to produce an output. In most modern applications of the term it would mean a mechanized apparatus to make some part or assist in the production of another material or product.

Macrogeometry   Large-scale consideration of form or shape. In popular usage, macrogeometry is concerned with size and shape that can be expressed with standard inspection instruments. Evaluation of squareness in shop applications of large machines usually is macrogeometry.

Macrometrology   Large-scale measurement and work such as the setup of large machinery, shipbuilding, land surveying, and so on. *See also* **macrogeometry.**

Macro processes   Broad, far-ranging processes that can often cross-functional boundaries.

Magnetic flux detection   Form of nondestructive test to locate internal cracks in metals that are difficult to X-ray. Test involves passing a current within the metal and tracing the resultant magnetic field using a powder of magnetic particles. This powder is sprayed or painted on the surface below which the current is passed. A discontinuity in the current will generally imply an internal crack and cause a proportional discontinuity in the magnetic field. The crack shows in the arrangement of the particles in the fluid.

Magnetic particle inspection (flux)   Nondestructive test used to find defects in ferromagnetic materials. A low-voltage electric current is passed through the material and magnetic particles are placed on the material to be tested. Particle clusters or lines indicate the location of the defect.

M

Magnification   Total magnification is the end result of the eyepiece magnification and the objective magnification. The eyepiece magnification is usually ×10. Thus coupled with an objective of ×43, for example, makes the total magnification 430 power.

Magnificent 7 tools   *See* **seven tools of quality.**

Main distribution   The main distribution is centered on an expected value of strengths, whereas a smaller freak distribution describes a smaller set of substandard products produced by random occurrences in a manufacturing process.

Main effect   Average change in the response by changing the level of a factor averaged over all (levels) of other factors in a designed experiment. The main effect is the controlling factor; interaction effects may provide an indirect effect.

Maintainability   Probability that a given maintenance action for an item under given usage conditions can be performed within a stated time interval, when the maintenance is performed under stated conditions using stated procedures and resources. Maintainability has two categories: serviceability (the ease of conducting scheduled inspections and servicing) and reparability (the ease of restoring service after a failure).

Maintenance   (1) That department of an organization that keeps buildings, equipment, and supporting processes functioning effectively by repairing and/or replacing nonfunctioning items. (2) Activities directed toward keeping current systems or processes in place and operating effectively.

Maintenance agreement (MA)   Customer's legal agreement with a manufacturer or third-party maintenance provider to provide certain services on the customer's products for a fee.

Major defect   Defect other than critical that may cause the product to fail, cause poor performance, shortened life, or prevent interchangeability.

Major nonconformity   Absence or total breakdown of the provisions required to cause product or system conformity or prevent product or systems to meet the needs and expectations of the customer. Absence means a lack of adequate provisions in theory and in practice. A total breakdown means adequate provisions are in place but they are not being implemented or used.

Malcolm Baldrige National Quality Award (MBNQA) Award established by the U.S. Congress in 1987 to raise awareness of quality management and recognize U.S. companies that have implemented successful quality management systems. Two awards may be given annually in each of five categories: manufacturing, service, small business, education, and health care. The award is named after the late secretary of commerce Malcolm Baldrige, a proponent of quality management. The U.S. Commerce Department's National Institute of Standards and Technology manages the award, and ASQ administers it. It currently has seven major categories: (1) leadership, (2) strategic planning, (3) customer and market focus, (4) information and analysis, (5) human resource focus, (6) process management, and (7) business results. By design, it is heavily slanted toward customer satisfaction and focus.

Malfunction analysis Study of a failure after it has occurred, either in order to develop correct future items designs where that malfunction will not occur or to perform corrective maintenance.

Malleable casting Casting made less brittle and tougher by annealing. *See also* **anneal.**

Mallows Cp statistic Regression parameter that is used to determine the smallest number of parameters that should be used when building a model. The number of parameters corresponding to the minimum of this statistic is the minimum number of parameters to include during the model-building process.

Management audit Planned examination of the management objectives, assignments, responsibilities, and methods of operation to assure these are achieving the desired results. These audits are conducted on behalf of management although not normally conducted by top management.

Management by exception Management approach in which managers concern themselves with only those variances that appear to be exceptionally significant.

Management by fact Business philosophy that decisions should be based on facts and data.

Management by objectives (MBO) Management approach developed by Peter Drucker that encourages managers to give their subordinates more freedom in determining how to achieve objectives. Performance reviews are then measured against those objectives. MBO gives the employees more flexibility than they would have under a traditional bureaucratic model, which specifies the methods as well as the outcome.

M

Management by policy	Organizational infrastructure and defined procedures that ensures the right things are done at the right time.
Management by walking around (MBWA)	Manager's planned, but usually unannounced, walk-through of the operation to gather information from employees and make observations. May be viewed in a positive light by virtue of giving employees the opportunity to interact with top management; has the potential of being viewed negatively if punitive action is taken as a result of information gathered.
Management plan	In project management, a documented plan that describes the overall guidelines for the project, how it is to be organized, administered, and managed in order to complete the project within the established constraints of the project.
Management planning tools	The seven commonly recognized management planning tools are (1) affinity diagram, (2) tree diagram, (3) process decision program chart (PDPC), (4) matrix diagram, (5) interrelationship diagram, (6) prioritization matrices, and (7) activity network diagram.
Management principles	Should include the following activities: planning, leading, controlling, organizing, staffing, and monitoring.
Management representative	The person management appoints to act on their behalf to manage the quality/environmental system. This person usually handles the interface with a registration body.
Management review	Periodic meeting of management at which it formally reviews the status and effectiveness of the organization's quality/environmental management system(s).
Management styles	Refers to the predominant personal styles used by managers; styles may be based on prevalent management theories or assumptions about people. Based on the manager and situation any of the following may be used: authoritarian, autocratic, combative, conciliatory, consensual, consultative-autocratic, democratic, disruptive, ethical, facilitating, intimidating, judicial, laissez-faire, participative, promotional, secretive, shared, or shareholder management style. See individual entries for each management style.
Management system	System for addressing the policies, objectives, principles, authority, responsibilities, accountability, and implementation plan of an organization.

Management training Usually refers to training and/or education provided to any management or professional-level person from front line supervision up to, but not including, executives.

Manager Individual charged with the responsibility for managing resources, personnel, and processes.

Managerial grid Management theory that a manager's style is based on his or her mindset toward people; it focuses on attitudes rather than behavior. The theory uses a grid to measure concern for production and a concern for people.

Manipulative error Error in measurement caused by handling the instrument and the part.

Mapping Process map designed to show how a process crosses several functions and touches certain levels in the organization. It has functional departments listed across the top of columns and the process steps down the rows. It then shows where these cross and/or combine.

Margin of safety (1) In measurement, the amount the measurement system exceeds the required amount of accuracy or precision. (2) In design, the amount of excess capability/abuse a product can withstand before failing or providing the opportunity for harm or injury.

Market-perceived quality Customer's opinion of your products or services as compared to those of your competitors.

Market segmentation Markets may be divided for various reasons such as geographical region, demographic use and age, buyer behavior, volume, brand name loyalty, price, and so on.

Market survey Collection and analysis of data from potential suppliers to determine the capability of satisfying customer requirements. It would typically include such activities as writing or calling knowledgeable persons, reviewing catalogs, websites and other informational sources, attending demonstrations, or conducting formal request for information.

Markov chain Method used to evaluate a system's mean time to failure. The system is modeled as a finite system with working systems, and a probability is associated to each transition between systems.

M

Mass	Quantity of matter forming a body with some feature of size and weight.
Mass customization	Concept that Alvin Toffler used in his keynote address at the 50th Annual Quality Congress in 1996 to explain the concept that as customer needs become more customized, their needs become more unique, and suppliers need to address these needs on a customer-by-customer basis. *See* **demassification.** See also *Powershift* (New York: Free Press, 1983).
Master Black Belt (MBB)	Six Sigma or quality expert responsible for strategic implementations within the business. The Master Black Belt is qualified to teach other Six Sigma facilitators the methodologies, tools, and applications in all functions and levels of the company and is a resource for utilizing statistical process control within processes.
Master flat	In metrology, an optical flat having surfaces of maximum precision. It is used to calibrate working flats.
Mastering	Setting to standards. Although it can apply to all types of measuring instruments, it is most often applied to air and electronic gages.
Material breach	In legal terms, it is the most serious form of a contract or moral breach. It is used to free the innocent party from any other binding obligations.
Material condition	In engineering dimensioning, an outside edge is less than 180° of material. An inside edge is more than 180°. These are the material conditions. When material is dimensioned, the part feature is said to be male. When the space between material is dimensioned, the part feature is said to be female.
Material requirements planning (MRP)	Planning and material-ordering technique based on the known or forecast final demand requirements of each item, the lead time required for each item to be fabricated, or purchased, taking into consideration inventory on hand.
Materials review board (MRB)	Quality control committee or team, usually employed in manufacturing or other materials-processing installation, that has the responsibility and authority to deal with items or materials that do not conform to fitness-for-use specifications. An equivalent, the error review board, is sometimes used in software development.
Material Safety Data Sheets (MSDS)	Compilation of information required under the Occupational Safety and Health Administration (OSHA) communication standards, on the identity of hazardous chemical, health, and physical hazards, exposure limits, and

precautions required. Used to notify employees and others of the real and potential risk associated with substances they come in contact with.

Matrix   Graphical planning tool for displaying the relationships among various data sets.

Matrix chart/ diagram   Management and planning tool that shows the relationships among various groups of data; it yields information about the relationships and the importance of tasks and method elements of the subjects. For each required task (listed along the left side of the diagram), the matrix diagram would show which departments were in charge, which had some involvement, and which had no involvement (listed across the top of the diagram). At each intersecting point the relationship is either present or absent. This is frequently used to determine who or what department has responsibility for the different elements of an implementation plan. One of the seven management and planning tools.

Matrix organization   Organizational structure in which the overall manager shares responsibility with the functional managers to assign and direct work as required.

Matrix structure   Describes company organized into a combination of functional and product departments; it brings together teams of people to work on projects and is driven by product scope.

Maturity   Balance of experience, courage, and consideration that enables a person to speak openly, give honest feedback, and demonstrate respect for the feelings of others.

Maximum material condition (MMC)   When a feature of size contains the maximum amount of material within its specified size limits. An external feature in its MMC would be at its upper size limit. An internal feature in its MMC would be at its lower size limit.

Mean down time   Measure of maintainability derived by dividing the sum of the elapsed clock time that a system is unavailable due to failures, by the number of occurrences over a selected time frame: hours, weeks, months, and so on.

Means (in the *hoshin* planning usage)   Step of identifying the ways by which multiyear objectives will be met, leading to the development of action plans.

Mean square   Sum of squares divided by degrees of freedom.

Mean time between failures (MTBF)	Average time interval between failures for a repairable product for a defined unit of measure (e.g., operating hours, cycles, or miles).
Mean time to repair (MTTR)	For a repairable unit, a stated period in the life of a functional unit, the average time required for corrective maintenance that will bring the unit back to a functional state.
Measure	Criteria, metric, or means to which a comparison is made with output.
Measured surface	(1) That surface of a measuring instrument that is movable and from which the measurement is taken (e.g., the spindle of a micrometer). (2) That area of a part on which a measurement is taken.
Measurement	Act or process of quantitatively comparing results with requirements. Measurement may be in any quality (length, weight, hardness, etc.) and lots may be in any units (inches, volts, picas, etc.). *See also* **metrology.**
Measurement accuracy	Extent to which the average value of a repeated measurement tends toward the true value of the measured quantity.
Measurement and test devices/ equipment (M & TE)	All the gages, measuring tools, and monitoring devices used to test, inspect, monitor, diagnose, or otherwise examine products, materials, supplies, and services to assure they conform to specified requirements.
Measurement capability	Ability of a measuring system or device to measure true values to the accuracy and precision required.
Measurement error	Difference between the actual value and the measured value of a measured quantity.
Measurement precision	Extent to which a repeated measurement gives the same result accurately.
Measurement pressure	Pressure applied to a measured surface by the measuring instrument. The pressure should be positive but not excessive; in many cases it is an important factor and should be maintained at the same pressure as that used when the instrument was calibrated.
Measurement standard	Standard of measurement that is a true value and recognized as the basis for comparison. Usually traceable to a national standard.

M

Measurement system Complete process of obtaining measurements. This includes the collection of equipment, operations, procedures, software, and personnel that affects the assignment of a number to a measurement characteristic.

Measurement system analysis (MSA) *See* **gage repeatability and reproducibility.**

Measurement uncertainty Variation observed when repeated measurements of the sample parameter on the same specimen are taken with the same device.

Measuring instrument Instrument or assemblage of equipment used to measure system output or make comparisons to standards, calibrated by the calibration system but not used in the process of calibration. A gage, indicator, meter, scale, and similar instruments.

Median Middle number or center value of a set of data in which all the data are arranged in sequence.

Median chart For variables data, a control chart of the median of subgroups.

Mediation Process of bringing two parties engaged in a dispute or disagreement to settle their differences through a meeting with a disinterested party, the mediator. Unlike in binding arbitration, the mediator has no authority to force a settlement.

Mentor Someone similar to a coach who provides a role model and guides an individual that is less experienced.

Merchantability Fitness for a particular purpose. Products are merchantable if they are reasonably fit for the ordinary purposes for which the product was intended. Used as a measure of implied warranties.

Meter Base unit of measure for length. The SI definition is the distance traveled by light in a vacuum during a time interval of 1/299,792,458 of a second. *See* **SI base units** for a complete listing of all SI base units.

Methane Colorless, nonpoisonous, highly flammable gas created by the decomposition of organic compounds. A major component of natural gas as is used in homes.

Methodology Standardized set of instructions or procedures used to accomplish a task.

M

Metric   Standard for measurement or evaluation method.

Metric system   Familiar name for Système Internationale d'Unités, the most recent of many so-called metric systems. It is based on the meter (length), kilogram (weight), second (time), degree Celsius (temperature), ampere (electrical), and candela (light).

Metrology   Science of measurement, including weights and measures or of measurement. In a modern sense, the science of measurement applied especially to calibrating measuring instruments in order to achieve accuracy.

Metrology laboratory   Laboratory for the calibration of standards and gages. It may be a department within a company or an outside service.

Mic   *See* **micrometer.**

Micro   One millionth of a factor. Expressed as 10 to the minus 6th power.

Microgeometry   Study and application of small-scale considerations of form or shape. The precision in microgeometry is expressed in "mikes." The evaluation of surface flatness of gages is microgeometry.

Micromanaging   Managing every little detail. For example, approving a requisition for paper clips.

Micrometer   Instrument that achieves its amplification as a result of the precision resolution of screw threads.

Micrometrology   Refers to very small work, much smaller than is found in most common workshops. *See also* **microgeometry.**

Micron   One millionth of a meter or one ten-thousandth of a millimeter.

Micro processes   Narrow processes made up of detailed steps and activities that could be accomplished by a single person.

Microscope   Optical instrument for greatly enlarging the view of a small part feature or item.

Midrange   In a statistical set of data, midrange is the arithmetic mean of the largest and smallest observed value.

Mike (1) Slang term for micrometer. (2) In the decimal-inch system of terminology, "mike" means millionths. However, in common use, "micro-inch" is the most common designation for millionths of an inch.

Mil In the decimal-inch system of terminology, "mil" means thousandths of an inch (.001).

Milestone In project management, a point in time when a critical event is to occur; a symbol is placed on a milestone chart to locate the point where a critical event is to occur.

Milestone chart Another name for a Gantt chart.

Mill Removal of material by means of passing the part under rotating cutters.

Milliampere One-thousandth of an ampere.

Millimeter Metric linear unit of measurement, equal to .039 of an inch, or 1/1000 of a meter.

MIL-STD Military standard. Most common MIL-STD sampling plans were 105E for attributes and MIL-STD-414 for variables, now obsolete.

MIL-Q-9858A Military standard that describes quality program requirements.

MIL-STD-45662A Military standard that describes the requirements for creating and maintaining a calibration system for measurement and test equipment.

MIL-STD-105E Military standard that describes the sampling procedures and tables for inspection by attributes.

MIL-STD-414 Military standard that describes the sampling procedures and tables for inspection by variables.

Mind mapping Technique for creating a visual representation (use of symbols) of a multitude of issues or concerns by forming a map of the interrelated ideas, to get a more complete and common understanding of a situation.

Minimum acceptable value (MAV) Lowest limit of compliance that can be approved for use. In tolerancing, the least dimension that can be used. In acceptance testing, the least amount of conformance that would be acceptable to provide conformity to regulations or to the customer.

M

Minimum material condition	Occurs when the male feature is at its smallest size and the female feature is at its maximum size. *See also* **tolerance.**
Minor defect	Defect that is not likely to reduce materially the usability of the product (e.g., a scratch on a household appliance).
Minor nonconformity	Any failure to meet one or more requirement of a standard that cannot be classified as a major or critical nonconformity.
Minor risk	Risk event that does not cause significant problems, no matter what its probability.
Mission	Organization's purpose. In quality award criteria, the term *mission* refers to the overall function of an organization. The mission answers the question, "What is this organization attempting to accomplish?" The mission might define customers or markets served, distinctive competencies, or technologies used.
Mission statement	Explanation of purpose or reasons for existing as an organization; it provides the focus for the organization and defines its scope of business. A mission statement should define the core purpose of the organization. It is seldom revised.
Mistake proofing	Engineering technique that makes a process or product so robust that it cannot fail. *See* **poka-yoke, error proofing,** and *kaizen.*
Mitigation	Risk response strategy that decreases risk by lowering the probability of a risk event's occurrence or reducing the effect of the event should it occur.
Mixture experiments	Variables are expressed as proportions of the whole and sum to unity. Measured responses are assumed to depend only on the proportions of the ingredients and not on the amount of the mixture.
Mock-up	Physical or virtual demonstration model, built to scale, and used in the early development of a project to verify proposed design, fit, critical clearances, operator interfaces, and other physical characteristics of the item to be produced.
Mode	Value occurring most frequently in a data set.
Model	Way to look at a situation or opportunity, generally by abstracting and simplifying it to make it understandable in a certain context.

Model for quality assurance   Standard or selected set of quality system elements combined to satisfy the quality assurance needs for a given situation. Examples may include the ISO 9001:2000 standard, the Malcolm Baldrige National Quality Award criteria, and so on.

Modified control limits   Control limits based on specification limits.

Modifiers   In engineering blueprints, the symbols for maximum material condition and least material condition. Their presence in the feature control frame "modifies" the size of the geometric tolerance and signifies that additional tolerance may be possible. *See* Appendix E.

Mold   Cavity formed by sand or some other material that forms an open area where molten metal is poured. In other applications such as plastics forming, a mold is made of metal and the material is forced into the mold under pressure to form the part.

Mole   Base unit of measure for substance. The SI definition is the amount of substance of a system that contains as many elementary entities as there are atoms in 0.012 kilogram of carbon 12. *See also* **SI base units** for a complete listing of all SI base units.

Moment of truth   As described by Jan Carlzon, the former CEO of Scandinavian Air Services, in the 1980s as "Any episode where a customer comes into contact with any aspect of your company, no matter how distant, and by this contact, has an opportunity to form an opinion about your company." See also *Moments of Truth* (New York: Harper Business, 1997).

Monte Carlo analysis   Scheduling or cost risk assessment technique that entails performing a project simulation many times to estimate the likely distribution of expected results.

Monte Carlo simulation   Modeling technique to predict the behavior of a system from the known random behaviors and interactions of the system's component parts.

Mothball   Storage method that attempts to minimize the degradation of an item while it is stored, often in a natural external environment in a dormant condition and usually for a long period of time, at times years. The items mothballed are usually large capital items, such as ships.

Monitoring   To periodically and systematically or provide continuous surveillance or testing to determine the level of compliance with engineering or regulatory requirements. It does not imply any action will be taken.

Motivating   Act of inducing a person to work toward goals established for themselves or by others.

Motivation theories   Theories that were developed to estimate what will motivate employees. See McClelland (motivational theories), Maslow (hierarchy of needs), and Herzberg (satisfiers and dissatisfiers).

Motivators   According to Herzberg's motivation-hygiene theory, the two sets of factors that must be considered to satisfy a person's needs are (1) those related to job satisfaction (motivators) and (2) those related to job dissatisfaction (hygiene or maintenance factors). To retain employees, managers must focus on improving negative hygiene factors (such as pay), but to get employees to devote a higher level of energy to their work, managers must use motivators (such as recognition). Others present similar list of motivators. See also *The Motivation to Work,* 2nd ed. (New York: John Wiley & Sons, 1959).

Monument   Point in a process that requires a product to wait in a queue before being processed any further; a barrier to continuous flow.

Moving averages/ ranges charts   Control chart that combines rational subgroups of data and plots the combined subgroup averages and ranges. Often used in continuous process industries, such as chemical processing, where single samples are analyzed.

MRO   Maintenance, repair, and operations. The supplies needed to run a company.

MRP2   Manufacturing resource planning. Closed-loop system integrating and managing all the resources used in the production of products and/or services.

Muda   Japanese for waste. Any activity that consumes resources but creates no value for the customer. Seven defined classes of waste are overproduction, delays, transportation, excess inventory, inappropriate processing, wasted motion, and defective parts.

Multiattribute evaluation   Simpler than QFD (quality function deployment), this process rank-orders and weights customer requirements relative to the competition. In addition it estimates the cost of each requirement in order to prioritize improvement actions.

Multicollinearity Exists when independent variables in a multiple regression analysis are corrected.

Multiple sampling Attributes sampling plan defining how a lot should be accepted or rejected after one or more samples are taken. Has the ability to accept good lots with less inspection and reject bad lots with less sampling.

Multivariate control chart Control chart for evaluating the stability of a process in terms of the levels of two or more variables or characteristics.

Multiview Engineering blueprint in which the part is represented in two or more views. *See* Appendix E.

Multivoting Group decision-making tool proposed by Peter Scholtes that enables a group to sort through a long list of ideas to identify priorities. After voting on an established shortened list they may be asked to vote again on a further shortened list.

Murmurs Technique from Japan used to gather information on consumer behavior by watching the customer use the product or service. *See also* **observation murmurs.**

Murphy's law Informal and unfounded principle of business stating that whatever can go wrong, will go wrong. Ed Murphy, a development engineer, coined the term in 1949 as a result of errors made by a laboratory technician.

Myers-Briggs type indicator (MBTI) Methodology and an instrument for identifying an individual's personality type based on Carl Jung's theory of personality preferences, developed by Katharine C. Briggs and Isabel Briggs Myers. It is based on four scales, each reflecting different dimensions of human behavior: extrovert-introvert, sensing-intuitive, thinking-feeling, and judging-perceiving. These scales comprise 16 different psychological types, each associated with a number of well-documented behavioral traits.

Mystery shopper Person who pretends to be a regular shopper in order to get an unencumbered view of how a company's service process works.

N

n Number of units in a sample.

N Number of units in a population.

Nano One-billionth. Expressed as 10 to the minus 9th power.

National Aeronautics and Space Administration (NASA) U.S. government agency charged with the U.S. space exploration program.

National Bureau of Standards (NBS) Now known as **National Institute of Standards and Technology (NIST).**

National Committee for Quality Assurance (NCQA) Nonprofit organization whose stated objective is "To become the most widely trusted source of information driving health care quality improvement."

National Institute of Standards and Technology (NIST) Agency of the U.S. Department of Commerce that develops and promotes measurements, standards, and technology. NIST manages the Malcolm Baldrige National Quality Award. The official standardization agency for the U.S. government.

National Quality Month (NQM) In October each year; used to promote quality in U.S. industry.

Z

Natural capability	Range of the resulting part sizes that can be expected during normal operation. The basis for statistical quality control by variables.
Natural process limits (NPL)	Limits that include a stated fraction of the individuals in a process or population that will contain random variation and/or defects.
Natural team	Team of individuals drawn from a single work group; similar to a process improvement team except it is not cross functional in composition and is usually permanent.
Natural tolerances of a process	Usually expressed as three standard deviations on either side of the mean.
Natural work team	Group of people with different responsibilities who are closest to the process or problem chosen to work on an identified problem or improvement opportunity.
Natural variation	Concept that there is variation in all processes, that making any product or providing any service with absolute consistency is impossible.
N-chart	Number defective chart. A simple chart for attribute data: A control chart of the number of defective units found in a subgroup of fixed size. The N-chart is used where each unit is inspected from a given lot.
Negative binomial	Defines the probability that "r" occurrences will require a total of "r + s" trials of an event that has a probability of occurrence of "p" on each trial (note that the total number of trials, "n", is "r + s"). The trials must be independent.
Negative skewness	In a distribution, where the tail is to the left and the hump is on the right.
Nested data	Experimental design where the trials are not fully randomized sets. In lieu of full randomization, trials are structured such that some factors are randomized within other factor levels.
Net present value (NPV)	In accounting, a discounted cash flow technique for finding the present value of each future year's cash flow. Takes into account the time value of money.

Network diagram	Schematic display of the logical relationships of a projects activities, usually drawn from left to right to reflect project chronology. Also called a "logic diagram," and often incorrectly referred to as a "PERT chart."
Networking	Act of contacting others with common interest, such as in professional groups, often with a view to training, obtaining information, and so on, for the mutual benefit of the members.
New seven	Sometimes referred to as the "Q seven": (1) relationship diagram, (2) affinity diagram, (3) tree diagram, (4) matrix diagram, (5) matrix data-analysis diagram, (6) process decision program chart (PDCA), and (7) arrow diagram. See individual entries for more information.
Next operation as customer	Concept of internal customers in which every operation is both a receiver and a provider.
Node	In various diagramming techniques, a junction point where activities are joined; an intersection, or where two or more lines in a network diagram converge.
Noise	(1) In process parameters, nuisance variables that are difficult, impossible, or very expensive to control. (2) In data analysis and problem solving, external influences that affect the data. (3) In communications, any influences that interfere with the communication process.
Nominal	Desired dimension for a product feature whose size is of concern: the desired mean value for the particular dimension. The target value.
Nominal chart	Control chart that plots the deviation from the nominal value. Often used when individual samples are taken in short-run, low-volume processes. Allows multiple part numbers manufactured by similar processes to be plotted on the same control charts.
Nominal group technique	Technique, similar to brainstorming, used by teams to generate ideas on a particular subject. Team members are asked to silently come up with as many ideas as possible, writing them down. Each member is then asked to share one idea, which is recorded. After all the ideas are recorded, they are discussed and prioritized by the group.
Nonconformity	Nonfulfillment of a specified requirement. The departure or absence of one or more quality characteristics or quality system element from specified requirements. See **blemish, defect,** and **imperfection.**

Nondestructive testing and evaluation (NDT, NDE)	Testing done without impairing subsequent usefulness of the product. It includes testing performed to detect flaws and measures of physical properties in materials and parts.
Nondisclosure agreement	Legally binding document in which an organization promises to use another's proprietary data only for specified purposes and not to reveal or disclose these data to any other organization or individual.
Nonferrous metals	Nonmagnetic metals such as aluminum, lead, copper, and brass.
Nonlinearity	(of a measuring instrument) Deviation of the instrument's response (indicated reading) from the actual measurement.
Nonlinear parameter estimation	Methodology whereby the arduous, labor-intensive, and distinctly frustrating task of multiparameter model calibration can be carried out automatically under the control of a computer.
Nonparametric tests	Nonparametric tests are often used in place of their parametric counterparts when certain assumptions about the underlying population are questionable. For example, when comparing two independent samples, the Wilcoxon Mann-Whitney test (see entry) does not require the population to be normally distributed, whereas its parametric counterpart, the two-sample t-test, does. Nonparametric tests may be, and often are, more powerful in detecting population differences when distributional assumptions are not satisfied. All tests involving ranked data (data that are ordered) are nonparametric.
Nonrepairable device	Term used to describe something that is discarded after it fails to function properly or is broken. A common lightbulb is nonrepairable and is discarded when it burns out.
Nonstationary process	Process with a level and variance that can grow without limit.
Non-value-added	Term that describes a process step or function not required for the direct achievement of process output. This step or function is identified and examined for potential elimination. Movement, storage, most inspections, and so on, are non-value-added.

Norm (behavioral)	Expectations of how a person or persons will behave in a given situation based on established protocols, rules of conduct, or accepted social practices.
Normal curve	Gaussian distribution. *See* **normal distribution (statistical).**
Normal distribution curve	Bell-shaped curve that results when a variable is changing by chance, such as in the throws of a dice. May also at times be called a histogram. *See also* **standard deviation.** *See* Appendix C.
Normal distribution (statistical)	Charting of a data set in which most of the data points are concentrated around the average (mean), thus forming a bell-shaped curve. Covers 99.73% at 3 sigma, 95.44% at 2 sigma, and 68.26% at 1 sigma. Also called the "Gaussian distribution." *See* Appendix C.
Normal inspection	Inspection, under certain sampling plans, that is used when no evidence exist that the quality level of the product being submitted is better or worse than the specified quality level.
Normalizing	In metalworking, heating material to a specified temperature and cooling it in air.
North American Free Trade Agreement (NAFTA)	Trade agreement among the countries on the North American continent whereby they agree not to place restrictions on trade within the participating countries of Mexico, the United States, and Canada.
North American Industry Classification System (NAICS)	Replacing the Standard Industrial Classification (SIC) and used to define organizations according to the products or services provided.
np-chart	For attribute data: a control chart of the number of defective units in a subgroup. Requires a constant subgroup size.
Nth sampling	Sampling technique in which you determine the total lot size, determine the quantity of samples you will take, and divide the lot by the sample size and take every designated sample as they come available. Lot size 100 sample size 5, you take every 20th part. This is in contrast to random sampling.
Nuclear embrittlement	Reduction in mechanical ductility and tensile strength caused in an item subjected to long-term neutron flux, such as near a nuclear reactor.

Z

Null hypothesis   Hypothesis tested in test of significance where there is no difference or effect. Used to test differences between processes or populations using samples. The null hypothesis cannot be proved true.

Number of affected units chart   Control chart for evaluating the stability of a process in terms of the total number of units in a sample in which an event of a given classification occurs.

Objective Specific statement of a desired short term condition or achievement; includes measurable end results to be accomplished by specific teams or individuals within time limits. *See also* **targets and objectives.**

Objective evidence Information that can be verified and proved true, based on facts or obtained through observation, measurement, test, or other means.

Observational error Error formed during the reading of an instrument. For instance, viewing a dial indicator from an angle will provide a distorted view compared to that viewed straight ahead.

Observation (audit) Item of objective evidence found during an audit, usually of lesser importance than a finding, but still in need of addressing. It may or may not require a corrective action response.

Observation murmurs Technique originated in Japan used to gather information on consumer behavior by watching the customer use the product or service.

Observation (statistics) (1) Process of determining the presence or absence of attributes or making measurements of a variable. (2) Result of the process of determining the presence or absence of attributes or making measurements of a variable. For variables measurements, the preferred term for the result usage is **observed value**.

Observed value Particular value of a characteristic determined as a result of a test or measurement.

Obsolete documents Documents that are no longer required for operational use. They may be useful for historical purposes, so many times they are retained.

Occupational Safety and Health Administration (OSHA)	U.S. government agency that sets and enforces regulatory guidelines on worker health and safety conditions in the workplace.
Occurrence	Specified event, usually in a sequence of events. A specific problem, or in an audit a specified noted deficiency.
Occurrence rating	In an FMEA, it is a rating scale from 1 to 10, used to evaluate how frequently a failure will occur. A high rating of 9–10 means a failure could occur very often. A low rating of 1–2 indicates a failure would occur rarely if ever.
Offline quality	Placing extra emphasis on the design and development phase of a project, providing trouble-free pilot production and finished product. Product can then be manufactured within defined parameters, making it error free and fully serviceable for its intended use.
Offline testing	Any test method that removes the unit to be tested from its actual production flow. Also called "shop testing."
Offset section view	On engineering blueprints, a sectional view in which the cutting plane is bent at a 90° angle to pass through features that do not lie in a straight line.
Off-the-job training	Training that takes place away from the job site.
One-tail test	Test of hypothesis that has only one critical value, either an upper or lower acceptance limit. Compare with a two-tail test: each assumes the other tail is impossible.
One-at-a-time experiment	Each factor is varied individually while holding the levels of other factors constant. For example, an individual tries to fix a problem by making a change then executing a test. Depending on the findings, something else may need to be tried.
One-to-one marketing	The concept of knowing a customer's unique requirements and expectations and marketing to these. *See also* **customer relationship management (CRM).**
Online testing	Any method of testing a unit in its operational environment, or simulated load testing.

On-the-job training (OJT)	Training conducted usually at the workstation, typically done one on one, by someone already skilled at the task.
Opacity	Amount of light obscured by particulate particles suspended in a medium. A clear window glass has zero opacity; a block wall is 100% opaque. Opacity is an indicator of changes in performance of particulate control systems.
Opaque	Quality of not letting light pass through.
Open book management	Approach to managing that exposes employees to the organization's financial information, provides instruction in business literacy, and enables employees to better understand their role and contributions and their impact on the organization.
Open door policy	Management approach that encourages employees to speak freely and regularly to management regarding any aspect of the business or operations.
Opening meeting	Meeting between the auditor(s) and representatives of the organization being audited. It is convened before the audit starts to confirm the audit scope and arrangements.
Operating characteristic curve (OC curve)	Graph to determine the probability of accepting lots as a function of the lots' or processes' quality level when using various sampling plans. There are three types: type A curves, which give the probability of acceptance for an individual lot coming from finite production (will not continue in the future); type B curves, which give the probability of acceptance for lots coming from a continuous process; and type C curves, which (for a continuous sampling plan) give the long-run percentage of product accepted during the sampling phase.
Operating procedure	Documented procedure used by employees that describes how specific tasks are to be performed.
Operational environment	Environment, including the stresses, loading, behaviors encountered while doing, preparing to do, or recovering from actual useful work.
Operational stress	Stresses that are present when a unit is functionally operating. Includes the operating conditions that may cause or accelerate any deterioration of components under prolonged operation.

Operational testing	Testing performed by the end user in its normal operating environment. The testing would include exposure to the realistic operating conditions, loads, and other circumstances that can be reasonably expected.
Operator sensitive	Part design or manufacturing process that the respective manufacturing or assembly personnel can cause to fail based on operator training, ability, fatigue, or motivation.
Opportunity	Future event or series of events that, if occurring, will have a positive impact on the business. Or an event with potential benefits to be realized by undertaking it.
Optical alignment	That branch of metrology that uses light waves to examine sizes and geometrical relationships over larger distances than are ordinarily required in shop and laboratory work.
Optical comparator	Measuring instrument that projects a greatly magnified image of a part feature onto a screen for examination.
Optical flat	Glass or quartz reference surface with one or both sides finished to be precisely flat and to have minimum surface imperfections. *Flats* is also the general term for such devices made from nontransparent materials such as steel or ceramics.
Optical micrometer	Mechanically adjustable means to offset an optical path in one axis. It is calibrated so the offset is known. Optical micrometers are frequently used in pairs at right angles to each other. They are not used alone but are incorporated into instruments such as line of sight telescopes.
Optical polygons	Polygons with precisely spaced faces that represent divisions of a circle. In other words, they represent angles. They are used with optical alignment instruments to set out and to measure angles.
Optical square	Means for turning all or some of the rays in the optical path to 90° from that path.
Optimal	State of a system or process where it is functioning at its maximum effectiveness and/or efficiency.
Optimization	Achieving planned process results that meet the needs of the customer and supplier alike and minimize their combined cost.

Ordering data Rearranging the data and listing them in ascending or descending order.

Ordinal number Any number in a series of numbers used to indicate order.

Organic Referring to or derived from living organisms. Naturally occurring plant or animal matter.

Organization Company, corporation, firm, enterprise, or institution, or a part thereof, that has its own functions and administration.

Organizational chart Graphic display of the management reporting relationships and structure, to provide a general framework of the organization.

Organizational development (OD) Organizationwide (usually) planned effort, managed from the top, to increase organization effectiveness and health through interventions in the organization's processes, using behavioral science knowledge.

Organizational effectiveness Measure of the ability of an organization to achieve maximum customer perceived value, stakeholder equity, profitability, and meet organizational goals.

Organizational goals Statement describing where an organization desires to be, in innovation, in social and environmental matters, in competition, and in financial health.

Organizational structure Set of formal and informal responsibilities, authorities and relationships, arranged in a pattern, through which an organization performs its functions.

Organizational structures Various models that have been developed based on need or management style of the top management, including flat, functional, geographical, historical, matrix, product, tall, team based, and quality. See individual entries for information on each style.

Orientation tolerance In engineering blueprints, the orientation tolerances control the relationship of a part feature to one or more datums. They specify how far the part feature is allowed to vary with respect to the datum. They are expressed as either perpendicularity, angularity, or parallelism. *See* Appendix E.

Original equipment manufacturers (OEM) Company that uses product components from one or more other companies to build a product it sells under its own company name and brand. Sometimes mistakenly used to refer to the company that supplies the components.

Original inspection First inspection of a lot as distinguished from the inspection of a lot that has been resubmitted after a previous rejection or hold status.

Orthogonal Literally, perpendicular or at right angles. (1) In popular use it has come to mean movement in two or three axes at right angles to each other. (2) In a DOE the property that ensures the effects can be determined independently.

Orthogonal array Refers to a device in which the functional parts act at right angles to each other.

Orthogonal contrasts In a designed experiment, two contrasts are orthogonal if the contrast coefficients of the two sets satisfy the condition that when multiplied in corresponding pairs, the sum of those products is equal to zero.

Orthogonal design Design in which all pairs of factors at particular versions (levels) appear together an equal number of times. Where the effects of one factor balance out the effects of the other factors.

Orthographic projection On engineering blueprints, a systematic method of representing a three-dimensional object in six two-dimensional views.

OSHA *See* **Occupational Safety and Health Administration.**

Outer array In a Taguchi-style fractional factorial experiment, the factors in a process being studied cannot be controlled (as opposed to an inner array where they can be controlled).

Outlier Data point that is unusually large or unusually small because of an erroneous reading or some other abnormal situation.

Out-of-box audit Process of inspecting a completed product that is packaged for shipment.

Out-of-control process Process in which the statistical measure being evaluated is not in a state of statistical control. In other words, the variations among the observed sampling results cannot be attributed to a constant system of chance causes. *See* **in-control process.**

Out of spec Term that indicates a unit does not meet a given requirement.

Outputs Products, materials, services, or information provided to customers (internal or external), from a process.

Outside diameter Distance measured across the full width of a round or spherical piece of material, such as a ball, a pipe, rod, and so on.

Outsourcing Strategy to relieve an organization of processes and tasks in order to reduce cost, improve quality, reduce cycle times, reduce the need for specialized skill, and increase efficiency.

Oxidation In an environmental sense, the chemical addition of oxygen to break down pollutants or organic waste; such as the destruction of chemicals like cyanides, phenols, and organic sulfur compounds in sewage by bacterial and chemical means.

Ozone layer Protective layer in the earth's atmosphere, about 15 miles above the ground, that absorbs some of the sun's ultraviolet rays, thereby reducing the amount of potentially harmful radiation that reaches the earth's surface.

P

Pad In casting or machining, a raised area used generally to provide a support surface.

Pairwise comparison A multivoting technique used to rank-order a set of factors (e.g., requirements, projects, and so forth) when the members of a group cannot reach agreement on the priorities of each of the factors. Each factor is compared with all other factors and voted on by the group to determine which is most important. *See also* **multivoting.**

Panels Groups of customers recruited by an organization to provide ad hoc feedback on performance or product development ideas.

Paradigm Set of standards, rules of behavior, attitudes, modes, mores, and so on, by which a group, business, or culture live.

Paradigm shift Advent and acceptance of a totally new model that is theory shattering and displaces and/or discredits older theories and models.

Parallax error Apparent shifting of an object caused by the shifting of the observer. For example, the act of viewing an indicator dial face from an angle when it should be viewed directly or from a straight line of sight.

Parallelism In engineering blueprints, a surface or center plane that is an equal distance at all points from a datum plane. An axis whose entire length is an equal distance from the datum plan or datum axis. A parallelism tolerance specifies how far the surface or center plane, is allowed to vary from the specified datum. *See* Appendix E.

Parallel structure Describes an organizational module in which groups, such as quality circles or a quality council, exists in the organization in addition to and simultaneously with the line organization. Also referred to as "collateral structure."

Parameter (1) Variable, measurable property whose value is determined by the characteristics of a system such as temperature, pressure, length, and weight. (2) Constant or coefficient that describes some characteristic of a population such as the standard deviation, average, regression coefficient, and so on.

Parameter design (Taguchi) Use of design of experiments for identifying the major contributors to **variation.**

Pareto chart Graphical tool for ranking causes from most significant to least significant. It is based on the Pareto principle, first defined by Joseph M. Juran in 1950. The principle, named after 19th-century economist Vilfredo Pareto, suggests most effects come from relatively few causes; that is, 80% of the effects come from 20% of the possible causes. The Pareto chart is one of the **seven tools of quality.**

Parity product Product of equal quality or value supplied by another supplier, or a substitute product supplied by the same supplier that will function equally well for the intended purpose.

Parkinson's law States that work expands to fit the organization developed to perform it, and there is a tendency for each work unit within an organization to try to build up its importance by expanding the number of jobs and personnel it controls.

Partial view On engineering blueprints, a portion of a whole view. It is used to save space on the blueprint or to clarify a detail without resorting to a whole view.

Participative management Style of managing whereby the manager tends to work from theory Y assumptions about people, involving the workers in decisions made.

Particulates In an environmental sense, (1) fine liquid or solid particles such as dust, smoke, mist, fumes, or smog, found in air or emissions. (2) Very small solids suspended in water, they can vary is size, shape, density and electrical charge.

Partitioning   In auditing, the concept of dividing up a large complex audit into smaller more manageable portions.

Partnering   When partnering with employees it shows a high form of trust by management of the employees; at times it may also include team concepts within an organization.

Partnership/ alliance   Both a strategy and a formal relationship between a supplier and a customer that engenders cooperation for the benefit of both parties.

Parts list   Itemized list of all the components in an assembly, including the name of the component, its material composition, part number, and quantity needed for the assembly.

Parts per billion (PPB)   Number of times an occurrence happens in one billion chances. In a typical quality setting, it usually indicates the number of times a defective part will happen in a billion parts produced. The calculation is projected into the future based on past performance.

Parts per million (PPM)   Number of times an occurrence happens in one million chances. In a typical quality setting, it usually indicates the number of times a defective part will happen in a million parts produced. The calculation is often projected into the future based on past performance.

Sigma Level	Parts Per Million
1	690,000
2	308,537
3	66,807
4	6,210
5	233
6	3.4

Parts per million opportunities (PPMO)   Same as PPM.

Pascal   Unit of pressure or stress equal to one newton per square meter.

Pass/fail test   Test used to determine acceptability with only two outcomes: accept or reject.

Passivation   Treatment of corrosion-resistant steel or electrical components with certain noncorrosive agents that will remove surface contaminants and produce a coating more resistant to corrosion or contamination.

Passive data analysis   Data is collected and analyzed as the process is currently performing. Process alterations are not assessed.

Path   Set of ordered tasks, in a logical sequence, in lines, or in nodes in a network diagram.

Path float   *See* **float.**

Path of steepest ascent   Methodology used to determine different factor levels to use in a follow-up experiment such that the expected response will be larger than previous responses.

Pathogens   Microorganisms such as bacteria, viruses, or parasites that can cause disease in humans, animals, and plants.

Patrol inspection   Inspector who has a routine or route to examine product directly from a machine or process.

Pattern   Model (usually made of wood or other easily replaced material) used to form a mold for casting or for repeated use in any number of similar applications.

Payback period   Number of years it will take the results of a project or capital investment to recover the investment from net cash flow.

P chart   *See* **percent chart.**

Peen   To draw, bend, or flatten by hammering with a peen (hammer) or as if a peen were used.

Peer review   Review of a project or performance by individuals with equivalent knowledge and background, but who are not in a superior position to the person or operation being reviewed.

Percent chart   For attribute data, a control chart for evaluating the stability of a process in terms of the percentage of the total number of units in a sample in which an event of a given classification occurs. The percent chart is also referred to as a "proportion chart."

Percent defective
Number of defective parts or units in any quantity of production. Calculated by 100 times the number of defective units divided by the total number produced.

Performance
Determination of achievement to measure and manage a project or service quality.

Performance appraisal
Formal method of measuring employees' progress against performance standards and providing feedback to them.

Performance improvement
Primary result of efforts extended to improve a situation or process, it may be increased output, higher quality, or improved individual learning skills and performance.

Performance management system
System that supports and contributes to the creation of high performance work and work systems by translating behavioral principles into procedures.

Performance objectives
Objectives that are set to evaluate performance. For managers to be effective they must observe certain concepts: (1) Know yourself. (2) Know your employees. (3) Have a positive attitude. (4) Share your goals. (5) Make your work and your employees' work interesting. (6) Communicate effectively. (7) Celebrate success.

Performance plan
Documented performance management tool that describes desired performance and provides a way to assess the performance objectively.

Performance standard
Metric against which a complete action is compared.

Performance study
Analysis of a process to determine the distribution of a run. The process may or may not be in statistical control.

Performance test
Assessment device that requires candidates to complete an actual work task in a controlled situation.

Performance variation
Degree to which a manufactured part or a process output deviates from its target value during the product life span, under different operating conditions and across different units of production. The smaller the variation from the target value, the greater the control is demonstrated and improved quality is implied.

Periodic assessment   Assessment in which the Quality/EMS system is subjected to system maintenance monitoring activities between periods of a complete reassessment.

Permeability   Rate at which liquids or gasses pass through a material in a specified direction.

Perpendicularity   Condition of a line in which all angles to a reference plane are at right angles. In surface plate work, perpendicular is generally synonymous to vertical.

Personality test   Assessment device that measures a person's interaction skills and patterns of behavior.

Personal protective equipment (PPE)   Clothing and equipment worn by persons who are or may be exposed to potentially hazardous chemicals and other pollutants.

PERT chart   Project network diagrams that graphically demonstrate the relationship among project elements. It shows the order in which elements are to be completed. May also include additional time information: earliest and latest time an element can be completed without affecting the project. Slack time may be included as well as a critical path. It is event oriented and requires time estimates for each activity.

pH   Expression of the intensity or the basic or acid condition of a liquid; it may range from 0 to 14, where 0 is the most acidic and 7 is the neutral point. Natural waters usually have a pH of between 6.5 and 8.5.

Phantom line   On blueprints, one long and two short dashes used in various applications: (1) to show where an existing structure needs modification, (2) to show alternate positions of an object, (3) to avoid showing unnecessary detail (to show all the coils in a spring), and (4) to show the direction of a unilateral profile tolerance zone in geometric tolerancing. *See* Appendix E.

Phase review   Management review process of monitoring and controlling the development of products at distinct stages, starting at conception/design and ending at production and shipment, or field evaluation.

Phenols   Organic compounds that are by-products of petroleum refining, tanning, and textile, dye, and resin manufacturing. Low concentrations cause taste and odor problems in water; higher concentrations can kill humans, animals, and aquatic life.

Photoelectric instruments Instruments used to avoid the subjective bias of the observer. Optical instruments that use photoelectric sensors to ascertain the reference and measured points. The most common and advanced of these use lasers as their light source.

Pico One-trillionth part of a factor. Expressed as 10 to the minus 12th power.

Pie chart Graphical representations that look like a cut pie. They are effective in showing problems in a Pareto fashion, showing how much each component of a set of values contributes to the whole. Or how much of the total problem is contributed by each element of the problem being considered.

Pilot lot First lot off of production tooling. Used to prove the capability of the production equipment and process.

Pilot process Small-scale operation used to develop new products or to test out process modifications before moving it up to full production operations. Used to identify risk associated with a process.

Pinch point Location in a mechanical mechanism where a pinch injury may occur.

Pitch Describes the number of threads or knurl teeth per inch. Also refers to the distance from a point on one thread or knurl to an adjacent thread or tooth.

Plackett-Burman design Two-level experimental design to screen for the few important controlled variables from a larger number of controlled variables. It is good for sifting out more than six variables for importance. It allows a larger number of control variables than a fractional factorial.

Plan Provisions made to achieve an objective.

Plan-do-check-act (PDCA) cycle Four-step process for quality improvement. In the first step (plan), a plan to effect improvement is developed. In the second step (do), the plan is carried out, preferably on a small scale. In the third step (check), the effects of the plan are observed. In the last step (act), the results are studied to determine what was learned and what can be predicted. The plan-do-check-act cycle is sometimes referred to as the "Shewhart cycle," because Walter A. Shewhart discussed the concept in his book *Statistical*

P

Method from the Viewpoint of Quality Control, and as the Deming cycle, because W. Edwards Deming introduced the concept in Japan. The Japanese subsequently called it the Deming cycle. Also called the "plan-do-study-act (PDSA) cycle." The basic foundation on which Six Sigma is based, which requires that problems be methodically evaluated and the root cause identified and eliminated or controlled, providing for continual improvement.

Plan-do-study-act cycle (PDSA)   Variation on the plan do check act (PDCA) cycle, with the variation indicating additional study is required after a change is made.

Plane   (1) Removal of material to make a flat surface by means of planing. (2) On blueprints, the plane in which the reference points lie. It is always perpendicular to the line of reference. The reference plane by definition must be flat. The reference plane is also known as the "datum plane." *See* Appendix E.

Plate   To put a thin layer of metal on a surface (such as chrome plate). *See also* **surface plate.**

Platykurtosis   For frequency distributions: a distribution that has longer, flatter tails than a normal distribution with the same standard deviation. *See also* **kurtosis.**

Plug gage   Nonadjustable gage for measuring holes. Often configured with a go end and a no-go end. May also be configured to various shapes to fit patterned holes.

Pneumatic metrology   Refers to any measurement system that uses pressure changes in a fluid (air or other gases) system, to amplify changes in part sizes or shapes.

Point estimate   Single value used to estimate a population parameter. Point estimates are commonly referred to as the points at which the interval estimates are centered; these estimates give information about how much uncertainty is associated with the estimate.

Poisson distribution   Distribution that can be equated to a limiting form of the binominal distribution. It is a discrete distribution that is applicable when there are many opportunities for the occurrence of an event, but a low probability (less than 0.10) on each trial. *See* Appendix C.

P95', P50', P10', P05', and so on   Submitted quality in fraction defective for which the probability of acceptance is 0.95, 0.50, 0.10, 0.05, and so on, for a given sampling plan. Note:

The exact value of P95', P50', P10', P05', and so on, depends on whether "submitted quality" relates to lot quality or process quality.

Poka-yoke   Japanese term that means mistake proofing or error proofing. A *poka-yoke* device prevents incorrect parts from being made or assembled, or easily identifies a flaw or error.

Polish   To produce a fine surface finish (such as by means of a very fine abrasive).

Policy   Guide to thinking, action, and decisions. An overarching plan (direction) for achieving an organization's goals.

Policy deployment   Process of developing, distributing, and enforcing policies in an organization, then turning those policies into goals for the various business units.

Pollutant   Generally, any substance introduced into the environment that adversely affects the usefulness of a resource or the health of humans, animals, or the environment.

Polymer   Natural or synthetic chemical structure where two or more like molecules are joined to form a more complex molecular structure, such as polyethylene in plastics.

PONC   Price of nonconformance; the cost of not doing things right the first time.

Population   Group of people, objects, observations, or measurements about which one wishes to draw conclusions. Also called a "universe."

Population (statistical)   Totality of items or units of material under consideration. The items may be measurements, and the population may be real or conceptual. Thus *population* may refer to all the items actually produced in a given day or all that might be produced if the process were to continue (in control) over a long period of time.

Porosity   Degree to which a material has pores or cavities through which liquids or gases can move into or through.

Portfolio analysis   Process of comparing the value of proposed projects or acquisitions relative to the financial impacts on current projects as well as the potential on resources of the proposed project or acquisition.

Position   In engineering blueprints, the theoretically exact location of a center, axis, or center plane or a feature in relation to another feature or datum. A position tolerance states how much the center plane is allowed to vary from its theoretically exact position. *See* Appendix E.

Positional tolerancing   Recognizes that the limits of clearances and fits between mating parts occur in circles, and not in rectangles that result from tolerancing with orthogonal relationships.

Positive skewness   Occurs in a distribution where the tail tapers to the right and the hump appears to the left of the distribution; also called "right skew."

Postmortem   Evaluation of a project after completion. To determine how the project went, each team member should provide input as to their evaluation of the process, what went well and what parts had problems, and how the process could be improved.

Potential nonconformity   Situation that if left alone will in time result in a nonconformity.

Potential process capability (P_{pk})   Used in the validation stage of a new product launch (uses a similar formula as C_{pk}, but a higher value is expected due to the smaller time span the samples are taken from). *See* **C_{pk} ratio**. *See* Appendix C for formula.

Pounds per square inch (PSI)   Measure of pressure indicating the force applied to a container by the buildup of pressure within the container.

Power curve   Graph of the relation between the probability of rejecting the hypothesis that a sample belongs to a given population with a given characteristic and the actual population value of that characteristic.

Pre-award survey   On-site survey of a supplier to evaluate its ability to supply acceptable products and to perform deliveries in accordance with a proposed contract.

Precedence diagramming method (PDM)   Network diagramming technique in which activities are represented by boxes (or nodes) and linked by precedence relationship lines to show the sequence in which the activities are to be performed. The nodes are connected with arrows to show the dependencies. Four types of relationships are possible: finish-to-finish, finish-to-start, start-to-finish, and start-to-start. Also called "activity-on-node (AON)" or "activity on arc."

Precision instruments Measuring instruments that provide enough amplification of the natural senses of sight and touch to provide a positive degree of accuracy and confidence in the measurement.

Precision (metrology) Aspect of measurement that addresses repeatability or consistency when an identical item is measured several times with the same instrument while obtaining the same accurate results.

Precision (statistical) Closeness of agreement between randomly selected individual measurements or test results. Note: The standard deviation of the error of measurement is sometimes called a measure of "imprecision."

Pre-control Control process, with simple rules based on tolerances, advocated by Dorian Shanin. It is proposed for any process where a worker can measure a quality characteristic (dimension, color, strength, etc.) and can adjust the process to change that characteristic, and where there is either continuous output or discrete output totaling three or more pieces.

Predecessor activity Activity that must begin or end before another activity or task can begin or end.

Prerequisite tree Technique used in the application of Eliyahu Goldratt's theory of constraints. It is used to identify obstacles to implementing any change.

Preventive action Action taken to remove or improve a process or to prevent potential future occurrences of a nonconformance.

Prevention cost Cost of all activities specifically designed to prevent poor quality in products or services. Those incurred for efforts intended to prevent problems at later stages in the life cycle of the product or service where the cost of a nonconformance would increase. Examples could include new product reviews, quality planning, supplier capability surveys, process capability studies, quality improvement team meetings, quality improvement projects, quality education and training. For a complete explanation of the principles of quality cost, see *Principles of Quality Costs* (Milwaukee: ASQ Quality Press, 1999).

Prevention of pollution In an environmental management system, the use of processes, practices, materials, or products that avoid, reduce, or control pollution. These activities may include recycling, treatment, process changes, control mechanisms, efficient use of resources, and material substitution.

Prevention versus detection   Term used to contrast two types of quality activities. Prevention refers to activities designed to prevent nonconformances in products and services. Detection refers to activities designed to detect nonconformances already in products and services. Another phrase to describe this distinction is "designing in quality versus inspecting in quality."

Primary   Processes that refers to the basic steps or activities that will produce the output without the "nice-to-haves."

Primary customer   Person or group who directly receives the output of a process.

Primary datum   In engineering blueprints, it is usually established by the largest or most important feature of the part. Part of the datum reference frame. *See* Appendix E.

Primary reference standard   For measurements, a standard maintained by the National Institute of Standards and Technology for a particular measuring unit. The primary reference standard duplicates as nearly as possible the international standard, used to calibrate other transfer standards, which in turn are used to calibrate measuring instruments for industrial use.

Principal view   On engineering blueprints, the six views that define the shape and features of a part. These include the front, top, right side, left side, bottom, and rear.

Print   Another name for an "engineering blueprint" or "mechanical drawing."

Priorities   Process of setting order to events by magnitude of importance or required sequence of activities.

Priorities matrix   Tool used to choose between several options that have many useful benefits, but where not all of them are of equal value. These choices are then prioritized based on known weighted criteria. The choices are then narrowed down to the most desirable or effective one(s) to accomplish the task or problem at hand. One of the seven management and planning tools.

Proactive   Taking the initiative to implement methodologies based on experience in order to anticipate the best ways to avoid defects, problems, or customer-perceived problems.

Probability (statistical)   Refers to the likelihood of occurrence of an event, action, or item.

Probability density function	Mathematical function that can model the variation density reflected in a histogram.
Probability distribution	Mathematical formula that relates the values of characteristics to their probability of occurrence in a population. *See* Appendix C.
Probability of detection	The likelihood, expressed as a percentage, that a test or examination method will correctly identify the error or defect.
Probability of rejection	Probability that a lot will be rejected.
Probability paper	Various types of graph paper used to plot the probability of an occurrence.
Probability theory	Set of mathematical theorems and practices dealing with uncertainty. Often used to describe the short-run likelihood of an event and to help determine whether a short run typifies the long run, especially in sampling matters.
Problem definition	Process of distinguishing between causes and symptoms to determine the scope of effort required to correct a problem or potential problem.
Problem solving	Act of defining a problem; determining the cause of the problem; identifying, prioritizing, and selecting alternatives for a solution; and implementing a solution. A *six-step* process would include: (1) identify the problem, (2) define the problem, (3) investigate the problem, (4) analyze the problem, (5) solve the problem, and (6) confirm the results. A *seven-step* process: (1) identify the problem, (2) list possible root causes, (3) search out the most likely root cause, (4) identify potential solutions, (5) select and implement a solution, (6) follow up to evaluate the effect, and (7) standardize the process.
Problem-solving tools	The primary seven quality tools are (1) cause-and-effect diagrams, (2) flow-charts, (3) check sheets, (4) histograms, (5) control charts, (6) Pareto charts, and (7) scatter diagrams. See individual entries.
Procedure	Itemized and documented steps in a process that detail how these steps are to be performed, when, where, by whom, what materials are used, and so on, for a defined process to fulfill customer's requirements.

P

Process	Set of interrelated work activities involving people, materials, machines, methods, energy, and environment, characterized by a set of specific inputs and value-added tasks that make up a procedure for a set of specific outputs.
Process analysis	Quantifying the process capability from data, which, in turn, are the results of measurement of work performed by the process.
Process analysis diagram	Cause-and-effect diagram for a process. Each step of the process and the factors contributing to it are shown, indicating all cause-and-effect relationships. This allows systematic tracing of any problems that may arise, to identify the source of the problem.
Process average quality	Expected or average value of process quality.
Process capability	Limits within which a tool or process operates based on minimum variability as governed by the prevailing circumstances. Note: The phrase "by prevailing circumstances" indicates that the definition of inherent variability or a process involving only one operator, one source of raw material, and so on, differs from one involving multiple operators, and many sources of raw materials, and so on. If the measure of inherent variability (*see* **statistical control**) is made within very restricted circumstances, it is necessary to add components for frequency occurring assignable sources of variation that cannot economically be eliminated. *See* C_{pk} and P_{pk}.
Process capability index	Value of the tolerance specified for the characteristic divided by the process capability. The several types of process capability indexes include the widely used C_{pk} and P_{pk}. *See* Appendix C for formulas.
Process control	Methodology for keeping a process within boundaries and minimizing the inherent variation of a process.
Process decision program chart (PDPC)	Management and planning tool that identifies all events that can go wrong and the appropriate countermeasures for these events. It graphically represents all sequences that lead to a desirable effect. One of the seven management and planning tools.
Process failure mode and effects analysis (PFMEA)	Diagram used to identify and evaluate the relative failure modes and/or negative interactions in a process.

Process flow diagram (chart)	Path or steps of work process, graphically displayed on a chart. Typically a diamond would represent storage; a blacked-out spot, a decision; an outlined arrow, transportation; a circle, handling; a circle with lines, add to step; a circle with a blackened dot, an origination step; and a square box, an inspection point.
Process improvement	Application of the plan-do-study-act (PDSA) philosophy to processes, used to produce positive improvement and better meet the needs and expectations of customers. *See* **plan-do-check-act cycle.**
Process improvement group (PIG)	Team-structured environment often made up of cross-functional members who work together to improve a process or operation. Usually the team is established by the quality management steering committee. A variation on the process improvement team concept.
Process improvement model	Five-step process: (1) Select the process to improve. (2) Review current performance. (3) Identify improvement needs or opportunities. (4) Implement process changes. (5) Evaluate the process change for desired effect.
Process *kaizen*	Improvements made within an individual process or in a specific area. Sometimes called "point *kaizen*."
Process management	Pertinent techniques and tools applied to a process to implement and improve process effectiveness, hold the gains made, and ensure process integrity in fulfilling customer requirements.
Process map	Type of flowchart depicting the steps in a process, with identification of responsibility for each step and the key measures required to maintain control.
Process organization	Form of departmentalization where each department specializes in one phase of the process.
Process owner	Person who coordinates the various functions and work activities at all levels of a process, has the authority or ability to make changes in the process as required, and manages the entire process cycle to ensure performance effectiveness.
Process performance management	Overseeing of process instances to ensure their quality and timeliness. Can also include proactive and reactive actions to ensure a good result.

P

Process quality	Value of percentage defective or of defects per hundred units in product from a given process. Note: The symbols "p" and "c" are commonly used to represent the true process average in fraction defective or defects per unit; and "l00p" and "100c" the true process average in percentage defective or in defects per hundred units.
Process quality audit	Analysis of the elements of a process an appraisal of the completeness, correctness of conditions, and probable effectiveness of a process.
Process reengineering	Strategy directed toward major rethinking and restructuring of a process; often referred to as the "clean sheet of paper" approach.
Process village	Refers to machines grouped by type of operation (contrast with a cell layout).
Procurement	Process of acquiring goods or services from outside the organization, beginning with determining the need for the supplies or services and ending with the receipt of the goods.
Procurement audit	Structured review of the procurement process from planning through contract administration to identify successes and failures. The lessons learned can be used later on other projects to improve the process.
Procurement management	Process that describes the management of the procurement processes, from contract origination, the bid process, order and receipt, to close out of the contract.
Producer's risk (α, also called alpha risk and type I error)	For a given sampling plan, refers to the probability of not accepting a lot, the quality of which has a designated numerical value representing a generally desirable level. Usually the designated value will be the acceptable quality level (AQL).
Product	Result of activities or processes. A product can be tangible or intangible, or a combination of both. Any products or services.
Production and reliability acceptance test (PRAT)	Test conducted under specified conditions, using delivered or deliverable production items to determine the producer's compliance with specified reliability requirements as a condition of customer acceptance.

Production part approval process (PPAP)   Ford, Chrysler, and General Motors automotive process that defines the generic requirements for approval of production parts, including production and bulk materials. Its purpose is to determine during an actual production run at the quoted production rates whether all customer engineering, design record, and specification requirements are properly understood by the supplier and whether the process has the potential to produce product consistently meeting these requirements. *See also* **QS-9000, ISO/TS 16949.**

Production permit   Written authorization for a product, prior to its production, to depart from originally specified requirements. May also be known as a "deviation or waiver."

Productivity   Ratio of output to input, where input consists of labor, material, capital, and utilities, and output consists of a product or service.

Product liability   (Per ISO A8402) Generic term used to describe the requirements on a producer or others to make restitution for loss related to personal injury, property damage, or other harm caused by a product.

Product life cycle   Total period of time that a product may exist in the marketplace. In production it is usually defined in stages such as design, manufacturing, assembly, installation, operation, and shutdown. *See* **life cycle of a product** or **a project.**

Product organization   Organization divided along product lines, with each product line supporting its needs for labor and materials.

Product orientation   Refers to a tendency to see customers' needs in terms of a product they want to buy, not in terms of the services, value, or benefits the product will produce.

Product or service liability   Obligation of a company to make restitution for loss related to personal injury, property damage, or other harm caused by its product or service.

Product quality audit   Quantitative assessment of the conformance to required product specifications and characteristics.

Product warranty   Organization's stated policy that it will replace, repair, or reimburse a buyer for a product in the event a product defect occurs under certain conditions and within a stated period of time.

Professional development plan   Individual development tool for an employee. Working together, employee and supervisor create a plan that matches the individual's career needs and aspirations with organizational demands.

Professional engineer (PE)	Engineer who through education and performance has demonstrated a proficiency in the engineering field and has been designated as a professional.
Proficiency testing	Per ISO Guide 25 1990 (E) now replaced by ANSI/ISO 17025-1999, the determination of the laboratory calibration or testing performance by means of interlaboratory comparisons.
Profile	Usually, an irregular shape or cut on a part by means of a template (or guide).
Profile of a line	Tolerance that controls the profile of the individual cross-section of the part, rather than the entire surface as a single entity. *See* Appendix E.
Profile of a surface	Profile of a surface tolerance controls the profile of the entire length and width of the part feature. *See* Appendix E.
Profile tolerances	In engineering blueprints, a profile is a two-dimensional outline of a part feature from a top, side, or front view. On a drawing, it is typically defined by basic dimensions in the form of sizes, radii, angles, or arcs. A profile tolerance specifies a uniform boundary along the true profile within which the part feature must lie. The two types are profile of a line and profile of a surface. *See* Appendix E.
Profilometer	Electronic instrument used to measure the surface finish of machined parts by moving a stylus across the surface and providing a reading, usually in AA or RMS.
Profound knowledge, system of	Defined by W. Edwards Deming, a system that consists of an appreciation for systems, knowledge of variation, theory of knowledge, and understanding of psychology. See also *Out of the Crisis* (Cambridge: MIT, Center for Advanced Engineering Study, 1986).
Program	Group of interrelated activities managed in a way to obtain results that are not achievable if they are attempted individually.
Program evaluation and review technique (PERT)	Event-oriented project management planning and measurement technique that utilizes an arrow diagram or road map to identify all major project events and demonstrates the amount of time (critical path) needed to complete a project. It provides three time estimates: optimistic, most likely, and pessimistic.

Project Short-term efforts extended to create a product or accomplish a goal, usually defined with a start and end date to show duration and completion.

Project audit Structured formal review of a project, at any time in the project life cycle, to assess progress performance relative to time, cost, and technical objectives; typically conducted by a third party.

Project control Activities associated with making decisions about present and future project activities and the collection and documentation of project information, through to completion.

Project life cycle Management of activities and events involved throughout a project's duration to include (1) concept, (2) planning, (3) design, (4) production, and (5) evaluation/closeout.

Project management Application of knowledge, skills, tools and techniques to a broad range of activities to meet the requirements of the particular project. Project management knowledge and practices are best described in terms of their component processes. These processes can be placed into five process groups (initiating, planning, executing, controlling, and closing) and nine knowledge areas (project integration management, project scope management, project time management, project cost management, project quality management, project human resource management, project communications management, project risk management, and project procurement management). Others call the cycle (1) planning, (2) organizing, (3) scheduling, and (4) controlling.

Project manager Person assigned to lead a project; duties include planning, scheduling, and controlling the project through completion.

Project plan All the documents that comprise the details of why the project is to be initiated, what the project is to accomplish, when and where it is to be implemented, who will have responsibility, how the implementation will be carried out, how much it will cost, what resources are required, and how the project's progress and results will be measured.

Project success Ten steps a manager should keep in mind to improve a project's success: (1) Keep the project visible. (2) Balance cost with performance. (3) Communicate openly with clients. (4) Use technology where applicable. (5) Maintain a schedule. (6) Use the right people. (7) Ensure top management support. (8) Prepare contingencies. (9) Don't be hasty to declare a success. (10) Remember that a project is only as good as its application.

Project team   Manages the work of a project. The work typically involves balancing competing demands for project scope, time, cost, risk, and quality, satisfying stakeholders with differing needs and expectations, and meeting identified requirements.

Promotional management style   Management approach in which the manager encourages team members to realize their full potential, cultivates team spirit, and lets team members know that good work will be rewarded.

Protocol   Series of formal and defined steps for conducting a process or test.

Prototype   Functioning, usually full-scale sample of a completed new product, used to evaluate the design of the product.

Protractor   Instrument for measuring angles by the displacement method. They usually have calibrated arcs as standards.

Psychographic customer characteristics   Variables among buyers in the consumer market that addresses lifestyle issues and includes consumer interests, activities, and opinions.

Pull system   Alternative to scheduling individual processes, in which the customer process withdraws the items it needs from a supermarket (storage area) and the supplying process produces to replenish what was withdrawn. Used to avoid push and excess inventory. *See **kanban.***

Punch   To cut, emboss, or perforate a part by means of forcing a rigid tool into or through a workpiece.

Punch list   List prepared for use at the end of a project to show items of work that still need to be completed before the project is closed out. Typically used for larger scale projects.

Punch press   Machine used to cut duplicate parts by means of a punch and die set (die), usually for high-volume precision pieces.

Punitive damages   Monetary compensation awarded by a court order, over and above the actual damages sought by an individual or company, used to punish someone or some company for wrongful acts.

Purchaser   The customer.

Purpose   In quality award criteria, the term *purpose* refers to the fundamental reason an organization exists. The primary role of purpose is to inspire an organization and guide its setting of values.

QA — Quality assurance, the planned activities implemented within a quality system, to provide confidence that defined requirements have been fulfilled. A term used to define a department in an organization, whose function is to provide guidance in quality practices in a proactive way to prevent problems and to assure products and processes meet customer requirements.

Q: Big Q, Little q — Terms coined by Joseph M. Juran to contrast the difference between managing for quality in all business processes and products (big Q) and managing for quality in a limited capacity—traditionally only in factory products and processes (little q). See also *Juran's Quality Handbook,* 5th ed. (New York: McGraw-Hill, 1999).

QC — Quality control. Term used to define a department in an organization whose function is to monitor and inspect parts and/or processes to assure that defective parts do not get to the customer. The operational techniques and procedures implemented in a quality system used to eliminate the causes of defects or unsatisfactory performance at all stages of production or service delivery. It is by nature a reactive process.

Q Chart (quality score chart) — Control chart for evaluating the stability of a process in terms of a quality score.

QEDS Standards Group — U.S. Standards Group on Quality, Environment, Dependability, and Statistics consists of the members and leadership of organizations concerned with the development and effective use of generic and sector specific standards on quality control, assurance and management, environmental management systems and auditing, dependability, and the application of statistical methods.

Q9000 series Refers to ANSI/ISO/ASQ Q9000 series of standards, which is the verbatim American adoption of the 2000 edition of the ISO 9000 series standards.

QS-9000 Quality management systems requirement developed by the Big Three automakers for the automotive sector. Currently being replaced by Technical Specification 16949 (ISO/TS 16949).

Q seven and the new seven The seven statistical tools (commonly referred to as the "Q seven") and seven additional tools (the "new seven") that have made an indispensable contribution to the constant evolution and improvement of the total quality control movement. The seven statistical tools are (1) Pareto diagrams, (2) cause-and-effect diagrams, (3) histograms, (4) control charts, (5) scatter diagrams, (6) graphs, and (7) check sheets. The new seven are (1) relationship diagram, (2) affinity diagram, (3) tree diagram, (4) matrix diagram, (5) prioritization matrix, (6) PDCA (process decision program chart), and (7) arrow diagram.

Quadratic Of or pertaining to a second order mathematical relationship.

Qualification Determination by a series of test and examinations of products or services, through related documents and processes, that the product or service meets all the specified performance capability requirements.

Qualification process Process of demonstrating whether an entity is capable of meeting specified requirements.

Qualified personnel Personnel who have been judged as having the necessary skills and or ability to carry out a particular task.

Qualitative assessment Gathering of information by an organization to measure and track performance. Items of interest may include sales figures, on-time delivery from supplier, employee satisfaction data, customer satisfaction data, and so on. Qualitative data is not easily used because of the subjective nature of the information. Much of what is gathered is used to make management decisions by converting the information into a numeric format by use of formulas, scales, or other types of rating systems.

Qualitative factor Factor that has discrete levels. For example, product origination where the factor levels are Supplier A, Supplier B, and Supplier C.

Quality Subjective term for which each person has his or her own definition. In technical usage, quality can have two meanings: (1) the characteristics of a product or service that bear on its ability to satisfy stated or implied needs; and (2) a product or service free of deficiencies.

Quality adviser Person (facilitator) who helps team members work together in a quality process and is a consultant to the team. The adviser is concerned about the process and how decisions are made rather than about which decisions are made.

Quality assessment Process of identifying business practices, attitudes, and activities that are enhancing or inhibiting the achievement of quality improvement in an organization.

Quality assurance/ quality control (QA/QC) Two terms that have many interpretations, but are often used interchangeably because of the multiple definitions for the words *assurance* and *control*. For example, *assurance* can mean the act of giving confidence, the state of being certain or the act of making certain; *control* can mean an evaluation to indicate needed corrective responses, the act of guiding or the state of a process in which the variability is attributable to a constant system of chance causes. (For a detailed discussion on the multiple definitions, see also *ANSI/ISO/ASQ A3534-2, Statistics—Vocabulary and Symbols—Statistical Quality Control*.) One definition of quality assurance is all the planned and systematic activities implemented within the quality system that can be demonstrated to provide confidence a product or service will fulfill requirements for quality.

Quality audit Systematic independent examination and review to determine whether quality activities and related results comply with planned arrangements and whether these arrangements are implemented effectively and are suitable to achieve the objectives.

Quality auditor Trained person who has the qualification status to perform quality audits. The person doing the quality audits.

Quality characteristics Characteristics that are important to the customer, and by which they judge the total quality of the product or service.

Quality circles Quality improvement or self-improvement study groups composed of a small number of employees (10 or fewer) and their supervisor. Quality circles originated in Japan, where they are called "quality control circles."

Quality control *See* **quality assurance/quality control.**

Quality costs   Methodology to categorize and prioritize quality improvement opportunities based on cost. These cost are usually divided up as four categories (1) prevention cost, (2) appraisal cost, (3) internal failure cost, and (4) external failure cost. See individual entries. For a complete explanation, see also *Principles of Quality Costs* (Milwaukee: ASQ Quality Press, 1999).

Quality cost reports   System of collecting quality cost that uses a spreadsheet to list the elements of quality cost against a spread of the departments, areas, or projects in which the cost occur and summarizes the data to enable trend analysis and decision making. The reports help organizations review prevention cost, appraisal cost, and internal and external failure cost.

Quality council   Also called "quality steering committee." The group driving the quality improvement effort and usually having oversight responsibility for the implementation and maintenance of the quality management system; operates in parallel with the normal operation of the business.

Quality culture   Consists of employee opinions, beliefs, traditions, and practices concerning quality within an organization.

Quality document   Document that contains either requirements for quality system elements for products and services or the results of these activities such as inspection or quality audit reports.

Quality engineering (QE)   Analysis of a manufacturing system at all stages to maximize the quality of the process itself and the products it produces.

Quality engineer in training (QEIT)   Former ASQ certification.

Quality evaluation   Systematic examination of the extent to which an entity (part, product, service, or organization) is capable of meeting specified requirements. A quality evaluation may be used to determine supplier quality capability. In this case, the result of quality evaluations may be used for the qualification, approval, registration, or accreditation purposes.

Quality evidence audit   Final part of the data-gathering phase of a quality audit in which data related to quality improvements is compiled, divided into key areas, and rated. The objective is to collect easily quantifiable data that can be clarified by follow-up interviews with select personnel.

Quality Excellence for Suppliers of Telecommunications (QuEST) Forum Partnership of telecommunications suppliers and service providers with more than 130 members. The QuEST Forum developed TL 9000 (see entry).

Quality function Entire collection of activities through which an organization achieves fitness for use, no matter where these activities are performed.

Quality function deployment (QFD) Structured method in which customer requirements are translated into appropriate technical requirements for each stage of product development and production. The QFD process is often referred to as "listening to (or capturing) the voice of the customer." Also called "the house of quality."

Quality gate Defined criteria for a task. May include an audit, a walk-through inspection, dimensional inspection, or other qualifying method to provide an assessment of the processes used or products as delivered.

Quality improvement Actions taken to increase the value to the customer by improving the effectiveness and efficiency of processes and activities throughout the organizational structure.

Quality Information Center (QIC) The ASQ library, staffed with professional information specialists. Its mission is to be a critical and relevant information resource that advances learning, quality improvement, knowledge exchange, ASQ members, and ASQ communities. It offers access to ASQ's quality-related resources and publications, the Quality InfoSearch database, subject matter experts, customized research, and document delivery services.

Quality inspection Any of a number of activities used to determine product or service attributes or dimensions. To make an informed judgment about the conformity to meet specifications or fitness for use.

Quality level agreement (QLA) Internal service/product providers assist their internal customers in clearly delineating the level of service/product quality required in quantitatively measurable terms. A QLA may contain specifications for accuracy, timeliness, quality/usability, product life, service availability, responsiveness to needs, and so on.

Quality loop   Conceptual model of interacting activities that influence quality at the various stages ranging from the identification of needs to the assessment of whether those needs are satisfied.

Quality losses   Losses caused by not realizing the optimum potential of resources in processes and activities.

Quality loss function   Parabolic approximation of the quality loss that occurs when a quality characteristic deviates from its target value. The quality loss function is expressed in monetary units: the cost of deviating from the target increases as the quality characteristic moves outside the target range. The formula used to compute the quality loss function depends on the type of quality characteristic being used. The quality loss function was first introduced in this form by Genichi Taguchi. See also *Introduction to Quality Engineering* (Dearborn, MI: American Supplier Institute, 1986).

Quality management (QM)   Oversight and application of quality principles in a management system used to guide overall operational process to achieve maximum customer satisfaction at the lowest overall cost to the organization while continuing to improve the process.

Quality management system (QMS)   Formalized system that documents the structure, responsibilities, and procedures required to achieve effective customer satisfaction levels.

Quality manual   Document stating the quality policy and describing the quality system of an organization. A quality manual will normally contain, or refer to, the quality policy, the relationships, and the responsibilities, authorities, and interrelationships of personnel who manage, perform, verify, or review work affecting quality. May also include procedures and work instructions.

Quality measure   Quantitative measure of the features and characteristics of a product or service. Note: Quantitative measures may take a variety of forms such as physical and chemical measurements, the percentage of product not conforming to specifications, the percentage of product conforming to specifications, a demerit index, and so on. Quality measures are used in technical applications in order to provide needed analytical information useful for control and acceptance purposes. Some are used to evaluate the conformance of individual units to specifications; others are used to interpret quality in terms of the percentage of conforming or nonconforming units in a lot, and so on.

Quality metrics Numerical measurements that give an organization the ability to set goals and evaluate actual performance versus plan.

Quality organizations Within each organization are various quality groups or departments whose primary function is to assure the integrity of the product or service provided.

Quality philosophy Established quality policies and procedures used to guide an organization's work that serve as the basis for judging the organization's products and/or services.

Quality plan (QP) Document or set of documents that describe the standards, quality practices, resources, and processes pertinent to a specific product, service, or project.

Quality planning Establishing and developing the objectives and requirements for quality and the requirements for the application of the quality system. According to Juran, these steps should include a quality council, quality policies, strategic quality goals, deployment of quality goals, resources for control, measurement of performance, and quality audits.

Quality policy Organization's general statement of its beliefs about quality, how quality will come about, and what is expected to result. A formalized document created to communicate the overall intentions and directions of the organization as they relate to quality. First step in creating an organization's formal quality system.

Quality predictor Measures for estimating the likelihood of conforming to the specifications identified and required to produce a product or to deliver a service.

Quality principles Rules or concepts that an organization believes in collectively. The principles are formulated by senior management with input from others and communicated and understood at every level on the organization.

Quality process review Process of using data to determine how the actual results compare with the quality specifications and requirements.

Quality program Organized efforts and actions taken to ensure the delivery of quality products and services to the customer.

Quality requirements Translation of customer needs into a set of quantitatively or qualitatively stated requirements for the characteristics of a product or service to enable its realization and examination. The requirements for quality should be initially expressed in functional terms and documented.

Quality score chart (Q chart) Control chart for evaluating the stability of a process in terms of a quality score. The quality score is the weighted sum of the count of events of various classifications in which each classification is assigned a weight. Also known as a "demerit chart."

Quality (statistical) Totality of features and characteristics of a product or service that bear on its ability to satisfy a given needs. Note: In order to be able to assure control or improve quality, it is necessary to be able to evaluate it. This definition calls for the identification of those characteristics and features bearing on the "fitness-for-use" of a proof, a product, or service. The ability "to satisfy given needs" reflects value to the customer and includes economics as well as safety, availability, design, and all other characteristics that the need for the product or service involves. The phrase "given needs" includes defining a price as well as stating what must be achieved, since it is usually possible to improve use characteristics if price is not a limitation.

Quality steering committee *See* **quality council.**

Quality surveillance Continuous monitoring and verification of the status of an entity (part, product, service, organization, etc.) and an analysis of records to ensure that requirements are being fulfilled.

Quality system Organizational structure, responsibilities, procedures, processes, and resources for implementing quality management. The quality system of an organization is designed primarily to satisfy the internal requirements of the organization and not limited to the quality assurance requirements for its customers. The development of a quality system should include (1) a quality statement, (2) a quality manual, (3) quality procedures, and (4) quality work instructions.

Quality system audit Documented activity performed to verify, by examination and evaluation of objective evidence, that applicable elements of the quality system are suitable and have been developed, documented, and effectively implemented in accordance with specified requirements.

Quality system review Formal evaluation by top management of the status and adequacy of the quality system in relation to the organization's quality policy and other relevant objectives.

Quality tokenism Practice of naming a department or individual as the quality assurance function for the purpose of satisfying a customer or a public relations requirement, but not using the department or individual to perform a legitimate quality assurance function.

Quality tool Instrument or technique to support and improve the activities of process quality management, and improvement. *See also* **seven tools of quality.**

Quality trilogy Documented by Juran, a three-pronged approach to managing for quality. The three legs are quality planning (developing the products and processes required to meet customer needs); quality control (meeting product and process goals); and quality improvement (achieving unprecedented levels of performance).

Quantitative factor Factor that is continuous. For example, a product can be manufactured within a process temperature range of 50°C and 80°C.

Quench To cool a heated piece of metal suddenly by immersion in water, oil, or other coolants.

Questionnaire *See* **survey.**

Queue processing Processing in batches (contrast with continuous flow processing).

Queue time Wait time of product awaiting the next step in a process.

Quincunx Tool that creates frequency distributions. Beads tumble over numerous horizontal rows of pins, which force the beads to the right or left. After a random journey, the beads are dropped into vertical slots. After many beads are dropped, a frequency distribution results. In the classroom, quincunxes are often used to simulate a manufacturing process. The quincunx was invented by English scientist Francis Galton in the 1890s.

R

Radar chart Visual method to show in graphic form the size of gaps among a number of both current organization performance areas and ideal areas; the resulting chart resembles a radar screen.

Radian Base unit of measure for an angle out from a plane. The SI definition is the plane angle with its vertex as the center of a circle that is subtended by an arc equal in length to the radius. *See* **SI base units** for a complete listing of all SI base units. In circular measurement, the radian is an angle whose arc length equals its radius. It is usually defined as 180° divided by *pi*, or in grads as 200 divided by *pi*. So 1 (one) radian is equal to 57.29578°, or 63.662 grads. *See* **grad** and **degree.**

Radiation Transmission of energy through space or through any medium. Also known as "radiant energy." Many of these units of energy are artificially generated and can be harmful to humans. They are regulated to limit exposure to the public.

Radio frequency interference (RFI) Form of electromagnetic interference at radio frequencies from 0.014 to 10,000 megacycles.

Radius Measure of the distance from the center of a circle to any point on its circumference.

RAM (1) In quality-related jargon it is reliability/availability/maintainability. See individual entries. (2) In computer jargon, it is random access memory, the memory used by the computer to run the various operating systems and programs.

Random Having no specific pattern as determined by chance.

Random cause   Cause of variation due to chance and not assignable to any factor.

Random effects (or components of variance) model   Factorial experiment where the variance of factors is investigated (as opposed to a fixed effects model).

Random error   Limits of variation in a measured value of unpredictable sign and magnitude occurring when measurements of the same quantity are made under effectively the same conditions.

Randomizing   Process used in statistics to avoid possible bias, due to the influence of systematic disturbances that are either known or unknown.

Random number generator   Used to select a stated quantity of random numbers from a table of random numbers; the resulting selection is then used to pull specific items or records corresponding to the selected numbers to comprise a "random sample."

Random sampling   Process of selecting units for a sample of size "n" in such a manner that all combinations of "n" units under consideration have an equal or ascertainable chance of being selected as the sample.

Range   For a set of numbers, the absolute difference between the largest and smallest values.

Range chart (R chart)   Control chart in which the subgroup range, R, is used to evaluate the stability of the variability within a process.

Range (statistical)   Measure of dispersion in a data set (the difference between the highest and lowest values in a given set of data).

Ranked sample analysis   Sample data listed in order relative to magnitudes.

Ratio   Statement that compares two numbers. When a pie is cut into eight pieces and one piece is removed, that piece has a ratio of 8:1 because the one piece removed is one of eight total pieces.

Ratio analysis   Process of relating isolated business numbers, such as sales margins, expenses, debt, and profits, to make them meaningful.

R

Rational subgroup	Subgroup expected to be as free as possible from assignable causes (usually consecutive items).
R-bar	Average range value displayed on a range control chart. Value is set when control limits are calculated.
R chart	Control chart of the range of variation among the individual elements of a sample.
Reaction plan	Part of a control plan that spells out how the organization will react if a failure mode does occur.
Readability	In inspection, it is the relative ease with which the measurement instrument scale can be distinguished. For example, both a vernier caliper and a dial caliper have the same discrimination, but the dial caliper is more readable.
Readiness	Measure of system effectiveness depending on availability and equal to system ability to carry out a specified task free of interruptions and catastrophes at a specified performance level when activated at any given time.
Ream	To enlarge slightly or shape precisely a hole with a precision tool (reamer).
Recall	Process used to contain damage, loss, or exposure to potential losses due to the failure of a product or the potential for liability due to unforeseen circumstances at the time of manufacture. Used to return products to the manufacturer for repair or replacement.
Reclamation	In recycling, the restoration of materials found in a waste stream to beneficial use. May be for purposes other than that of its original intended use.
Reconfigure	To change an internal hardware configuration. This usually either avoids using a failed hardware component or redistributes throughput requirements to meet new load requirements or to operate as effectively as possible despite reduced performance.
Record	Document that furnishes objective evidence of activities performed or of results achieved. A quality record provides objective evidence of the extent of the fulfillment of the requirements for quality or the effectiveness of the operation of a quality system element. Some of the purposes of quality records are for the demonstration and traceability of corrective actions. Records can be stored on any data medium.

R

R

Record retention	Period of time established by an organization that records are kept for reference, for legal requirements, or for good business practice.
Records management	Procedures established by an organization to identify, index, store, and control the distribution of records, in order to have the required records available to those who need them at the proper time and location and then to remove obsolete records.
Recurring cost	Production cost such as labor, utilities, and materials that varies with the volume of production.
Red bead experiment	Experiment developed by W. Edwards Deming to illustrate the impossibility of putting employees in rank order of performance for the coming year based on their performance during the past year, because performance differences must be attributed to the system, not to employees. Four thousand red and white beads in a jar (20% red) and six people are needed for the experiment. The participants' goal is to produce white beads because the customer will not accept red beads. One person begins by stirring the beads and then, blindfolded, selects a sample of 50 beads. That person hands the jar to the next person, who repeats the process, and so on. When everyone has his or her sample, the number of red beads for each is counted. The limits of variation between employees that can be attributed to the system are calculated. Everyone will fall within the calculated limits of variation that could arise from the system. The calculations will show no evidence that one person will be a better performer than another in the future. The experiment shows that it would be a waste of management's time to try to find out why, say, John produced 4 red beads and Jane produced 15; instead, management should improve the system, making it possible for everyone to produce more white beads.
Red flag report	Reports issued in connection with customer satisfaction data-gathering mechanisms, in which a request is issued that a sales or customer service representative call on a customer who is experiencing problems within a relatively short period of time.
Red line	Position of an indicator on a monitoring dial or readout showing an unacceptable condition specified on the dial or readout. Operating in this range compromises either performance capability or safety.
Reduced inspection	Used with a defined sampling plan, where a product with an acceptable quality level is inspected using smaller sample sizes than for normal inspection.

Redundancy   Means to provide more than one method of accomplishing a given task in such a way that more than one method must fail before the complete system fails.

Reengineering   Fundamental rethinking and redesign of operating processes and organizational structure, focused on the organization's core competencies to achieve dramatic improvements in organizational performance. The results should show dramatic changes and improvements in the process, such as cost, quality, service, and speed.

Reference dimension   Dimension on an engineering blueprint, usually without tolerance used for information purposes only. A reference dimension is a repeat of a dimension or is derived from other values shown on the blueprint or related blueprints. It is considered auxiliary information only and does not govern production or inspection operations. *See* Appendix E.

Reference material   Material or substance used in gage calibration, with which one or more properties are sufficiently well established, to assign values to the materials or substance.

Reference plane   On engineering blueprints, the plane in which the reference points lie. It is always perpendicular to the line of reference. The reference plane by definition must be flat. The reference plane is also known as the "datum plane." *See* Appendix E.

Reference point   Position on a part feature from which a dimension is expressed. Usually, but not necessarily, it is expressed as zero.

Reference standard   In gage calibration, a standard generally of the highest metrological quality at a given location, from which measurements at that location are made.

Referent authority   Influence based on a person referring to a higher authority as supporting his or her position or recommendation (when someone states that your boss specifically requested that this is done this way).

Reflection   Change of direction of light when it is directed on a suitable surface.

Refraction   Change in a path of light when it passes from one transparent medium into a different medium.

Regardless of feature size (RFS)   In engineering blueprints, this principle is used in geometric tolerances when the tolerance is not modified by the MMC or LMC symbol. It remains the specified size, regardless of the actual size of the part feature. *See* Appendix E.

R

Registrar Accreditation Board (RAB) Board that evaluates the competency and reliability of registrars (organizations that assess and register companies to the appropriate ISO 9000 series standards and to the ISO 14000 environmental management standard). RAB provides ISO course provider accreditation. Formed in 1989, RAB is governed by a board of directors from industry, academia, and quality management consulting firms and by a joint oversight board for those programs operated with the **American National Standards Institute (ANSI).**

Registration Act of including an organization, product, service, or process in a compilation of those having the same or similar attributes.

Registration to standards Process in which an accredited independent third party organization conducts an on-site audit of a company's operations against the requirements of the standard to which the company wants to be registered. Upon successful completion of the audit, the company receives a certificate indicating it has met the standard requirements.

Regrade In ISO terms, the alteration of the grade of a nonconforming product, in order to make it conform to requirements differing from the initially intended ones.

Regression analysis Statistical technique for determining the best mathematical expression describing the functional relationship between one response and one or more independent variables.

Regulation Written description of the product, process, or service requirements and the needed compliance with applicable administrative, trade association, or governmental requirements.

Regulatory requirements Requirements established by law pertaining to products or services.

Reinforcement Process of providing positive consequences (positive reinforcement) when an individual is applying the correct knowledge and skills to the job. It has been described as "catching people doing things right and recognizing their behavior." Caution: Less than desired behavior can also be reinforced unintentionally (negative reinforcement).

Rejection number In relation to sampling plans, the smallest number of defectives (or defects) in the sample or samples under consideration that will, when reached, require the rejection of the lot.

Reject quality level (RQL) Level of quality that is considered unsatisfactory when developing a sampling plan or when using a sampling plan.

Related results Results that arise out of performing an activity or making a decision. In the context of quality/environmental management system activities, they may be documents, records, approval and acceptance decisions, and reject decisions for various processes, products, or services.

Relative frequency diagram *See* **histogram.**

Release (1) In an environmental sense, any spilling, leaking, pumping, dumping, or disposing into the environment of a hazardous or toxic chemical or extremely hazardous substance. (2) In ISO terms, the permission to proceed to the next stage of a process. (3) In the context of documents, the revision level of the document. *See also* **engineering change notice.**

Reliability Probability of a product's performing its intended function under stated conditions without failure for a given period of time. The four phases in planning for reliability are (1) designing, (2) manufacturing, (3) testing (or validation), and (4) maintaining.

Reliability assessment (1) Process of determining the achieved level of reliability of an existing system or system component. (2) Estimate of the achieved reliability calculated using data gathered during test and performance measurement.

Reliability assurance (1) Management and technical integration of the reliability activities essential in maintaining reliability achievements including design, production, and product assurance. (2) Deliberate positive measures to provide confidence that a specified reliability will be achieved.

Reliability availability and serviceability (RAS) System effectiveness features included to support system operations and support activities, to keep a system in operation as intended.

Reliability engineering Science of including those factors in the basic design that will assure the required degree of reliability, availability, and maintainability.

R

Reliability function   Reliability expressed as a function of time, cycles, stress loads, or other defined parameters.

Reliability life test   Testing units under specified conditions for a planned sequence or for a predetermined number of failures, to estimate the failure rate at a specified confidence level.

Relief   In machining, an offset in the surface to allow for clearance.

Remedial action   Action proposed or taken to remove a nonconformity. The action applied to the affected item, process, or activity. The action applied to rectify the affected item. *See also* **corrective action** and **preventive action.**

Remedy   Something that eliminated or counteracts a problem cause; a solution.

Removed section   On engineering blueprints, a sectional view that is not in direct alignment with the cutting plane view but has been moved to a more convenient location to the drawing.

Repair   Action taken on a nonconforming item so it will fulfill the intended usage requirements although it may not conform to the originally specified requirements. *See also* **rework.**

Repeatability   Variation in measurements obtained with one measurement instrument when used several times by one appraiser while measuring the identical characteristic on the same part.

Repeatability and reproducibility (R&R)   Measurement validation process to determine how much variation exists in the measurement system (including the variation in the product, the gage used to measure, and the operator using the gage). *See* **gage R & R.**

Replication   Test trials that are made under identical conditions.

Representative sample   Sample in which the number of units selected in proportion to the size of the sublots are identified by some rational criteria and selected at random.

Reproducibility   Variation in the average of the measurements made by different appraisers using the same measuring instrument when measuring the identical characteristics on the same part.

Requirements   Ability of an item to perform a required function under stated conditions for a stated period of time. Or that an identified feature conforms to stated dimensional constraints.

Requirements   Requirements including laws, statutes, rules and regulations, codes, envi-
of society   ronmental considerations, health and safety factors, and conservation of energy and materials.

Residual   (1) In a designed experiment, the differences between experimental responses and predicted values that are determined from a model. (2) In an environmental sense, the amount of pollutant remaining in the environment after a natural or technological process has taken place; such as the sludge remaining after an initial wastewater treatment or particulates that remain in the air after it passes through a filter or scrubbing process.

Residual error   In a designed experiment, the difference between the observed result and the predicted value (estimated treatment response) for that result, based on the empirically determined assumed model.

Residual value   Value of fixed assets after depreciation charges have been subtracted from its original cost.

Resistance to   Person's unwillingness to change due to their beliefs, habits, and ways of
change   doing things.

R

Resolution   Ability to distinguish visually with the unaided eye between separate items, usually lines. It is the ratio of the width of one scale division on the face of the dial to the width of the indicating hand.

Resolution   Smallest unit of measure that an instrument is capable of indicating.
(of a measuring
instrument)

Resource   Designating of the amount and type of resources to be assigned to a
loading   specific activity for a certain time frame.

Resource   Having fewer resources available than are required to complete a project.
overloading

Resource   Process of determining resource requirements (people, equipment, facilities,
planning   materials, etc.) needed in specific quantities, at a specific time, to perform the work.

Resource requirements matrix   Tool to relate the resources required to predict tasks requiring them (used to indicate types of individuals needed, material needed, subcontractors, etc.).

Resources   Labor, facilities, equipment, materials, supplies, and utilities required or used to perform an activity.

Responsibility   Obligation of an individual or group to perform assigned task or to perform activities and care for the operation of a process or system with reasonable care and be accountable for that care.

Responsible care   Set of guidelines for environmental management systems adopted by the Chemical Manufacturers Association (CMA) in 1988. Participation by individual businesses is an obligation of membership in the CMA.

Resubmitted lot   Lot that had previously been rejected or held for some nonconformance and then submitted again for inspection after having been sorted, reprocessed, reworked, and so on.

Results   Effects that relate to what is obtained by an organization, in terms or product or service provided, at the conclusion of a time period.

RETAD   Rapid exchange of tooling and dies. Refers to the ability to change out tooling and or dies rapidly and thus keep machines running. *See* **single minute exchange of dies.**

Retention *(of training)*   It is commonly held that we retain 10% of what is read, 20% of what is heard, 30% of what is seen, 50% of what is seen and heard, and 70% of what is seen and spoken.

Return on equity (ROE)   Net profit after taxes, divided by last year's tangible stockholders' equity, and then multiplied by 100 to provide a percentage (also referred to as "return on net worth").

Return on investment (ROI)   Umbrella term for a variety of ratios measuring an organization's business performance and calculated by dividing some measure of return by a measure of investment and then multiplying by 100 to provide a percentage. In its most basic form, ROI indicates what remains from all money taken in after all expenses are paid. ROI is always expressed as a percentage.

Return on net assets (RONA)   Measure of the earning power of the firm's investment in assets, calculated by dividing net profit after taxes by last year's tangible total assets and then multiplying by 100 to provide a percentage.

Revenue   Amount of money earned as a result of completing a project, selling a product, or providing a service.

Reversal technique   Method for detecting or canceling small changes by comparing a variable with itself but with reversed algebraic sign.

Reverse engineering   Developing design specifications by inspection and analysis of an existing product.

Review   In the ISO concept, those activities undertaken to determine the suitability, adequacy, and effectiveness of the subject matter to achieve established objectives.

Revision block   On engineering blueprints, typically, the area in the upper right corner of the sheet, where revisions to the blueprint are documented. *See* Appendix E.

Revolved section   On an engineering blueprint, a sectional view that has been revolved 90° to the plane of the blueprint. Used to show the true shape of ribs, spokes, and other features that would not be obvious in other views.

Reward and recognition system   Management-supplied incentives used to promote or reinforce desired employee behavior. It is conveyed through various means such as bonuses, awards, prizes, days off, and so on. It is usually linked to established guidelines for behavior and/or job performance.

Rework   Actions taken on a nonconforming item so it will fulfill the originally specified requirements. *See* **repair.**

Rib   In casting or machining, additional material used for extra support or strength in a part.

Right the first time   Term used to convey the concept that it is beneficial and more cost effective to take the necessary steps up front to ensure a product or service meets its requirements than it is to provide a product or service that will need rework or not meet customer needs. In other words, an organization should engage in defect prevention rather than defect detection.

Risk   Refers to a potential hazard or quality deficiency associated with a product, services, or process.

Risk assessment/ management	Process of determining what risks are present in a situation (e.g., in a project or proposal) and what actions might be taken to eliminate or mediate them.
Risk identification	Process of determining the risk events that are likely to affect a product or project and then classifying them according to their cause or source.
Risk management	Process of evaluating and selecting alternative responses to the risk. The selection requires the consideration of legal, economic, technology, process limits, and other social factors.
Risk priority number (RPN)	Product of severity, occurrence, and detection rankings within a failure modes and effects analysis (FMEA), which prioritizes design concerns; those with high RPNs require increased attention in order to address issues to lower the risk associated with the identified characteristic. However, even issues with a low RPN may still deserve special attention if the severity ranking is high.
RMS	Abbreviation for "root mean square." The average of the sum of squares of the deviations of the high and low values, typically used in measuring the roughness of machined parts. Compare to **AA.**
Roadblock	Anything that hinders progress, provides an obstruction, or prevents people, teams, or organizations from meeting their objectives.
Robust design	Design capable of properly performing its intended functions under a wide range of conditions, including some anticipated level of customer or user abuse.
Robustness	Condition of a product or process design that remains relatively stable, with a minimum of variation, even though factors that influence operations or usage, such as environment and wear, are constantly changing.
Rocking	Movement of a measuring instrument, such as a micrometer or caliper, by feel of contact, so its axes are oriented parallel to the line of measurement. Sometimes called "centralizing."
Rockwell test	Widely used type of test for metal hardness of two basic types: "superficial" and "regular." The test uses a defined point (indenter) and various combinations of loads (scales) to measure the depth of penetration caused by the test.
Role playing	Training technique whereby participants perform in an assigned scenario to determine how they would handle an identified situation.

R

Rollout   Widespread phased introduction of a product or service into or from an organization.

Root   The base of the thread or gear tooth on screw threads and gears.

Root cause   Factor that caused a nonconformance and should be permanently eliminated through process improvement.

Root cause analysis   Quality tool used to distinguish the source of defects or problems. It is a structured approach that focuses on the decisive or original cause of a problem or condition.

Root mean square (RMS)   Average of the sum of squares of the deviations of the high and low values, typically used in measuring the roughness of machined parts. Compare to **AA.**

Roughness   In surface finish measurement, closely spaced irregularities on the surface being measured. Contrast with waviness, which are more widely spaced irregularities.

Roughness average   In surface finish measurement, the arithmetic average (AA) of the absolute values of the profile height deviations. Sometimes referred to by its earlier term: *centerline average.*

Roundness   Characteristic that all parts of a circle are identical. *See also* **lobing.** *See* Appendix E.

R

Routing   Sequence of processes, operations, transportations, and storages to be followed and the machines, tools, workstations, and any other equipment to be used to produce a particular part or product.

Royalty   Payments made by one party to another for the use of its inventions, intellectual assets, and so on, based on a percentage of sales, production, or other criteria agreed to by the parties.

Rule   Measuring device with graduations that are as near to the designated divisions of its unit of length as practicable. For example, readings from a rule are taken from its scale. *See* **scale.**

Run   As used in SPC, the consecutive points showing a particular characteristic, such as consecutive points on one side of the centerline of an SPC chart. Beyond a certain consecutive number of these points (statistically based), the pattern becomes unnatural and is worthy of attention.

Run chart   Chart showing a line connecting numerous data points collected from a process running over a period of time. Used to show variation in a process over time.

Run-in   Procedure to put usage on a machine for the purpose of capturing early failures.

Runout   In engineering drawings, the deviation of a part surface from the desired form and orientation as it is rotated 360° around a datum axis. The controlled surface may be cylindrical, tapered, or perpendicular to the datum axis. A runout tolerance specifies how much the part surface is allowed to vary in relation to the datum axis. There are two types: circular and total runout. *See* **total indicator reading/runout (TIR).** *See* Appendix E.

Rupture   In testing for strength or integrity of a component, the minimum value at which the component physically comes apart. Usually associated with pressure testing.

S

Sabotage — Intentional disruption of a function or destruction of a critical part to render a component or assembly unusable. The user is usually unaware of the problem and many times is put at risk of injury.

Safe — In an environmental sense, conditions of exposure under which there is a practical certainty that no harm will result to exposed individuals.

Safety *(Per ISO A8402)* — The state in which risk of harm (to persons) or damage is limited to an acceptable level.

Safety margin — (1) Difference between the highest expected stress level and an item's rated operating stress level expressed in units of the rating. Also called "margin of safety" or "margin for error." (2) Amount of intentional derating of an item's capability to allow for user abuse.

Sales leveling — Strategy of establishing a long-term relationship with customers to lead to contracts for fixed amounts and scheduled deliveries in order to smooth the production flow and eliminate surges or seasonal fluctuations.

Salting samples — Practice of placing a known quantity of nonconforming materials in with a lot of materials in order to find out if the established inspection process will identify the nonconformities.

Salvage — Utilization of nonconforming products or other waste materials for a productive purpose.

Sample — In acceptance sampling, one or more units of product (or a quantity of material) drawn from a lot for purposes of inspection to reach a decision regarding acceptance of the lot.

Sample frequency	Ratio of the number of units of production randomly selected for inspection purposes to the number of units of product passing the inspection station.
Sample plan	Documented plan scheduling the number of samples to be taken from a lot to be used as the basis of acceptance or rejection of a lot. There are a number of standard sampling plans such as the Dodge-Romig plans, MIL-STD-105 for attributes and MIL-STD-414 for variables.
Sample size	[n] Number of units in a sample.
Sample standard deviation chart (s-chart)	Control chart in which the subgroup standard deviation, "s", is used to evaluate the stability of the variability within a process.
Sample variation	Variation of a sample's properties from those of the population from which it was drawn.
Sampling	Process of drawing conclusions about a population based on values obtained from a part of the population.
Sampling at random	As commonly used in acceptance sampling theory, the process of selecting sample units so all units under consideration have the same probability of being selected. Note: Actually, equal probabilities are not necessary for random sampling. What is necessary is that the probability of selection be ascertainable. However, the stated properties of published sampling tables are based on the assumption of random sampling with equal probabilities. An acceptable method of random selection with equal probabilities is the use of a table of random numbers in a standard manner.
Sampling, double	Sampling inspection in which the inspection of the first sample leads to a decision to accept a lot, reject it, or take a second sample; the inspection of a second sample, when required, then leads to a decision to accept or to reject the lot.
Sampling, multiple	Sampling inspection in which, after each sample is inspected, the decision is made to accept a lot, reject it, or to take another sample; but there is a prescribed maximum number of samples, after which a decision to accept or reject the lot must be reached. Note: Multiple sampling as defined here has sometimes been called "sequential sampling" or "truncated sequential sampling."
Sampling, single	Sampling inspection in which the decision to accept or to reject a lot is based on the inspection of a single sample.

Sampling, unit   (1) Sequential sampling inspection in which, after each unit is inspected, the decision is made to accept a lot, reject it or to inspect another unit. (2) Sampling unit is also used in the concept of sampling theory and in survey research, which indicate that the term *sampling unit* can also indicate a portion of a population.

Sand blast   Blowing sand at high speed with compressed air or steam pressure to clean, cut, or engrave castings, forgings, and other materials.

Satisfied customers   Customers who are content with the quality of product or service they receive. A satisfied customer may tell 3–5 others about the experience, but a dissatisfied customer will tell 9–10 others. Those who are happy with their purchase.

Satisfier   Term used to describe the quality level received by a customer when a product or service meets expectations.

Saturation   Condition of a material when it has taken into itself the maximum possible quantity of another given substance at a given temperature and pressure. May also include a liquid that has taken into solution the maximum quantity of another substance at a given temperature and pressure.

Scale   (1) On engineering blueprints, the size of the blueprint with respect to the size of the part it represents often expressed as a ratio (e.g., a scale of 1: 4 means 1 inch on the blueprint is equal to 4 inches on the part). (2) Measuring device whose graduations are proportional to a unit of length for either reduction or enlargement. A rule, in contrast, has graduations that are as near as practical to the designated divisions of its unit of length. In addition, the word *scale* designates that portion of an instrument that has rulings. For example, the readings from a rule are taken from its scale.

Scatter diagram   Graphical technique to analyze the relationship between two variables. Two sets of data are plotted on a graph, with the y-axis being used for the variable to be predicted and the x-axis being used for the variable to make the prediction. The graph will show possible relationships (although two variables might appear to be related by cause and effect, they might not be: those who know most about the variables must make that evaluation). The scatter diagram is one of the **seven tools of quality.**

Scenario planning   Strategic planning process that generates multiple stories about future conditions, allowing an organization to look at the potential impact on them and different ways they could respond.

Schedule Time-sequenced plan of events or activities.

Scientific approach Making decisions based on data. The common steps are (1) collect meaningful data, (2) identify root causes of problems, (3) develop appropriate solutions, and (4) plan and make the needed changes. *See* **PDCA cycle.**

Scientific management/ approach Term referring to the intent to find and use the best way to perform tasks to improve quality, productivity, and efficiency. The philosophy of Frederick Taylor.

Scientific wild anatomical guess (SWAG) Best guess. Estimate by a person based on his or her experience, typically done in haste, and usually of questionable accuracy. Usually by someone who should have knowledge of the situation, but without considering all the facts and consequences. Not considered very accurate.

Scope Total sum of products, operations, or services under consideration or review.

Scope creep Gradual increase of control or influence over a project, job, or situation that expands responsibilities and usually also expands the work load.

Scorecard Evaluation device, usually in the form of a questionnaire that specifies the criteria customers will use to rate your business's performance in satisfying their requirements. *See also* **Balanced scorecard**.

Scrap In ISO terms, action on a nonconforming product to preclude its originally intended use. Materials that are discarded from the manufacturing process but may still be suitable for reprocessing purposes.

Screening Technique used to review, analyze, rank, and select the best alternative for a proposed action plan.

Screening experiment First step of a multiple factorial experiment strategy, where the experiment primarily assesses the significance of main effects. Two-factor interactions are normally considered in the experiments that follow a screening experiment.

Screening inspection Inspection in which each item or part is inspected for designated characteristics and all defective items are removed.

S curve   Graphic display of cumulative cost, labor cost, and other resource cost plotted in time. It usually starts off fairly flat, then expands in the center and tapers off again as the project nears completion.

Second   Base unit of measure for time. The SI definition is the duration of 9,192,631,770 cycles of the radiation associated with a specified transition of the cesium-133 atom. It is realized by tuning an oscillator to the resonance frequency of cesium-133 atoms as they pass through a system of magnets and a resonant cavity into a detector. *See also* **SI base units** for a complete listing of all SI base units.

Secondary customer   Groups or individuals who are outside the process boundaries and who receive the output of a process indirectly. Used car buyers are secondary customers.

Secondary datum   In engineering blueprints, this is established by at least two points of contact between a datum feature and the machine tooling or inspection surface. Part of the datum reference frame. *See* Appendix E.

Secondary failure   Failure of a system because one or more components failed due to excessive conditions, such as heat or vibration.

Secondary reference standards   In calibration, the standards used to perform instrument and equipment calibration. They are lower (second level) standards, usually compared to and calibrated to primary standards.

Second-party audit   Audits carried out by customers on their suppliers.

Secretive management style   Management style in which the manager is neither open or outgoing in speech, actions, or purpose, to the detriment of the organization.

Sectional view   On engineering blueprints, a view of the parts interior. Used when other views would not show the interior detail clearly. *See* Appendix E.

Section lines   On blueprints, light solid lines, usually at 45°, used to show the surface of a part that has been sectioned or cut off to show hidden detail. *See* Appendix E.

Sediments   In an environmental sense, the soil, sand, and minerals washed from land into water, usually after rain. They pile up in reservoirs, rivers, harbors, and lakes destroying fish and wildlife habitat and at times navigable waterways.

Segmenting customers Refers to the concept that customers from different groups or backgrounds have unique requirements. May be divided up by various criteria, income, purchasing volume, profitability, age, industry, geographic region, price, and so on.

Segregation of material Process of removing material from the normal flow, usually due to some defect or assigned reason to set the material aside, so it will not be used with the normal flow of material. Many times this material is identified by tags and placed in a quarantine area.

Selective listening People hear what they are predispositioned to hear and ignore the true message being relayed.

Self-assessment Assessments of any efforts, activities, systems, and so on, when the assessors are a part of or exert influence over those items or practices under evaluation.

Self-declaration (environmental claims) Environmental claim by an organization that is made without independent third-party verification or certification.

Self-directed learning Where the person doing the learning determines the material and pace at which to study. *See* **learner-controlled instruction.**

Self-directed/managed work team (SDWT) Type of team structure in which much of the decision making regarding how to handle the team's activities is controlled by the team members themselves.

Self-inspection Process by which employees inspect their own work according to specified rules and criteria.

Semantics Relationships of characters or groups of characters to their meanings, independent of the manner of their interpretation and use.

Senior leaders In quality award criteria, refers to an organization's senior management group or team. In many organizations, this consists of the head of the organization and his or her direct reports.

Sensitivity (of a measuring instrument) Smallest change in the measured quantity of which the instrument is capable of detecting.

Sensor In an inspection or monitoring system, a device that detects a condition out of the normal and supplies a signal to provide notification that the changed condition exists.

Sequential testing Items are tested in sequence. Decisions are made continually to determine if the test should be continued as each lot or unit is accepted or rejected based on its individual test.

Service To perform an activity for another person or organization. The delivery or use of tangible products may also be linked to service. The supplier or customer may be represented at the interface by personnel or equipment. A service may be part of the manufacture and supply of tangible or intangible products.

Service level agreement Formal agreement between an internal provider and an internal receiver (customer).

Service quality Aspects of service that satisfy customers so they return for repeat business. The goal should be to deliver exceptional quality of service to delight the customer.

Service recovery Five-step program to handle and recover from customer complaints: (1) Apologize (fast and honest). (2) Restate (restate the problem as the customer relates it). (3) Empathize (make sure you communicate your concern for the customer). (4) Make restitution (take immediate action to resolve the problem, offer a concession if possible). (5) Follow up (see if the actions taken have satisfied the customer). This last step is where most programs fail.

Setup time Time taken to change over a machine or process to run a different product or service. *See* **single minute exchange of dies** and **RETAD.**

Seven management tools of quality Tools used primarily for planning and managing are (1) activity network diagram and/or arrow diagram, (2) affinity diagram (KJ method), (3) interrelationship diagram, (4) matrix diagram, (5) priorities matrix, (6) process decision program chart (PCDC), and (7) tree diagram. For a complete description of these tools, see Michael Brassard's *The Memory Jogger Plus* (Methuen, MA: GOAL/QPC, 1989), available through ASQ Quality Press.

Seven statistical tools (1) Pareto diagram, (2) cause-and-effect diagram, (3) histograms, (4) control charts, (5) scatter diagrams, (6) graphs (run chart), and (7) check sheets.

See individual entries for more information. Note: These are referred to as statistical tools in general, even though not all are truly statistical in application.

Seven tools of quality   Tools that help organizations understand their processes and improve them. The seven tools are (1) **cause-and-effect diagram,** (2) **check sheet,** (3) **control charts,** (4) **flowcharts,** (5) **histogram,** (6) **Pareto chart,** and (7) **scatter diagram** (see individual entries).

Seven types of waste   According to Taichi Ohno, the opposite of value is waste, and seven wastes affect productivity and quality: (1) overproduction, (2) waiting, (3) transporting, (4) inappropriate processing, (5) excess inventory, (6) unnecessary motions, and (7) defects. See also *Toyota Production System—Beyond Large Scale Production* (Portland, OR: Productivity Press, 1988).

Severity   Consequences of a failure, usually associated with occurrences that are hazardous or cause greater financial loss.

Severity rating (SR)   In an FMEA, the severity rating scale is a value from 1 to 10 used to evaluate the relative severity of the consequences of a failure. A low rating of 1–2 would indicate the impact would be minimal or unnoticed. A high rating of 9–10 would indicate the consequences or impact would be great.

Sexagesimal system   Measurement system based on the number 60. It is used for various features, for example: the circle = (360°), a degree = 60 minutes (60'), a minute = 60 seconds (60").

S: five S's   Five terms beginning with "S" utilized to create a workplace suited for visual control and lean production. *Seiri* means to separate needed tools, parts, and instructions from unneeded materials and to remove the latter. *Seiton* means to neatly arrange and identify parts and tools for ease of use. *Seiso* means to conduct a cleanup campaign. *Seiketsu* means to conduct *seiri, seiton,* and *seiso* at frequent, indeed daily, intervals to maintain a workplace in perfect condition. *Shitsuke* means to form the habit of always following the first four S's. *See **kaizen.***

Shall   In ISO standards, a required element that needs to be fulfilled in order to meet the standard.

Shape   (1) Pattern or outline formed by the relative position of a large number of individual values obtained from a process. (2) Removal of metal using a shaper.

Shared leadership Management approach in which the manager believes the many functions of leadership can be effectively spread among various teams or individuals.

Shareholder Owner of one or more shares of a corporation usually evidenced by the holding of certificates or other formal documents.

Shareholder management Management approach that provides little information exchange within the team, but the team must take final authority for the decisions it makes.

Shear To cut metal by forcing it to separate across its cross-sectional area.

Shewhart control chart Commonly known as "X-bar" and "R charts." Plotting is normally based on +/– three sigma limits. *See* **Walter A. Shewhart** in Appendix A.

Shewhart cycle *See* **plan-do-check-act (PDCA) cycle.**

Shift Abrupt change in an important variable in a process such as a broken tool, a part slipped, or a missed ingredient in a mix.

Shim Thin pieces of material used to take up space between mating parts or to level or adjust.

Ship-to-stock program Arrangement with a qualified supplier whereby the supplier ships materials directly to the buyer without the buyer's incoming inspection; often a result of evaluating and approving the supplier for approval on a certain part or materials.

Shock test (1) Subjecting a unit to one or more singly applied acceleration pulses at a frequency of less than 1 hz. (2) Subjecting a unit to one or more singly applied deceleration test (such as a commonly applied 3-foot drop test).

Shop standard Standard used in the shop environment, calibrated against a secondary standard. Usually used to qualify parts for workmanship, dimensional, or other characteristics.

Should In ISO standards, a provision that would provide benefit for the organization, but is an option.

SI base units Basic units of measure from which all other units can be derived: meter (length), kilogram (weight), second (time), ampere (electrical), Kelvin (temperature), mole (amount of substance), candela (light), radian (degrees of a circle, plane angle), and steradian (solid angle). See individual entries.

SIC (Standard Industrial Classification)   Replaced by NAICS. *See* **NAICS** in Appendix B.

Sigma   Greek letter (Σ) that stands for the estimated standard deviation of a process. For a normal process, 1 sigma will include 68.26% of the output; 2 sigma, 95.44%; and 3 sigma, 99.73%. *See* **Six Sigma.**

Sigma limits   Interval about the mean expressed in units of standard deviation in a normal distribution. *See* **Sigma.**

Signal-to-noise ratio (S/N ratio)   Mathematical equation that indicates the magnitude of an experimental effect above the effect of experimental error due to chance fluctuations.

Significance   Statistical statement indicating that the level of a factor causes a difference in a response with a certain degree of risk of being in error.

Significant digits   Those digits within a number that express a meaning and are therefore necessary.

Silent happy customer syndrome   Normal, often wrong assumption that customers who do not complain are happy. The producer assumes that as long as there are no complaints the customers must be satisfied.

Silo   (as in "functional silo") Organization where cross-functional collaboration and cooperation is minimal and the functional "silos" tend to work toward their own goals to the detriment of the organization as a whole. *See* **stovepipe.**

Simulation *(modeling)*   Using a mathematical model of a system or process to predict the performance of the real system.

Simultaneous engineering   *See* **concurrent engineering.**

Sine bar   Bar to which two identical cylinders are attached with a known separation and a known relation to the reference surface of the bar. The bar becomes the hypotenuse of a triangle for angle measurement.

Sine plate   Wide sine bar. Also known as "sine block."

Sine table   Sine device incorporated into a worktable of an inspection device or machine tool.

Single-factor analysis of variance   One-way analysis of variance with defined levels (or treatments) used to determine if there is a significant difference between level effects.

Single minute exchange of dies (SMED)   Change of complex tooling (dies) is accomplished in a very short period of time. A goal to be achieved is reducing the setup time required for a changeover to a new process; the methodologies employed in devising and implementing ways to reduce setup. *See* **RETAD** (rapid exchange of tooling and dies).

Single-piece flow   Method whereby the product proceeds through the process one piece at a time, rather than in large batches, eliminating queues and costly waste.

Single-sided test   Statistical consideration in which, for example, an alternative hypothesis is that the mean on a population is less than a stated value.

SIPOC analysis   Macro-level analysis of the suppliers, inputs, processes, outputs, and customers.

Site   In an environmental program, the land and structures on which activities are carried out.

Situation analysis   Review of the process used to identify and define facts and variables that might influence a situation.

Situational leadership   Leadership theory that maintains leadership style should change based on the person and the situation, with the leader displaying varying degrees of directive and supportive behavior.

Six boxes   Organizational diagnosis method proposed by Marvin Weisbord, used to collect data on a company and to help with improvement. The six boxes are (1) purposes (what business are we in, do we understand the goals); (2) structure (how are we organized, by function, by product, etc.); (3) relationships (how do people cooperate or deal with conflict); (4) rewards (how does the rewards system help the individual to achieve); (5) leadership (what is the character of our leaders, are they visionary or participative); and (6) helpful mechanisms (how do we track and implement changes). See also *Organizational Diagnosis: A Workbook of Theory and Practice* (Reading, MA: Addison-Wesley, 1978).

Six M's   As used in cause-and-effect diagrams (fishbone diagram): man, machine, material, method, measurement, and mother nature (also labeled as environmental).

Six Sigma   Methodology that provides businesses with the tools to improve the capability of their business processes. This increase in performance and decrease in process variation lead to defect reduction and improvement in profits, employee morale, and quality of product. 1 sigma = 690,000 PPM; 2 sigma = 308,537 PPM; 3 sigma = 66,807 PPM; 4 sigma = 6,210 PPM; 5 sigma = 233 PPM; and 6 sigma = 3.4 PPM.

Six Sigma quality   Term generally used to indicate a process is well controlled (±6 sigma from the centerline in a control chart). The term is usually associated with Motorola, which named one of its key operational initiatives "Six Sigma quality."

Six Sigma quality steps   Measure, analyze, improve, control.

Six thinking hats   Concept proposed by Edward DeBono. For creative thinking in meetings, (1) White hat = (pure facts and figures), (2) Red hat = (emotion and feelings), (3) Black hat = (devil's advocate, critical and negative), (4) Yellow hat = (optimistic viewpoints), (5) Green hat = (a signal for creativity), and (6) Blue hat = (indication of control in the meetings). See also *Six Thinking Hats* (Boston: Little, Brown, 1985).

Skewed distribution   Pattern of variation, which is not normal; when plotted graphically, it appears to be pushed over to one side.

Skewness   Measure of a distribution's symmetry. A skewed distribution that has a longer tail on its right or left side, with its hump (probability) pushed to the opposite side.

Skill   Ability to use one's knowledge, technical proficiency, and developed or acquired ability to devise an efficient method to accomplish a given objective.

Skip-level meeting   Evaluation technique that occurs when a member of senior management meets with persons two or more organizational levels below, without the intervening management present, to allow open expression about the effectiveness of the organization.

Skip-lot sampling In acceptance sampling, a plan in which some set number of lots in a series are accepted without inspection. When the set number of lots are received, without inspection, the next lot is then inspected, unless problems surface that merits all lots be inspected until the problem is eliminated and confidence is restored.

Slack time The time an activity can be delayed without delaying the entire project; it is determined by calculating the difference between the latest allowable date and the earliest expected date (*see* project evaluation and review **PERT chart**). Also defined as "float" in project management.

Small quantity generator Under the guidelines of the Environmental Protection Agency (EPA). Persons or enterprises that produce 220 to 2200 pounds per month of hazardous waste. They are required to keep records on how they control and dispose of the hazardous waste they generate.

Smoothing In conflict resolution, the process of emphasizing areas of agreement, and deemphasizing areas of disagreement. A joint problem-solving approach is sought. This is often used where common interest between companies have high values.

Snap gage **Go/no-go** type gage that is preset to a given dimension. Often made with two settings, one to admit acceptable parts and one to reject out-of-tolerance parts. An attribute gage.

Societal loss Concept presented by Taguchi that financial losses can be implanted to the public in general by the harmful side effects of certain products or production methods.

Society of Automotive Engineers (SAE) International membership organization for the exchange of ideas advancing the engineering of mobility systems (powered transportation systems).

Software quality assurance (SQA) Planned and systematic approach to the evaluation of the quality of and adherence to software product standards, processes, and procedures. SQA includes the process of assuring that standards and procedures are established and are followed throughout the software acquisition life cycle.

S

Solder   Metallic compound used to seal joints between surfaces, and pipes. Until recently most solder contained 50% lead. Use of solder containing more than 2% lead is now prohibited in pipes carrying drinking water.

Solid waste   In an environmental sense, nonliquid, nonsoluble materials ranging from municipal garbage to industrial wastes that contain complex and some-times hazardous substances. Solid waste also includes sewage sludge, agri-cultural refuse, demolition wastes, and mining residue.

Solubility   Amount of mass of a compound that will dissolve in a unit of volume of a solution. Aqueous solubility is the maximum concentration of a chemical that will dissolve in pure water at a reference temperature.

Spaghetti diagram/map (chart)   Before improvement chart showing the existing steps in a process and the many back-and-forth interrelationships (can resemble a bowl of spaghetti); used to see the redundancies and other wasted movements of people and material. Often used in lean thinking activities.

Span of control   Refers to how many subordinates a manager can effectively and efficiently manage. Number varies, but generally a manager should have no more than 10 direct reports.

Special causes   Causes of variation that arise because of special circumstances. They are not an inherent part of a process. Special causes are also referred to as "assignable causes." *See* **common causes.**

Specification   Document that states the requirements to which a given product or serv-ice must conform.

Specified requirement   Requirements prescribed by the customer in a contract or by standard industry specifications such as material, grade, and so on.

Spin-off   (Spinout) Creation of a new organization with ties to and many times financial dependency on the parent organization, usually to address new business interest.

Spline   In a mechanical sense, a keyway or series of keyways cut into a hub, or on a shaft, especially to maintain alignment and to keep the mating parts from turning on each other.

Sponsor   Person who supports a team's plans, activities, and outcomes; the team's backer.

Sporadic cause   Sudden adverse change in a process requiring a solution that will return the process to its original condition or state.

Sporadic problem   Sudden adverse change in the status quo that can be remedied by restoring the status quo. For example, actions such as changing a worn part or proper handling of an irate customer's complaint can restore the status quo.

Spotface   Shallow counterbore usually used to provide a good seat for a bolt head.

Sprue   In casting or injection molding, the extra material left attached to the part after it has been removed from the sand cast or mold. The extra material left on the part after removal from the mold.

Square   Tool for aligning workpieces at a right angle.

Squareness   Condition of being at a right angle to a line or plane. Also, a right angle in material form. *See* **perpendicularity.** *See* Appendix E.

Stability   (1) Of a gage, it is the ability of a gage to retain its accuracy over time and usage. (2) Of a process, a process is said to be stable if it shows no recognizable pattern of change.

Stable process   Process that is in control with only common causes of variation.

Stage   For optical instruments, such as a microscope or optical projector, *stage* is the term that corresponds to the worktable on most other instruments.

Stages of creativity   One model presented gives the following stages: generate, percolate, illuminate, and verify. Another model presents creativity this way: visualization, exploration, combination, and modification. Each process follows a basic PDCA process.

Stages of team growth   Four stages identified by Peter Scholtes in *The Team Handbook* that teams move through as they develop maturity over time: forming, storming, norming, and performing. See also *The Team Handbook* (Madison, WI: Oriel, Inc., 2003).

Stakeholder   Any individual, group, or organization that will have a significant impact on or will be significantly impacted by the quality of the product or service an organization provides. In quality award criteria, the term *stakeholder* refers to all groups that are or might be affected by an organization's actions and success or failure. Examples of key stakeholders would include customers, employees, partners, stockholders, local communities, and governmental and regulatory agencies.

Stakeholder management   Management approach used to avoid activities by stakeholders that would interfere with a project or operation.

Standard   Metric, specification, gage, statement, category, segment, grouping, behavior, event, or physical product sample against which the outputs of a process are compared and declared acceptable or unacceptable. A standard is a copy and traceable back to the national standard.

Standard deviation (statistical)   Computed measure of variability indicating the spread of the data set around the mean. The square of the standard deviation is called the variance. *See* **Sigma.** *See* Appendix C for formula.

Standardize, Do, Check, Act, (SDCA)   Variation on the PDCA cycle in which management decides first to establish the standard before the regular PDCA function.

Standard error   Square root of the variance of the sampling distribution.

Standard for calibration   *See* **calibration standards.**

Standard operating procedure (SOP)   Usually a written document that details methods and procedures for performing specific operations or activities. Most commonly denotes officially reviewed and approved procedures, especially for repetitive actions or tasks.

Standard values   Representative values based on the experience record of the process.

Standard work   Precise description of each work activity specifying cycle time, takt time (see entry), the work sequence of specific tasks, and the minimum inventory of parts on hand needed to conduct the activity.

Statement of work (SOW)   Description of actual work to be accomplished. It is derived from the work breakdown structure and, when combined with the project specifications, becomes the basis for the contractual agreement on the project (also referred to as "scope of work").

State of statistical control   Process is considered to be in a state of statistical control if the variations among the observed sampling results can be attributed to a constant system of chance causes.

Stationary process	Process with an ultimate constant variance.
Statistic	Quantity calculated from a sample of observations, most often to form an estimate of some population parameter.
Statistical confidence	(Also called "statistical significance") Level of accuracy expected of an analysis of data. Most frequently it is expressed as either a "95% level of significance" or "5% confidence level."
Statistical inference	Process of drawing conclusions about a population on the basis of statistics from a sample from the population.
Statistical process control (SPC)	Application of statistical techniques to control a process. The term is often used interchangeably with **statistical quality control.** A process of measuring and recording the results on defined charts to detect process changes. These charts are used to signal changes required to keep a process from making defective units.
Statistical quality control (SQC)	Application of statistical techniques to control quality. The term is often used interchangeably with **statistical process control,** although statistical quality control includes acceptance sampling and statistical process control.
Statistical thinking	Philosophy of learning and action based on these fundamental principles: (1) All work occurs in a system of interconnected processes. (2) Variation exists in all processes. (3) Understanding and reducing variation are vital to improvement.
Statistical tolerance limits	Engineering tolerances based on statistical analysis of product variation. Can also mean the limits of the interval for which it can be stated with a given level of confidence that it contains at least a specified proportion of the population.
Statistics	Field that involves the tabulating, depicting, and describing of data sets; a formalized body of techniques characteristically involving attempts to infer the properties of a large collection of data from inspection of a sample of the collection.
Status	Condition or progress of a project or process at any given point in time.
Steering committee	Special group set up by management for guiding and tracking team efforts. The group will usually contain the key leaders of the organization (i.e.,

S

CEO, quality manager, operations manager, engineering manager, controller, etc.).

Stem and leaf plot   Variation on the dot plot, with the stem and leaf plot a line (stem) drawn vertically, with the units of variation marked vertically down the left side of the line and the actual measurements taken plotted horizontally in line on the right side with the corresponding stem.

Steradian   Base unit of measure for an angle out from a sphere. The SI definition is the solid angle with its vertex at the center of a sphere that is subtended by the area of the spherical surface equal to that of a square with sides equal in length to the radius. *See* **SI base units** for a complete listing of all SI base units.

Stimulus   Any effort, energy, or force applied to a system or device to produce a result.

Stopgap measure   Short-term fix to a problem, usually until the main cause of the problem can be eliminated. It may include sorting and/or repairing a product to keep production running.

Storyboarding   Technique that visually displays thoughts and ideas and groups them into categories, making all aspects of a process visible at once. Often used to communicate to others the activities performed by a team as they improve a process.

Stovepipe   Company operating unit concentrating on a narrow piece of a process. The people involved tend to look inward toward their own process and upward to their boss. *See* **silo.**

Straightness   On engineering blueprints, a straightness tolerance specifies how much a surface is allowed to vary from the perfect straight line implied by the blueprint. *See* Appendix E.

Strain   Deformation in a solid body caused by external forces.

Strain gage   Device used to measure the deformation in a solid body.

Strategic fit review   Process by which managers assess the future of each project to a particular organization in terms of its ability to advance the mission and goals of that organization.

Strategic goals Goals that are defined, specific, and scheduled (e.g., become ISO 9001 registered by year end). These may be for a longer duration, even years.

Strategic partnership Voluntary formation of a business relationship among or between independent organizations in support of a long-term strategy of mutual interest and benefit.

Strategic planning Process by which an organization envisions its future and develops strategies, goals, objectives, and action plans to achieve that future. Common steps in this process may include develop a vision, develop a mission, develop guiding principles, develop strategic objectives, and develop the tactical goals.

Strategic quality audit Audit performed to verify that the strategic plan of the organization addresses current and future legal, environmental, safety, and market quality requirements.

Strategy Action plan to set the direction for the coordinated use of resources through programs, projects, policies, procedures, and organizational assets to advance future business interest.

Stratification Layering of objects or data. The process of classifying data into subgroups based on characteristics or categories.

Stratification *(of a sample)* If a sample is formed by combining units from several lots having different properties, the sample distribution will show a concentration or clumping about the mean value for each lot; this is called stratification.

Stratified random sampling Technique to segment (stratify) a population prior to drawing a random sample from each stratum. The purpose is to increase precision when information is needed on each stratum.

Stratified sampling Process of selecting units deliberately from various locations within a lot or batch or from various phases of or periods of a process to obtain a sample.

Strengths, weaknesses, opportunities, and threats analysis (SWOT) Analysis methodology used to determine where to apply special efforts to achieve desired outcomes. The process involves listing (1) strengths, and how to take the best advantage of them; (2) weaknesses, and how to minimize their impacts; (3) opportunities that may be presented by various influences, and how to take the best advantage of them; and (4) threats, and how to deal with them.

Stress test Testing a device outside its usual operating conditions in an attempt to find marginal design or manufacturing parameters.

Stretch goals Set of goals designed to position the organization to meet future requirements.

Structural variation Variation caused by regular, systematic changes in output, such as seasonal patterns and a blip in long-term trends. Errors caused by temporary workers hired to take care of rush orders.

Student's distribution Another name for the *t* distribution used in testing a hypothesis when the sample size is small (typically less than 30).

Stylus method Used for surface smoothness examination, it resembles a record needle drawn across a surface. Its movement is amplified and recorded. A profilometer uses a stylus to record surface roughness of a machined surface.

Subassembly Two or more parts used in combination to make up an assembly.

Subcause In a cause-and-effect diagram, the specific items, steps, or processes that are identified as being a factor or potential cause of the problem.

Subcontractor Organization that provides a product or service to the supplier.

Subgroup (1) In an object sense, a set of units or quantity of material obtained by subdividing a larger group of units or quantity of material. (2) In a measurement sense, a set of groups of observations obtained by subdividing a larger group of observations. For control charts, a sample of units from a given process, all taken at or near the same time.

Suboptimization Need for each business function to consider overall organizational objectives, resulting in higher efficiency and effectiveness of the entire system, although performance of a function may be suboptimal.

Sum of squares Summation of the squared deviations relative to zero, to two level means, or the grand mean of an experiment.

Sump Pit or tank that catches liquid runoff for drainage or disposal.

Sunk cost Cost that once expended cannot be recovered, such as utilities and labor.

Superfund Program operated under the legislative authority of the Environmental Protection Agency (EPA). It is designed to include activities relating to investigating sites, determining the priority they should receive, and supervising cleanup and other remedial actions.

Supplier Source of materials, service, or information input provided to a process.

Supplier audits Reviews that are planned and carried out to verify the adequacy and effectiveness of a supplier's quality program, drive improvement efforts, and increase value.

Supplier certification Process of evaluating the performance of a supplier with the intent of authorizing the supplier to self-certify shipments if such authorization is justified.

Supplier corrective action request (SCAR) Formal documented program that requests a corrective action response from suppliers when their product or performance does not meet expected requirements.

Supplier quality assurance Confidence a supplier's product or service will fulfill its customers' needs. This confidence is achieved by creating a relationship between the customer and supplier that ensures the product will be fit for use with minimal corrective action and inspection. According to J. M. Juran, there are nine primary activities needed: (1) define product and program quality requirements, (2) evaluate alternative suppliers, (3) select suppliers, (4) conduct joint quality planning, (5) cooperate with the supplier during the execution of the contract, (6) obtain proof of conformance to requirements, (7) certify qualified suppliers, (8) conduct quality improvement programs as required, and (9) create and use supplier quality ratings.

Supplier selection strategy and criteria Selection of new suppliers based on the type and uniqueness of the materials, product, or service to be purchased and the total cost. Suppliers of commodity-type items and basic supplies may be selected from directories and catalogs. For more sophisticated products and services, more stringent evaluation criteria may be established.

Supply chain Series of suppliers relating to a given process.

Supply chain management (SCM) Acts of integrating and managing components of the supply chain.

Support operations Those indirect activities that have some effect on the product or services the organization provides such as shipping, receiving, material control, storage, traffic, human resources, advertising, maintenance, information services, and so on.

Support systems   Starting with top management commitment and visible involvement, support systems are a cascading series of interrelated practices of improvement. Such practices/actions may include mission statement, transformation of company culture, policies, employment practices, compensation, recognition and rewards, employee involvement, rules and procedures, quality level agreements, training empowerment, methods and tools for tracking quality, tracking-measuring-evaluating-reporting systems, maintenance activities, and so on.

Surface metrology   Study and examination of surface finish and geometry (roundness, flatness, etc.).

Surface plate   Smooth work surface, usually heavy and stable, made of granite or cast iron. Used to provide a reference plane for inspection work. It must also provide an adequate and convenient surface for the support of the part and measuring instruments.

Surface runoff   In an environmental sense, rain, snow melt, or irrigation water in excess of what can be absorbed into the soil surface and stored in small surface depressions.

Surface texture specimens   Known standards used to make comparisons with the surface being examined. There are two types: one, called a roughness comparison sample, is used to make visual comparisons with the workpiece. The second, a precision reference sample, is used to calibrate an inspection instrument, such as a profilometer.

Surveillance   Continual monitoring of a process; a type of periodic assessment or audit conducted to determine whether a process continues to perform to a predetermined standard.

Surveillance audits   Regular audits conducted by registrars to confirm that a company registered to the ISO series of standards still complies; usually conducted on a six-month or yearly basis.

Survey   Act of examining a process or of questioning a selected sample of individuals to obtain data about a process, product, or service. A survey is generally conducted on a selected sample of a population to obtain information about predetermined questions. A customer satisfaction survey is one type used to gain information for a company on their products or service.

Survivability Product or system capable of withstanding a measure of abuse without sustaining impaired ability to accomplish its intended use.

Symmetry In engineering blueprints, a part feature that can be divided into two equal halves is described as being symmetrical. Perfect symmetry exists when the median points of the features correspondingly located surfaces lie in the same plane. *See* Appendix E.

Symptom Observable phenomenon arising from and accompanying a defect.

Synergy Simultaneous actions of separate groups or agencies, which, together, have a greater total effect than the sum of their individual effects.

System Group of interdependent processes and people that together perform a common mission.

Systematic In quality award criteria, the term *systematic* refers to approaches that are repeatable and use data and information so improvement and learning are possible.

Systematic failure Failure that has a high probability of recurrence due to inadequacy in the system and for which corrective action can be taken to eliminate the cause and prevent recurrence.

Systematic management Deals with the extensive use of procedures so all processes are carried out in defined sequences.

Systematic variation *(of a process)* Variations that exhibit a predictable pattern. The pattern may be cyclic (i.e., a recurring pattern) or it may be progressive (trend).

System audit Audit carried out to establish whether the quality/enviromental management system conforms to a prescribed standard in both its design and in its implementation.

System effectiveness Ability of a system to achieve its stated purpose and meet its stated objectives.

System interfaces Physical interfaces among connecting parts of a system, or performance ties among various functional or complementary departments or groups.

System *kaizen*   Improvement aimed at an entire production or management stream.

System of profound knowledge   *See* **profound knowledge, system of.**

Systems approach to management   Management theory that views the organization as a whole. Where activities in one part of the organization affects all parts of the organization (also known as "systems thinking").

T

Tacit knowledge Knowledge that relies on past experiences and judgments whether used by an individual or organization. The knowledge and experience that comes from years of experience in a certain field, knowledge that does not normally come from classroom type training. See also *The Rise and Fall of Strategic Planning* (New York: Free Press, 1994).

Tactical goals Detailed short duration goals that meet a specific objective (e.g., provide SPC training to the quality department employees within one month).

Tactical plans Short-term plans, usually of one to two years duration, that describe actions the organization will take to meet its strategic business plan.

Tactics Strategies and processes that help an organization meet its objectives.

Taguchi loss function Pertains to where product characteristics deviate from the normal aim and losses increase according to a parabolic function. Merely attempting to produce a product within specifications does not prevent loss because additional loss may be inflicted on society after shipment of a product, even if all specifications have been met. See also *Introduction to Quality Engineering* (Dearborn, MI: American Supplier Institute, 1986).

Taguchi methods The American Supplier Institute's trademarked term for the quality engineering methodology developed by Genichi Taguchi. In this engineering approach to quality control, Taguchi calls for offline quality control, online quality control, and a system of experimental design to improve quality and reduce costs.

Tailings Residue of raw materials or waste separated out during the processing of minerals or crops.

Takt time   Rate of customer demand. Takt is the heartbeat of a lean system. Takt time is calculated by dividing production time by the quantity the customer requires in that time.

Tall organizations   Vertical organizations are known as "tall," meaning there are numerous layers in the management structure. Decision making is controlled and approvals are required for most events other than the routine activities required to conduct business.

Tally sheet   Another name for a **check sheet**.

Tampering   Action taken to compensate for variation within the control limits of a stable system. Tampering increases rather than decreases variation, as evidenced in the funnel experiment.

Tamper seal   Unreplaceable seal that shows evidence of unauthorized access to areas that could invalidate results. Usually this is a tape or seal crimped lead wire that must be broken, torn, or removed leaving highly visible evidence that access has been gained and that additional checking or other measures must be taken to assure product integrity.

Tangible asset   Assets that have physical substance and value that is expected to be held by the organization for some time, usually well beyond the current accounting cycle.

Tap   Tool used to cut internal threads in a workpiece. The process of cutting internal threads.

Taper   Gradual decrease in diameter, thickness, or width of an object.

Taper reamer   Tool that produces an accurate tapered hole when required.

Targets and objectives   Objectives are the overall goals set by an organization for itself, whereas targets are the detailed performance requirements with time schedules for achieving objectives.

TARP   U.S. Office of Consumer Affairs/Technical Assistance Research Programs. Among other things it studies how effective complaint handling can affect customer loyalty and affects repeat business.

Task   Specific, definable activity to perform an assigned function often finished within a certain time frame.

Taxonomy Classification of items or objects. As presented by Benjamin S. Bloom in his *Taxonomy of Educational Objectives* (1956), these are the six levels: (1) knowledge, being able to remember or recognize terminology, definitions, facts, ideas, and so on; (2) comprehension, being able to read and understand descriptions, communication, regulations, reports, and so on; (3) application, being able to apply ideas, principles, theories, and so on; (4) analysis, being able to break down information into its basic elements and understand their relationships; (5) synthesis, being able to put the elements together so the patterns and structure are evident and basic conclusions can be obtained; and (6) evaluation, being able to make informed judgments and decisions from the information collected.

t-distribution Used for a sample with size "n", drawn from a normally distributed population, with a mean X-bar and standard deviation "s". The true population parameters are unknown. The t-distribution is expressed as a table for a given number of degrees of freedom and alpha risk. As the degrees of freedom get very large, it approaches a Z-distribution.

Team Group of individuals organized to work together to accomplish a specific objective.

Team-based organization Management style that supports the team concept, encouraging employee involvement and suggestions. At times the team may make hiring and firing decisions.

Team-based structure Describes an organizational structure in which team members are organized around performing a specific function of the business, such as handling customer complaints or assembling an engine.

Team building/ development Process of transforming a group of people into a team and developing the team to achieve its purpose. Phases of team building according to Peter Scholtes in *The Team Handbook* are forming, storming, norming, and performing. See also *The Team Handbook* (Madison, WI: Oriel, Inc., 2003).

Team dynamics Interactions that occur among team members under different conditions.

Team facilitation Process of dealing with both the role as facilitator on the team and promoting the techniques and tools for facilitating the team. *See also* **facilitator**.

Team leader Team leader's roles should include organizing team meetings, keeping the efforts on track, providing updates on team progress to management, addressing team dynamics issues, serving as liaison between the team and other parts of the organization, helping solve problems, and handling administrative duties.

Team problems   As defined in *The Team Handbook* by Peter Scholtes, the 10 common problems encountered in a team environment are (1) foundering, (2) overbearing participants, (3) dominating participants, (4) reluctant participants, (5) unquestioned acceptance of opinions as facts, (6) rush to accomplishment, (7) attribution, (8) discounts and "plops," (9) wanderlust: digression and tangents, and (10) feuding members. For a complete discussion on these topics, see Scholtes, *The Team Handbook* (Madison, WI: Oriel, Inc., 2003).

Team process   As defined in *The Team Handbook* by Peter Scholtes, the 10 ingredients for a successful team are (1) clarity of team goals, (2) an improvement plan, (3) clearly defined roles, (4) clear communications, (5) beneficial team behaviors, (6) well-defined decision procedures, (7) balanced participation, (8) established ground rules, (9) awareness of the group process, and (10) use of the scientific approach. For a complete discussion on these topics, *The Team Handbook* (Madison, WI: Oriel, Inc., 2003).

Team types   Could include many varieties such as work groups, self-managed, process improvement, quality improvement, project implementation, and so on.

Team structure   Type of organization based on teams.

Team success strategy   A successful team must have proven ingredients, Peter Scholtes, in *The Team Handbook*, suggests these 10 requirements: (1) clarity in team goals, (2) an improvement plan, (3) clearly defined roles, (4) clear communications, (5) beneficial team behaviors, (6) well-defined decision procedures, (7) balanced participation, (8) established ground rules, (9) awareness of the group process, and (10) use of the scientific approach. See also *The Team Handbook* (Madison, WI: Oriel, Inc., 2003).

Technical expert   As defined for an audit team, a technical expert provides specific knowledge or expertise to an audit team but does not participate as an auditor.

Telecommuting   Completing job assignments away from the primary location through the use of computer technology and telecommunication devices.

Temper   In metalworking, the reheating of steel to bring it to a certain degree of hardness or softness.

Temperature, effects of Nearly all materials change size when their temperature changes. Most increase their size as temperature increases and decrease size as temperature decreases. When measuring in tenth to mil or finer increments, temperature becomes an increasingly important consideration. For close tolerance inspection and calibration work results should be taken at 68°F or the results corrected for the ambient temperature.

Template Guide used to cut or apply shapes into the workpiece or assist in inspecting the piece.

Tender Written offer to supply products or services at a stated cost.

Tensile strength Minimum nominal tension stress or pull a specimen will take before fracturing.

Ten-to-one rule Rule used in calibration to enhance the reliability of the measurements being performed. It states that the calibration instrument should be able to divide the part tolerance into 10 parts. It means that in calibration the master should be 10 times more accurate than the instrument being calibrated and traceable to NIST masters.

Tera One trillion. Expressed as 10 to the 12th power.

Tertiary datum In engineering blueprints, a tertiary datum requires at least one point of contact between the part feature and the machine tooling or inspection surface. Part of the datum reference frame. *See* Appendix E.

Tertiary standard Transfer standard, usually used to provide assurance from the primary standard at a location to the working standards used at a workplace location.

Test Technical operation that consists of the determination of one or more characteristics or performance of a given product, material, equipment, organism, physical phenomenon, process, or service according to a specified procedure.

Test coverage Percentage of possible combinations of group sizes to be used on a pass/fail or other functional test.

Testing Means of determining the capability of an item to meet specified requirements by subjecting the item to a set of physical, chemical, environmental, or operating actions or conditions.

Theory   Unproved assertion as to reasons for the existence of some phenomenon. Usually, several theories are presented to explain the presence of the phenomenon.

Theory of constraints (TOC)   Eliyahu Goldratt in *Theory of Constraints* identifies bottlenecks as a major hurdle to overcome in the continuous improvement process. Also called "constraints management." He also identifies a set of five tools that examines the entire system for continuous improvement: the current reality tree, conflict resolution diagram, future reality tree, prerequisite tree, and transition tree. See individual entries. See also *Theory of Constraints* (Great Barrington, MA: North River Press, 1990).

Theory of knowledge   Belief that management is about prediction, and people learn not only from experience but also from theory. When people study a process and develop a theory, they can compare their predictions with their observations with profound learning results.

Theory W   Proposed theory that provides an approach to software development, where the project manager tries to make winners of everyone involved in the software development process.

Theory X and theory Y   Theory developed by Douglas McGregor that maintains there are two contrasting assumptions about people, each of which are based on the manager's view of human nature. Theory X managers take a negative view and assume most employees do not like to work and try hard to avoid it. Theory Y managers take a positive view and believe employees want to work, will seek and accept responsibility, and can offer creative solutions to organizational problems. See also *The Human Side of Enterprise* (New York: McGraw-Hill, 1960).

Theory Z   Coined by William G. Ouchi and refers to a Japanese style of management that is characterized by long-term employment, slow promotions, considerable job rotation, consensus-style decision making, and a concern for employees as a whole. See also *Theory Z* (Reading, MA: Addison-Wesley, 1981).

Thermal fatigue   Mechanical breakdown of materials that have been subjected to varying cycles of heating and cooling.

Thermal shock   Subjecting a material to rapid and wide range changes in temperature to ascertain its ability to withstand those rapid changes. Tests resistance of finished items to rapid and severe changes in environmental temperature.

Third-angle projection On engineering blueprints, a system of orthographic projection commonly used in the United States.

Third party Any individuals, groups, or organizations fully independent of the organization (e.g., a consulting or registration firm).

Third-party audit External audits carried out by personnel who are neither employees of the customer nor of a supplier but are usually employees of certification bodies or of registrars.

Three-sixty-degree (360°) feedback process Evaluation method that provides feedback from the perspective of self, peers, direct reports, superiors, customers, and suppliers. A personal quality improvement tool used by organizations to provide performance feedback.

Throughput time Total time required (processing + queue) from concept to launch or from order received to delivery, or raw materials received to delivery to the customer.

Tier When *tier* is used in the context of quality/environmental management system documentation, it usually lists out four levels. In the ISO format, documentation is structured so it covers all levels of the management system being described. Typically the levels are tier 1, quality system manual (this may include a corporate manual as well as divisional or unit manuals); tier 2, quality procedures, quality plans, training manuals, operational procedures, and so on; tier 3, work instructions; tier 4, the forms, specification sheets, drawings, and other documents required by your system. Records may be applicable to any level in the documentation structure; they show something was accomplished.

Tightened inspection Inspection under a sampling plan using the same quality level as that of a normal inspection plan, but requiring a more stringent acceptance criteria, usually a larger sample size or less rejects.

Timeline chart Identification of the specific start, finish, and amount of time required to complete an activity.

Time plots Chart used to examine data for trends or other patterns that develop over time. It consists of data plotted in the sequenced time in which they occur.

Time study Procedure by which the actual elapsed time for performing a given task, with its subelements, is determined by the use of a suitable timing device and recorded. The procedure usually includes the adjustment of the actual time due to the operator's performance rating and any allowed delays.

Time value of money   Economic concept stating that money now available is more valuable than the same amount of money at some later date, it is not tied directly to inflation, but more to the potential earning power of the money.

Title block   On engineering blueprints, the box in the lower right corner where basic information about the blueprint and the part it represents is shown, such as part number, material, tolerances, and so on. *See* Appendix E.

TL 9000   Quality management standard for the telecommunications industry built on ISO 9000. Its purpose is to define the requirements for the design, development, production, delivery, installation, and maintenance of products and services. Included are cost and performance-based measurements that measure reliability and quality performance of the products and services.

Tolerance   The maximum and minimum limit values a product may have and still meet engineering or customer requirements.

Tolerance design   Concept proposed by Genichi Taguchi that provides a rational grade limit for components of a system; determines which parts and processes need to be modified and to what degree it is necessary in order to increase their control capacity; a method for rationally determining tolerances. See also *Introduction to Quality Engineering* (Dearborn, MI: American Supplier Institute, 1986).

Tolerance limits   Total allowable variation from the specified dimension for an individual unit of manufacturing output or service operation.

Tolerance stack up   Accumulation of errors that occur when dimensions are made in sequence with each dimension having its own tolerance. Consider a bar 6 inches long with a series of holes at 1-inch intervals, each with a +/- tolerance of .010 to the previous hole. This method of tolerancing could in theory allow the fifth hole to be up to +/- .050 (tolerances stacked) from the starting point. With true position tolerancing, all holes including the fifth hole would need to be within +/- .010 of the starting point. *See* **accumulation of errors** or **chain dimensioning**.

Tolerance zone   In engineering blueprints, the tolerance zone is the distance between two parallel planes, two parallel straight lines, or two uniform boundaries as with hole centers.

Tool Any implement held by hand used for cutting, hitting, shaping, removing, polishing, and so on, or used in a machine to accomplish the same activities.

Tooling and Equipment (TE) Supplement Interpretation of **QS-9000** (see entry) developed by the Big Three automakers for tooling and equipment suppliers.

Tool life Minimum amount of production that can be expected from a tool.

Tools and techniques Equipment, mechanisms, and procedures applied to process for the purpose of creating a product or service.

Top management Under the ISO systems, the person or group of people who direct and control an organization.

Top-management commitment Participation of the highest level officials in their organization's quality improvement efforts. Their participation includes establishing and serving on a quality committee, establishing quality policies and goals, deploying those goals to lower levels of the organization, providing the resources and training lower levels need to achieve the goals, participating in quality improvement teams, reviewing progress organizationwide, recognizing those who have performed well, and revising the current reward system to reflect the importance of achieving the quality goals.

Topography In an environmental sense, the physical features of a surface area including relative elevations and the position of natural and manufactured features.

Torque Amount of twist (force) used, based on the principle of the lever. When torque is applied to the rotation of a screw thread, force results. Force can be expressed as torque = force $\times$ length of lever. A force of 1 pound applied at a distance of 1 foot = 1 foot pound (1 ft. lb.).

Tort In law, wrongful acts that are neither a crime nor a breach of contract but renders the person committing the act liable to the victim for damages. An example would be the owner of a property failing to repair a public stair, causing someone to fall and suffer an injury. Tort laws provide a remedy for the injuries suffered.

Total indicator reading/runout (TIR) On a dial indicator, the swing of the needle between its lowest reading and its highest reading. Also known as the "full indicator movement," or FIM. *See* Appendix E.

Total predictive/ productive maintenance (TPM) Series of methods, originally pioneered by Nippondenso (a member of the Toyota group), to ensure every machine in a production process is always able to perform its required tasks so production is never interrupted. The aim is to maximize equipment effectiveness by a preventative maintenance program throughout the life of the equipment.

Total quality Strategically integrated system for achieving customer satisfaction that involves all managers and employees and uses quantitative methods to continuously improve an organization's processes.

Total quality control (TQC) Feigenbaum's concept of a system that integrates quality development, maintenance, and improvement of the parts of an organization. It helps a company manufacture its product and deliver its services economically. See also *Total Quality Control,* 3rd rev. ed. (New York: McGraw-Hill, 1991).

Total quality management (TQM) Term initially coined by the Naval Air Systems Command to describe its Japanese-style management approach to quality improvement. Since then, TQM has taken on many meanings. Simply put, it is a management approach to long-term success through customer satisfaction. TQM is based on the participation of all members of an organization in improving processes, products, services, and the culture in which they work. The methods for implementing this approach are found in the teachings of such quality leaders as Philip B. Crosby, W. Edwards Deming, Armand V. Feigenbaum, Kaoru Ishikawa, and Joseph M. Juran.

Total runout (TR) Specifies how much the surface of a part feature may vary as it rotates 360° around a datum axis. *See* Appendix E.

Touch probe Electronic contact measuring device that is mounted on a machine tool, gage, or coordinate measuring machine. The touch probe sends a signal to the instrument that contact has been made, which in turn indicates a dimension.

Toxic chemical Any chemical listed by the Environmental Protection Agency (EPA) in its rules as "Toxic Chemicals Subject to Section 313 of the Emergency Planning and Community Right-to-Know Act of 1986." Any chemical known to harm humans or animals.

Toxicity Degree to which a substance or mixture of substances can harm humans or animals. Acute toxicity involves harmful effects in an organism through a single or short-term exposure. Chronic toxicity is the ability of a substance or mixture of substances to cause harmful effects over an extended period.

Toxic substance Chemical or mixture that may present an unreasonable risk of injury to health or to the environment.

Toxic waste Any waste that can produce injury if inhaled, swallowed, or absorbed through the skin.

Trace (1) In an internal audit sense, *trace forward* is to start the audit trail at the beginning of production or receiving inspection and following the process through to finished product testing and shipment. Trace backward starts with the finished goods and traces back to receiving. (2) In a reliability sense, it is the ability to provide an audit trail that records the execution of a computer program showing the sequence in which the instructions were executed, providing a means to debug a programming error.

Traceability (1) As used in calibration terminology, the property of a result of a measurement whereby it can be related to appropriate standards, generally international or national standards, through an unbroken chain of comparisons. (2) As used in parts traceability, it is in the sense of being able to follow the materials used in the product from the source through the manufacturing or processing stages to final delivery. In some applications it includes the paper trail documentation that follows the entire process.

Traceability of gages Ability to verify each successively higher standard in the calibration process to the next higher standard, until it reaches the NIST standard.

Traceability of product Ability to trace the history, application, or location of a product or service by means of recorded identifiers. Traceability may refer to a product, to materials, and so on.

Tracer technique Technique used with an optical comparator, where a tracer is moved along a feature being inspected. The tracer simultaneously moves a similar member in the optical path so it can be compared to the path on the chart. This is useful when the feature to be inspected cannot be placed directly in the optical path, such as with an inside feature.

Tracing In auditing, tracing can be either forward or backward, literally meaning that you start in the audit process at the start and work forward through the process until you have completed the scope of the audit or you can start at the end of a process and trace forward until you have completed the process and you come to the starting point. Note: You could also start at any place in the process and audit forward or backward. The use of flow-charts is a useful tool in following the process flow.

Trademark   Nationally or internationally recognized logo or insignia that differentiates one company and its products from another.

Trade-off   Giving up or accepting one advantage or disadvantage for another to gain more value to the decision maker.

Traditional organizations   Those organizations not driven by customers and quality policies. Also refers to organizations managed primarily through functional units. Bureaucracies are called traditional organizations.

Training   Refers to the skills employees need to learn in order to perform or improve the performance of their current job or tasks, or the process of providing those skills.

Training cycle   Steps required to deliver effective training are (1) determine training need, (2) design the training program, (3) deliver the training, (4) evaluate the effectiveness, (5) measure the improvement to see if it has met the goals, and (6) maintain the improvement.

Training design   Major factors in training design are who (gives training and receives training), why, what (method, place, media), where, when, what (are the expected results and how measured).

Training environment   To obtain the best results for training efforts expended, the training environment must provide adequate control over certain conditions. Things to consider would include good lighting, room temperature and ventilation, good acoustics, proper line of sight, adequate seating, proper timing for the students, clean surroundings with enough room, and a good physical location.

Training evaluation   Techniques and tools used within the process of evaluating the effectiveness of training.

Training implementation plan   Donald Kirkpatrick identifies a 10-step plan in *Evaluating Training Programs* as (1) determining needs, (2) setting objectives, (3) determining subject content, (4) selecting participants, (5) determining a schedule, (6) selecting training facilities, (7) selecting instructors, (8) selecting and preparing training aids, (9) coordinating the program, and (10) evaluating the training as provided. See also *Evaluating Training Programs* (Westport, CT: Greenwood Press, 1987).

Training needs assessment — Process, techniques, and tools used to determine an organization's training needs.

Training retention — According to D. L. Goetsch and S. B. Davis in the book *Quality Management: Introduction to Total Quality Management for Production, Processing, and Services,* we retain only 10% of what we read, only 20% of what we hear, 30% of what we see, 50% of what we see and hear, 70% of what we see and speak of, and 90% of what we do while talking about it. See also *Quality Management: Introduction to Total Quality Management for Production, Processing, and Services,* 4th ed. (Upper Saddle River, NJ: Prentice Hall, 2002).

Transaction data — Detailed data pertaining to a given event occurring in a process. Examples are the data obtained from an individual checking out building supplies (the shopping process) and the data obtained from testing an assembled product (the final product inspection step in the production process).

Transactional leadership — Concept used to categorize a style of leading whereby the leader sees the work as being done through clear definitions of tasks and responsibilities and the provision of resources as needed.

Transfer standard — Master gage or standard used to check for the accuracy of a reference standard and a working standard used in the shop.

Transformational leadership — Style of leading whereby the leader articulates the vision and values necessary for the organization to succeed.

Transition fit — Type of fit that results when the specified size limits of mating part features produces interference at their maximum material condition and clearance at some point as they approach their least material condition.

Transition tree — Technique used in applying Eliyahu Goldratt's *Theory of Constraints*. It is used to identify the details required to implement a change. See also *Theory of Constraints* (Great Barrington, MA: North River Press, 1990).

Translation — In measurement, it refers to the comparison of an unknown dimension to a known standard.

Trash   In an environmental sense, any material considered worthless or offensive that is thrown away. Generally defined as dry waste materials, but in common usage it is a synonym for garbage, refuse, or rubbish.

Treatment   As related to design of experiments, the combination of the versions (levels) of each of the factors assigned to an experimental unit. *See also* **levels.**

Tree diagram   Management tool that depicts the hierarchy of tasks and subtasks needed to complete an objective. This tool systematically maps out in increasing detail the paths and task needed in order to achieve a primary task as well as smaller related task. The finished diagram bears a resemblance to a tree. One of the seven management and planning tools.

Trend   (1) As used on SPC charts, a trend is the graphical representation of a variable's tendency, over time, to increase, decrease, or remain unchanged. Like runs, attention should be given to these patterns when they exceed a (statistically based) predetermined number. (2) In quality award criteria, the term *trends* refers to numerical information that shows the direction and rate of change for an organization's results. Trends provide a time sequence of an organization's performance.

Trend analysis   Refers to the charting of data over time to identify a tendency or direction.

Trend control chart   Control chart in which the deviation of the subgroup average, X-bar, from an expected trend in the process level is used to evaluate the stability of a process.

Trend-line chart   Identification on a graph of the specific start, finish, and amounts of time required to complete an activity.

Trepan   To cut a hole into a workpiece without having to waste the material being removed.

Trial   One of the factor combinations in an experiment.

Trigonometry   Branch of mathematics dealing with the relationships of sides of triangles to the angles formed by them. Trigonometric functions are the ratios of pairs of triangle sides. They are useful to designate angles.

Trilogy   Concept proposed by Joseph M. Juran that requires (1) quality planning, (2) quality control, and (3) quality improvement.

Trivial many   Term used in Pareto analysis referring to the many items that fall in the 80% range. Includes many problems that contribute only a very small quantity by themselves. Contrast with the **vital few.** See also *Juran's Quality Handbook,* 5th ed. (New York: McGraw-Hill, 1999).

TRIZ   Problem-solving approach or "the theory of problem solving" that describes three steps to solve technical problems: (1) various tricks, (2) methods based on utilizing physical effects and phenomenon, and (3) complex methods.

True position   Exact location of a point, line, or plane with respect to a datum or other feature. *See* Appendix E.

Truncated sample   Sample in which items are removed from observation before they fail where the total number of nondefective items removed is not known.

Truncation   Deleting portions of a distribution greater than or less than a certain value. A sorted lot of defective parts will leave a truncated distribution.

t-test   Assesses whether the means of two groups are statistically different from each other. Used to compare the means of two groups.

t-type matrix   Management tool used to identify the root cause or problems that ultimately result in a design change. Helps to determine why the problem occurred, why it was not detected earlier in the process, and how the process can be improved.

Turbidity   In an environmental sense, haziness in air caused by the presence of particles and pollutants. It may also be a cloudy condition in water due to suspended silt or other organic matter.

Turn   In machining operations, to produce a diameter on a lathe.

Two-tailed test   Test of hypothesis that has two critical values, both an upper and a lower acceptance limit. A two-tailed test is used more frequently and has more applications than a one-tailed test.

Type I error   Incorrect decision that a process is unacceptable when, in fact, perfect information would reveal it is located within the "zone of acceptable processes." The decision to reject something (such as a statistical hypothesis or a lot of products) when it is in fact acceptable. Concluding that a process is unstable when in fact it is stable. Also known as the "(α) alpha risk."

Type II error   Incorrect decision that a process is acceptable when, in fact, perfect information would reveal it is located within the "zone of rejectable processes." The decision to accept something when it is unacceptable. Concluding that a process is stable when it is in fact unstable. Also known as the "(β) beta risk."

Type III error   Answering the wrong question.

U

U chart   Count per unit chart. Attribute control chart used to show the average number of defects in a sample; uses variable sample size. Compare with a **C chart**, which uses a fixed sample size.

UL (Underwriters Laboratories)   Develops and publishes standards for materials, products, and systems. Also tests products for compliance with these standards and for products that meet the requirements. Only then are they approved and awarded the UL mark, called "listing."

Ultrasonic inspection (UI)   Nondestructive test used to detect defects in a material. It uses an ultrasonic frequency subjected to the part; these are reflected to a microphone and analyzed.

Ultraviolet rays   Radiation from the sun that can be either helpful or potentially harmful. In its helpful state it enhances plant life; in its harmful state it can cause skin cancer or other tissue damage. The ozone layer in the earth's atmosphere partly shields the earth from ultraviolet rays.

Unacceptable risk   Exposure to risk that is significant enough to jeopardize an organization's strategy, present dangers to humans, or present a significant financial exposure, which the organization is not willing to accept.

Uncensored data   All sample data combined have a reading, without any filtering (sorting or adjustments made to the data).

Uncertainty   Indication of the variability associated with a measured value that takes into account two major components of error: (1) bias and (2) random error attributed to the imprecision of the measurement process. *See* **bias** or **random error.**

Unconditional guarantee Organizational policy of providing customers an unquestioned remedy for any product or service deficiency.

Unified national system System for classifying screw threads based on their diameter and pitch. The most commonly used are UNF Unified National Fine and UNC Unified National Coarse.

Uniform precision design Type of central composite response surface design in which the number of center points is chosen such that there is more protection against bias in the regression coefficients.

Unilateral tolerance Has one limit at the nominal dimension and expresses the other limit in its entirety as a deviation in one direction from the nominal only.

Unimodal Distribution that has one peak, such as a normal distribution.

Unit (1) Object on which a measurement or observation can be made. Note: Commonly used in the sense of a "unit of product," the entity of product inspected in order to determine whether it is defective or not defective. (2) In "unit of length," the smallest whole division of a standard of length.

Unit of command Concept that a subordinate should be responsible to only one superior.

Universe Group of populations, often reflecting different characteristics of the items or material under consideration. *See* **population.**

Upper control limit (UCL) Control limit for points above the central line in a control chart.

Upper specification limit (USL) Maximum limit for dimensions as specified for a product to be acceptable.

Upper tolerance limit (UTL) Maximum limit for dimensions as specified for a product to be acceptable.

Upset In metalworking, the process of forming a particular shape on the ends of a bar (such as a screw head) by hammering it between two dies.

Usage   During a life test, the measure of time on test. This measurement could, for example, be in units of power—on hours, test days, cycles, or system operations.

USDA   United States Department of Agriculture. Branch of the U.S. government that oversees the quality of life of the American public by supporting safe production of agriculture.

Useful life   Amount of time a product will provide a return or value to its owner or user.

Utility theory   Theoretical approach to the measurement of a person's willingness to take a risk in light of the different levels of reward, whether that reward is for the person taking the risk or for other potential beneficiaries of the reward.

Validation   Act of confirming, through the provision of objective evidence, that the requirements for a specified intended use or application have been fulfilled. The establishment and confirmation by objective evidence of the fulfillment of requirements. This is generally accomplished by inspection and testing of the unit or item to prove it will fulfill its intended purpose.

Validity   (1) Ability of a feedback instrument to measure what it was intended to measure. (2) Degree to which inferences derived from measurements are meaningful. There are three ways of measuring this: (1) criterion related, (2) construct related, and (3) content related.

Value   In quality award criteria, the term *value* refers to the perceived worth of a product or service, process, asset, or function relative to possible alternatives and the cost of each.

Value added   Parts of the process that add worth from the perspective of the external customer.

Value added per employee (VAE)   Contribution made by each employee toward the value of a product or service. In most cases this should be nearly double the wages paid per employee.

Value adding process   Activities that transform input into a customer usable output. The customer can be internal or external to the organization.

Value analysis   Assumes a process, procedure, product, or service is of no value unless proven otherwise. It assigns a price to every step of a process and then computes the worth-to-cost ratio of that step.

Value chain   *See* **supply chain.**

Value engineering   Approach to design that examines each element of a product or system to determine whether there is a more effective and less expensive way to achieve the same results. Value engineering points the way to elimination and reengineering of products, processes, and services.

Value research   Related to value engineering, for a given feature of the service or product value research helps determine the customers' strongest "likes" and "dislikes" and those for which customers are neutral. It focuses attention on strong dislikes and enables identified "neutrals" to be considered for cost reductions.

Values   Fundamental beliefs that drive organizational behavior and decision making.

Value stream   All activities, both value added and nonvalue added, required to bring a product from a raw material state into the hands of the customer, bring a customer requirement from order to delivery, and bring a design from concept to launch. Often used in lean manufacturing planning.

Value stream loops   Segments of a value stream with boundaries broken into loops are a way to divide future methods implementation into manageable pieces.

Value stream manager   Person responsible for creating a future methods map and leading door-to-door implementation of the future methods for a particular product family. Makes change happen across departmental and functional boundaries.

Value stream mapping   Pencil-and-paper tool used in two stages: (1) Follow a product's production path from beginning to end, and draw a visual representation of every process in the material and information flows. (2) Then draw a future methods map of how value should flow. The most important map is the future methods map. Often used in lean thinking operations.

Variable control charts   X-bar and R chart (when data is readily available). Run charts (with limited single point data). MX bar–MR charts (limited data). X-MR charts (with limited data). X-bar and S chart (when sigma is readily available). Median charts and Short-Run charts (very limited data).

Variable cost   Cost that varies with production quantity, such as material and direct labor.

Variable data Measurement information that is subject to change. Control charts based on variable data include average (X-bar) chart, range (R) chart, and sample standard deviation (s) chart.

Variable gage Gages capable of measuring the actual size of a part (e.g., dial indicator, micrometer, and dial caliper).

Variables Quantities that are subject to change.

Variable sampling plan Plan in which a sample is taken and a measurement on a specified quality characteristic is made on each unit. The measurements are summarized into a simple statistic, and the observed value is compared with an allowable value, as defined in the plan.

Variance Measure of dispersion on observations based on the mean of the squared deviations from the arithmetic mean. The square of the standard deviation, given by formula.

Variant Item or event classified differently from others of its type or kind.

Variation Change in data, characteristic, or function caused by one of four factors: **special causes, common causes, tampering,** or **structural variation** (see individual entries).

V-block method Most common method to measure round parts is to support them in a V-block, which also provides the reference points. Unfortunately, this is affected by any lobing that may exist.

Vendor In the context of quality processes, a supplier of commonly available hardware items and various goods and/or services where the requirements and specifications are well defined. *See also* **supplier.**

Vendor audits External audit of a supplier by its customers.

Verification Act of confirmation, through the provision of objective evidence, that specified requirements have been fulfilled. The establishment by examination that a process or activity provides the required acceptable output to assure the specified requirements have been met. *See also* **inspection.**

Vernier Instruments in which the vernier scale used is the outstanding characteristic. There are many instruments not so classified that also use verniers in their method of amplification.

Vernier scale   Scale used on a measuring instrument, to amplify by one division more, the main scale, by dividing or amplifying a given length as read on the main scale.

Version   (1) Issue of a commercial software application that reflects a major change in features. (2) Revision level of a procedure, instruction sheet, blueprint, and so on, to indicate changes made from the original issue.

Vertical   At a right angle to the plane of the horizon. In metrology, this is altered to state it is in the direction of the pull of gravity. For convenience, the X- and Y-axes are said to be in the horizontal axis, and the Z-axis is said to be in the vertical axis.

Vertically integrate   To bring together more of the steps involved in producing a product in order to form a continuous chain owned by the same firm; typically involves taking on activities that were previously supplied by an external source and making them in house.

Virgin materials   Resources extracted from nature in their raw form, such as timber or metal ore.

Virtual condition   Maximum material condition size of a part feature, plus or minus any applicable geometric tolerances. For an external feature, virtual condition is the MMC of the feature plus the geometric tolerance. For an internal feature, virtual condition is the MMC of the feature minus the geometric tolerance.

Virtual team   Remotely situated individuals affiliated with a common organization, purpose, or project who conduct their joint effort via electronic communication.

Viscosity   Measure of a fluid's resistance to flow. A viscosity cup is the typical method used to measure the flow rate for a given length of time through a designated size opening in the viscosity cup.

Visible line   On engineering blueprints, a thick solid line, which represents an edge or contour that is visible in a given view. *See* Appendix E.

Visible management   Technique in which management provides information about elements of a job in a clearly defined (visible) manner, so workers are aware of what is happening, how their work affects others, and can maximize their productivity.

Vision   Basic theme or value of an individual or organization that is important and meaningful to the person or members of the organization and shows a common focus of purpose.

Vision statement   Statement that explains in measurable terms what an organization wants to become and what it hopes to achieve. It should be brief, inspire and challenge, describe an ideal condition, appeal to all stakeholders, and provide direction for the future of the organization.

Visual control   Technique of positioning all tools, parts, production activities, and performance indicators so the status of a process can be understood at a glance by everyone. Also used to provide visual clues; to aid the performance in correctly processing a step or series of steps, to reduce cycle time, to cut cost, to smooth flow of work, to improve quality. Used in lean thinking. May also be used with Andon boards in an electronic display.

Vital few, useful many   Term coined by Joseph M. Juran to describe his use of the Pareto principle, which he first defined in 1950. (The principle was used much earlier in economics and inventory control methodologies.) The principle suggests most effects come from relatively few causes; that is, 80% of the effects come from 20% of the possible causes. The 20% of the possible causes are referred to as the "vital few"; the remaining causes are referred to as the "useful many." When Juran first defined this principle, he referred to the remaining causes as the "trivial many," but realizing that no problems are trivial in quality assurance, he changed it to "useful many." See also *Juran's Quality Handbook,* 5th ed. (New York: McGraw-Hill, 1999).

Voice of the customer   Expressed requirements and expectations of customers relative to products or services, as documented and disseminated to the members of the providing organization.

Volt   Practical unit of measure of electromotive force or difference in potential between two points in an electrical field that requires one joule of work to move a positive charge of one coulomb from one point of lower potential to another point of higher potential.

Volumetric accuracy   Accuracy of a measuring instrument when measuring along all axes simultaneously.

Vulnerability   (1) Organizational characteristics that leave an organization open to hazard threats due to natural causes (e.g., storms, floods, and power outages) or to manufactured hazard threats (e.g., theft, vandalism, or bodily harm to employees). (2) System characteristics that cause it to degrade or be unable to perform its designed functions, as a result of having been subjected to a certain level of stressful effects in a natural, manufactured, or hostile environment.

Waiver   Written authorization to release a product that does not conform to the specified requirement. Also may be called a **concession** or **deviation**.

Walkabout   Visual group technique used in resolving resource planning and resolving conflicts among organizational elements.

Walk the talk   Popularized by Philip B. Crosby, a concept that means not only talking about what one believes in but also be observed acting out those beliefs. Employees' buy-in of the TQM concept is more likely when management is seen involved in the process every day. See also *Quality Is Free* (New York: McGraw-Hill, 1979).

Walk-through   Peer review and examination of the requirements, for design, and implementation of a project, or presentation, to ensure the intended objectives will be met. The rehearsal of an operational procedure or presentation, with all its steps.

Wanderlust   As defined by Peter Scholtes in *The Team Handbook,* the tendency of team members to move away from the subject at hand by talking about subjects they like such as vacations, hobbies, and sports, rather than the subject a meeting was called for. As a result, when the meeting is over nothing was accomplished. See also *The Team Handbook* (Madison, WI: Oriel, Inc., 2003).

Warning limits   Often used on control charts near the two-sigma bands. These are limits set to call attention to the possibility of out-of-control conditions, but further action is not necessarily required.

Warrant   Documented confirmation provided by the supplier that required testing and inspections have been performed and the product conforms to stated requirements. Often required on new or revised tooling or processes.

Warranty   Expressed warranties are those provided by the manufacturer in writing, whereas implied warranties are those provided by law.

Warranty of merchantability   Promise by the manufacturer or distributor that the goods are reasonably fit for the purpose for which they are sold and represented by the seller.

War room   Command and control center for an organization that usually serves as a conference area for a project team, senior management, or other stakeholders.

Warusa-kagen   Term used in TQC that refers to things that are not yet problems, but are still not quite right. If left unattended they may develop into serious problems. It is often the starting point for improvement activities.

Waste   (1) In a productivity sense, anything that consumes resources and produces no added value to the product or service a customer receives. As proposed by Taichi Ohno, the opposite of value is waste, and seven wastes affect productivity and quality: overproduction, waiting, transporting, inappropriate processing, excess inventory, unnecessary motions, and defects. (2) In an environmental sense, the unwanted materials left over from a manufacturing process or from places of human or animal habitation. The Japanese term for waste is ***muda***. See also *Toyota Production System—Beyond Large Scale Production* (Portland, OR: Productivity Press, 1988).

Waste stream   In an environmental sense, the total flow of solid waste from homes, businesses, institutions, and manufacturing plants that is recycled, burned, or disposed of in landfills

Watt   Practical unit of measuring electrical power, it is equal to one joule per second or to the power developed in a circuit by a current of one ampere flowing through a potential difference of one volt. It is equal to one seven hundred and forty-sixth of a horsepower.

Waviness   In surface finish measurement, waviness is the widely spaced irregularities on the surface being measured, in contrast to roughness, which are more closely spaced irregularities.

Wear blocks   Thin gage blocks used on the ends of stacks from a master gage block set to absorb wear. By using wear blocks, which are replaced as they wear, the master set is made to have a longer useful life.

Wear-out Process of derogation of a part or assembly through use, which results in an increase in failure rates with increasing usage or age.

Web In metalworking, the same as a rib.

Weibull distribution Distribution of continuous data that can take on many different shapes and is used to describe a variety of patterns; used to define when the "infant mortality rate" has ended and a steady state has been reached (chance failure), and finally wear-out. *See* Appendix C.

Weighed voting Way to prioritize a list of issues, ideas, or attributes by assigning points to each item based on its relative importance.

What-if analysis In project planning, a process of evaluating alternative strategies, by changing certain variables and assumptions to predict the outcome while considering the stated changes.

Whisker From Multivari or box plot chart, it displays minimum and maximum observations within 1.5 IQR (75th to 25th percentile span) from either the 25th or 75th percentile. Outliers are those that fall outside of the 1.5 range.

White paper Expanded narrative on any topic advancing the thoughts and opinions of the author, the purpose of which may be have readers test the author's idea. Often written and distributed anonymously. In the government it indicates the official government position on a particular issue.

WIIFM (What's In It For Me?) Concept of process change or motivational techniques that must answer the question "What's in it for me?" for those affected by the change, in order for them to go along with the change.

Wilcoxon Mann-Whitney test Used to test the null hypothesis that two populations have identical distribution functions against the alternative hypothesis that the two distribution functions differ only with respect to location (median). It does not require the assumption that the two populations are normally distributed. In many applications, it is used in place of the two sample t-test when the normality assumption is questionable. This test can also be applied when the observations in a sample of data are ranks, that is, data set in order rather than from direct measurements.

Win-lose Outcome of a negotiation that typically makes use of the power available to each party and treats the disagreement as a zero-sum game. One side gains and the other loses.

Win-win	Outcome of a negotiation that results in both parties being better off.
Wisdom	Use and application of data to provide information. This is transformed into knowledge, which in is turn transformed into wisdom. The effective use and application of information and knowledge to provide greater opportunities for humankind.
Work analysis (work balance analysis)	Analysis, classification, and study of the way work is done. Work may be categorized as value-added work (necessary work), nonvalue added (rework, unnecessary work, idle time, and so on). Collected data may be summarized on a Pareto chart, showing how people within the studied population work. The need for and value of all work is then questioned and opportunities for improvement identified. A time use analysis may also be included in the study.
Workbook	Collection of exercises, questions, or problems to be solved during training; a participant's repository for documents used in training (e.g., handouts).
Work breakdown structure (WBS)	Project management technique by which a project is divided into tasks, subtasks, and units of work to be performed.
Work environment	In ISO terms, the set of conditions under which work is performed.
Workflow diagram	*See* **flowchart.**
Work group	Group composed of people from one functional area who work together on a daily basis and whose goal is to improve the process of their function. *See also* **work team.**
Work improvement team (WIT)	Employees who work in an assigned area who perform similar functions and work to improve the work environment, production process, or product.
Working drawings (blueprints)	Set of blueprints or drawings containing all the information needed to manufacture and assemble a part. It includes the assembly blueprint, the parts list, and a detail blueprint for each component in the assembly.
Working papers	In ISO audit terms, all the documentation required for the audit, such as procedures, work instructions, check sheets, check list, and notes taken during the audit.

Working standards	Standards used to perform equipment calibration. They are lower (third) level standards, usually compared to secondary standards.
Work instruction	Instructions that prescribe how work is to be executed, who is to do it, when it is to start, and how it is to be completed. *See also* **procedure.**
Workmanship	Degree of quality that employees put into the product they manufacture; often defined as a standard of good quality.
Work sheet	Form used to record inspection information and data.
Work systems	In quality award criteria, refers to how employees are organized into formal and informal units; how job responsibilities are managed; and the processes for compensation, recognition, communication, hiring, and training used to align the components and enable and encourage all employees to contribute effectively and to the best of their ability.
Work team	Team comprising members from one work unit. Also called a "natural team." Work teams usually operate under the direction of a team leader, with little involvement by upper management.
World-class quality	Term used to indicate a standard of excellence; the best of the best that can compete with the best processes or quality available worldwide.
Worst-case scenario	(1) In project planning, anticipating problems that can delay the project or cause unnecessary expenses; then planning ahead to make allowances to overcome these problems. (2) In engineering design, the concept of anticipating problems and planning ahead for methods to reduce or eliminate that possibility.
Worst-case tolerance	Overall tolerance that can be expected if all mating components were at their worst-case conditions.
Wring	To bring two surfaces of micro-inch flatness together so they adhere with only a micro-inch separation. Gage blocks are wrung together to make up a set for a precise dimension.

X-axis   The horizontal axis; the side-to-side movement on a measuring system such as a **capability maturity model (CMM).**

X-bar chart   *See* **average chart.**

X-bar and R chart   For variables data, control charts for the averages and range of subgroups of data. *See also* **control chart.**

X-bar and S chart (sigma)   For variables data, control charts for the averages and standard deviation of subgroups of data. *See also* **control chart.**

X-ray testing   Nondestructive testing method used to check for hidden defects. Cracks and other hidden defects show up on film. Often used to detect defects in critical welds.

Y

Y-axis The vertical axis on a graph; the front-to-back movement on a measuring system such as a **capability maturity model (CMM).**

Yield Ratio between salable goods produced or process output and the quantity of raw materials and/or components put in at the beginning of the process.

Yoden square Type of experimental design that eliminates the possible effects of the position in a block design. Used to reduce the tendency to overestimate any experimental error in the test.

Z

Z-axis   On a measuring system such as a **capability maturity model (CMM),** the up-and-down movement from the reference plane or base plate.

Zenith sight   That point directly above the point of reference at infinity.

Zero defects   Performance standard and methodology developed by Philip B. Crosby that states if people commit themselves to watching details and avoiding errors, they can move closer to the goal of zero errors or defects. See also *Quality Is Free* (New York: McGraw-Hill, 1979).

Zero investment improvement   Another name for a ***kaizen* blitz or event.**

Zero of ignorance   Unnecessary division of a dimension. The addition of zeros in a table to make all values come out neatly to the same length. However, at times they are added fraudulently to make work appear more precise than it is. For example, in 0.25000, the last two zeros are the zeros of ignorance when the actual value is 0.250.

Zone control chart   Special use control chart used to plot chronologically the cumulative sum of deviations of normally distributed observations from the target value.

Zone of indifference   Process levels located between the "zone of acceptance" and the "zone of rejection." These represent processes in which the quality measures can be considered borderline and it is a matter of "indifference" whether these processes are accepted or rejected based on the current sample information.

Z score   Used to measure how extreme a value is in relation to the average, stated in standard deviation units.

Z-test   Test of statistical hypothesis that the population mean "U" is equal to the sample mean X-bar, when the population standard deviation is known.

Z-theory   Japanese style of management characterized by long-term employment, slow promotions, job rotation, consensus-style decisions, and concern for the employee.

Z value   When measuring capability of a process, the Z value is defined as the area outside of specification and can be determined by the Z value on a Standard Normal Table.

Appendix A
Influential People in the Quality Field

Albrect, Karl Proponent of customer service and author of *Service America* and *At America's Service*. He advanced the key concept of the "inverted pyramid," encouraging leaders to turn their organizations upside down and become more customer focused. His six basic customer-centered values are (1) spirit of service, (2) shared fate, (3) codetermination, (4) mutuality, (5) empowerment, and (6) creative dissatisfaction. He also described customer expectations in these four steps: (1) basic (the essential elements of the product or service); (2) expected (normal features of the product or service); (3) desired (worthwhile but not necessarily provided as a part of the package); and (4) unanticipated (features that go beyond what the customer expected). He defines the term *moment of truth*, as coined by Jan Carlzon, as "Any episode where a customer comes in to contact with any aspect of your company, no matter how distant, and by this contact, has an opportunity to form an opinion about your company." See also *At America's Service* (New York: Warner Books, 1988).

Alderfer, Clayton Proposed the EGR (existence-growth-relatedness) theory of motivation, similar to Maslow's hierarchy of needs. But Alderfer only proposed three levels: (1) existence (basic needs: food, water, shelter, pay, working conditions); (2) growth (needs for a higher creative and productive existence); and (3) relatedness (social and interpersonal needs).

Babbage, Charles English inventor called the "Father of Computers." Developed the analytical engine, the precursor of modern computers. Babbage was the first person to realize economy of appropriate skill level as a benefit of the division of labor.

Baldrige, Malcolm   The late secretary of commerce and a proponent of quality management. The U.S. Commerce Department's National Institute of Standards and Technology manages the Malcolm Baldrige National Quality Award, and ASQ administers it. It currently has seven major categories: (1) leadership, (2) strategic planning, (3) customer and market focus, (4) information and analysis, (5) human resource focus, (6) process management, and (7) business results. By design it is heavily slanted toward customer satisfaction and focus.

Bennis, Warren   Providing a strong connection to the education field, Bennis defines the differences between leadership and management as leadership is doing the right thing (leadership = effectiveness) versus management doing things right (management = efficiency). See also *The Planning of Change,* 3rd ed. (New York: Holt, Rinehart and Winston, 1986).

Berry, Leonard   In the book *On Great Service,* Berry identifies the characteristics of great service as service wisdom, belief in others, love of the business, and integrity. He also advocates improving service using six basic guidelines: take a holistic approach, automate efficient systems, solve genuine problems, offer more not less control, optimize basic technologies, and combine high tech with high touch. See also *On Great Service* (New York: Free Press, 1995).

Blanchard, Ken   Wrote about ethics in business in *The Power of Ethical Management* in which he posed three questions: (1) Is it legal? (2) Is it balanced? (fair to all involved) (3) How will it make me feel about myself? See also *The Power of Ethical Management* (New York: Ballantine Press, 1988).

Bloom, Benjamin S.   Author of *Taxonomy of Educational Objectives,* in which Bloom categorizes three specific areas in the learning process: (1) cognitive (or mental skills); (2) affective (growth in feelings, emotional areas); and (3) psychomotor (manual, physical skills). See also **learning objectives.** See also *Taxonomy of Educational Objectives: The Classification of Educational Goals* (New York: Longman Group, 1999).

Box, George   Developer of response surface analysis and major contributor to SPC and DOE. A native of England, Box began his career during World War II with the British Army Engineers, where he learned statistics. He studied at University College, became head of the statistical techniques research section at Imperial Chemical Industrials, and obtained a doctorate. He moved to the United States and was a founder of *Technometrics,* published by ASQ and the American Statistical Association. A retired professor from the University of Wisconsin, Box is an honorary member of ASQ. See also *Statistics for Experimenters* (New York: John Wiley & Sons, 1978).

Breyfogle, Forrest W., III Published many articles on statistical methods and provides consulting and training in Six Sigma. See also *Implementing Six Sigma Smarter Solutions, Using Statistical Methods* (New York: John Wiley & Sons, 1999).

Brumbaugh, Martin A. Founder and first editor of *Industrial Quality Control* magazine. A former professor of statistics at the University of Buffalo, Brumbaugh published regularly on applied statistics. Brumbaugh was instrumental in getting two separate quality organizations—the Federated Societies and the Society for Quality Control—merged into one national organization: ASQ (then ASQC). Brumbaugh was an ASQ honorary member.

Campanella, Jack ASQ fellow and former chair of the ASQ Quality Cost Technical Committee. Edited the ASQ book *Principles of Quality Costs,* 3rd ed. (Milwaukee: ASQ Quality Press, 1999). Campanella has published numerous articles on quality cost as well as various other quality-related subjects.

Carlzon, Jan Coined the phrase *moment of truth* and advocates a culture of customer service principles. The term is further defined by Karl Albrect as "Any episode where a customer comes in to contact with any aspect of your company, no matter how distant, and by this contact, has an opportunity to form an opinion about your company." See also *Moments of Truth* (New York: Harper Business, 1997).

Champy, James Along with Michael Hammer promoted the concept of process improvement. Authored the books *Reengineering the Corporation* and *Beyond Reengineering,* promoting TQM for small process improvements and BPR (business process reengineering) for breakthrough improvements. They observe, "Companies today consist of *Functional Silos,* or *Stovepipes,* vertical structures built on narrow pieces of a process.... People involved in a process look inward toward their department and upward toward their boss, but no one looks outward toward the customer. The contemporary performance problems that companies experience are the inevitable consequences of process fragmentation." See also *Total Quality: A User's Guide for Implementation* (Reading, PA: Addison-Wesley, 1992).

Ciampa, Dan Defines total quality as total dedication to the customer and states that a company with a total quality mind-set is totally dedicated to the customer and promotes customer satisfaction in every way. See also *Total Quality: A User's Guide for Implementation* (Reading, PA: Addison-Wesley, 1992).

Collier, Simon ASQ president who led the society during a critical growth period in 1952–53. His term was marked by numerous milestone events, including a membership increase of 22% and the formation of 11 new sections and the first divisions. Collier, an ASQ honorary member, was a chemist who began his career at the National Bureau of Standards (now the National Institute of Standards and Technology). Later he worked at Johns-Manville Corp., where he produced a quality training film used by more than 300 companies.

Conway, William E. Developed the "right way to manage" concepts based on Deming's principles. He looks at the total picture of quality improvement to include the "development, manufacture, administration, and distribution of consistent low cost products and or services that meet the customers wants and/or needs. He identifies "six tools" of quality improvement: (1) human relations, (2) surveys, (3) simple statistics, (4) SPC, (5) imagineering, and (6) industrial engineering. He advocates the elimination of waste, including time and excess inventory. He stresses the importance of gathering and analyzing data to determine the best possible solutions, selecting the best possible solution, and implementing it.

Covey, Stephen R. Founder and chairman of Covey Leadership Center, publisher of *Executive Excellence* magazine; and founder of the Institute for Principle-Centered Leadership. Covey wrote the book *The 7 Habits of Highly Effective People*. These principles are considered to be the natural laws or self-evident characteristics that most major religions or ethical societies would consider basic. Examples of these basic principles would include fairness, integrity, honesty, human dignity, patience, encouragement, and service. See also *The 7 Habits of Highly Effective People* (New York: Simon & Schuster, 1989).

Crosby, Phillip B. Developed the "zero defects" program during the 1960s. Founder and chairman of the board of Career IV, an executive management consulting firm. Crosby also founded Philip Crosby Associates Inc. and the Quality College. He wrote many books including *Quality Is Free, Quality Without Tears, Let's Talk Quality,* and *Leading: The Art of Becoming an Executive*. Crosby, who originated the zero defects concept, was an ASQ honorary member and past president. According to Crosby, the sequence of improving quality in an organization is determination, education, and implementation. He believed quality is a significant part of an organization and senior managers must take charge of it. He taught that the four absolutes of quality management are as follows: (1) Quality means conformance to requirements. (2) Quality comes from prevention. (3) Quality performance standard is zero defects. (4) Quality measurement is the price of conformance. See also *Quality Is Free* (New York: McGraw-Hill, 1979).

William H. Davidow and Bro Uttal Presented a comprehensive six-step plan for customer service in *Total Customer Service*. A simpler systems-based approach might include leadership, service capability, service delivery, measurement, and customer data. See also *Total Customer Service: The Ultimate Weapon* (New York: Harper & Row, 1989).

DeBono, Edward Proposed a collection of critical and creative thinking techniques. See *Six Thinking Hats* (Boston: Little, Brown, 1985) and *Lateral Thinking: Creativity Step by Step* (New York: Harper Colophon Books, Harper & Row, 1973).

Deming, W. Edwards Honorary member of ASQ. Advocate of quality and productivity improvement through SPC. A prominent consultant, teacher, and author on the subject of quality. After Deming shared his expertise in statistical quality control to help the U.S. war effort during World War II, the U.S. War Department sent him to Japan in 1946 to help that nation recover from its wartime losses. Deming published more than 200 works, including the well-known books *Quality, Productivity,* and *Competitive Position* and *Out of the Crisis*. Deming developed the 14 points for management. His last book, *The New Economics in Government, Industry and Education,* is the definitive work on profound knowledge. He also developed the concept of seven deadly management diseases. He taught there is a "chain reaction" of events that improve quality. They are as follows: decrease cost (by less rework, fewer delays, etc.), then productivity improves; in turn you can capture more market share with better quality and pricing; this will allow you to stay in business and provide jobs. He also stressed the importance of individual responsibility. He indicated that 85% of problems are management controlled and 15% are operator controlled (see separate entries). See also *Out of the Crisis* (Cambridge: Massachusetts Institute of Technology, Center for Advanced Engineering Study, 1986).

Dodge, Harold F. An ASQ founder and honorary member. His work with acceptance-sampling plans scientifically standardized inspection operations provided for controllable risks. Although he is usually remembered for the Dodge-Romig sampling plans developed with Harry G. Romig, Dodge also helped develop other basic acceptance-sampling concepts (consumer's risk, producer's risk, average outgoing quality level), and several acceptance-sampling schemes. He coined the phrase "You can't inspect quality into a product."

Drucker, Peter   Writes about management practices in various books such as *The Effective Executive* and *Management Challenges for the 21st Century*. He points out that different levels of management will view a business problem differently. Supervisors and managers view situations differently than a CEO or president. Some of the management tasks defined by Drucker are (1) Decide on the mission of the company: what is its purpose? (2) Determine the values of the company. What is its conscience? (3) Develop the human side of the business. (4) Establish the working relationships needed to run the business, within the operating units, with customers, with suppliers and other stakeholders. (5) Be available for ceremonial functions. (6) Be responsible for the company. He believed that if a person applied knowledge to new tasks it would increase innovation. See also *Management: Tasks, Responsibilities, Practices* (New York: Harper & Row, 1974).

Edwards, George D.   First president of ASQC. Edwards was noted for his administrative skills in forming and preserving the society. He was the head of the quality engineering department and the director of quality assurance at Bell Telephone Laboratories. He also served as a consultant to the Army Ordnance Department and the War Production Board during World War II. Edwards was an ASQ honorary member. He coined the term *quality assurance*.

Fayol, Henri   French industrialist who proposed that the elements of management consist of five functional aspects: (1) planning, (2) organizing, (3) commanding, (4) coordinating, and (5) controlling. He also proposed the management concept of centralization-decentralization, depending on the amount of control exercised by upper management.

Feigenbaum, Armand V.   Founder and president of General Systems Co., an international engineering company that designs and implements total quality systems. Feigenbaum originated the concept of total quality control in his book *Total Quality Control*, originally published in 1951. The book has been translated into many languages, including Japanese, Chinese, French, and Spanish. The TQC philosophy maintains that all areas of an organization must be involved in the quality efforts. Feigenbaum is an ASQ honorary member and served as ASQ president for two consecutive terms. See also *Total Quality Control*, 3rd rev. ed. (New York: McGraw-Hill, 1991).

Fisher, Sir Ronald Aylmer   A founder of classical statistical analyses. Introduced the statistical methods of ANOVA and DOE. See also *The Design of Experiments* (Edinburgh: Oliver & Boyd, 1942).

Ford, Henry   Used standardized parts and the introduction of industrial engineering principles in a coordinated assembly line to mass-produce quality affordable automobiles. Ford is generally credited with refining and improving the assembly-line method for complex assemblies.

Gantt, Henry L.   Disciple of Fredrick Taylor who made numerous contributions to the field of scientific management in the early 1900s. He developed the Gantt charts, a technique used to display data required for scheduling purposes. It is an effective tool for management planning and control activities. One drawback to Gantt charts is that they do not show any interdependencies of the various activities. See **Gantt chart.**

Goldratt, Eliyahu   Proposed the theory of constraints, which included the elimination of bottlenecks to increase production. As an advocate of the "thinking process," he included a five-step approach to eliminate bottlenecks: (1) identify the constraint; (2) decide how to exploit the constraint; (3) subordinate everything else to the above decision; (4) evaluate the system's constraints; (5) return to step 1 and continue the cycle. See also *The Race* (Great Barrington, MA: North River Press, 1996); *The Goal,* 2nd ed. (Great Barrington, MA: North River Press, 1992); *Theory of Constraints* (Great Barrington, MA: North River Press, 1990); Goldratt & H. William Dettmer, *Theory of Constraints: A Systems Approach to Continuous Improvement* (Milwaukee: ASQ Quality Press, 1997).

Golomski, William   ASQ past president and honorary member and president of W. A. Golomski and Associates, a technical and management consulting firm. He was an educator, consultant, and author of more than 300 papers and 10 books. Golomski also co-founded the ASQ Food, Drug & Cosmetics Division, was founding editor of ASQ's *Quality Management Journal,* and served on the initial judging panel for the Malcolm Baldrige National Quality Award. He developed quality systems in many industries.

Goodman, John   Wrote *Consumer Complaint Handling in America.* His aim is to shed light on complaint handling and cost associated with lost customers. See also "Maximizing the Value of Customer Feedback" (*ASQ Quality Progress* [December 1996]: 35–39). See **TARP.**

Grant, Eugene L.   Grant was part of a small team of professors assigned during World War II to introduce statistical quality control concepts to improve manufacturing production. He wrote many textbooks, including *Principles of Engineering Economy* and *Statistical Quality Control,* editions of which he co-authored with W. Grant Ireson and Richard S. Leavenworth. He was an ASQ honorary member and a professor of economics engineering at Stanford University. See also *Statistical Quality Control,* 6th ed. (New York: McGraw-Hill, 1988).

Gryna, Frank M. Director of the Center for Quality and professor of business administration at the University of Tampa. From 1982 to 1991, he was with the Juran Institute as senior vice president. Prior to 1982, he was active in industry, government, and university settings. He was manager of Reliability and Quality Assurance for the Space Systems Division of the Martin Company. At Bradley University, he was Distinguished Professor of Industrial Engineering and also served as acting dean of the College of Engineering and Technology. In addition, he was also a consultant on the managerial and statistical aspects of quality and reliability. His books include co-authoring *Quality Planning and Analysis* with J. M. Juran (New York: McGraw-Hill, 2001), and *Work Overload! Redesigning Jobs to Minimize Stress and Burnout* (Milwaukee: ASQ Quality Press, 2004). He was associate editor of the second, third, and fourth editions of *Juran's Quality Control Handbook* (New York: McGraw-Hill).

Hammer, Michael With James Champy promoted the concept of process improvement. Authored the books *Reengineering the Corporation* and *Beyond Reengineering,* promoting TQM for small process improvements and BPR (business process reengineering) for breakthrough improvements. They observe, "Companies today consists of *Functional Silos,* or *Stovepipes,* vertical structures built on narrow pieces of a process. . . . People involved in a process look inward toward their department and upward toward their boss, but no one looks outward toward the customer. The contemporary performance problems that companies experience are the inevitable consequences of process fragmentation." See also *Reengineering the Corporation: A Manifesto for Business Revolution* (New York: Harper Business, 1992).

Harrington, James H. Wrote *Business Process Improvement,* where he identified five customer types: (1) primary, (2) secondary, (3) indirect, (4) external, and (5) end user. He wrote that in order for a company to survive it must have (1) an ROA of 6% or more; (2) a VAE above $74,000; (3) 76% of its customers rate the company highly; and (4) an increasing market share. He also proposed five management styles: coach, teacher, boss, leader, and friend. See also *Business Process Improvement: The Breakthrough Strategy for Total Quality, Productivity, and Competitiveness* (Milwaukee: ASQC Quality Press, 1991)

Hayes, Bob Author of *Measuring Customer Satisfaction: Development and Use of Questionnaires,* which provides a discussion on determining customer requirements prior to implementing a survey. See also *Measuring Customer Satisfaction: Survey Design, Use, and Statistical Analysis Methods*, 2nd ed. (Milwaukee: ASQC Quality Press, 1997).

Herzberg, Fredrick Identified *hygienic factors* that create dissatisfaction if not present but do not create satisfaction if present. These are wages, working conditions, challenging work, growth and learning, group identity, and participation in work planning. His *Motivational Factors* considered more freedom in the work environment, more responsibility, and greater recognition as the factors that should motivate a person. See also *The Motivation to Work*, 2nd ed. (New York: John Wiley & Sons, 1959).

Hunter, Stuart J. An honorary member of ASQ, Hunter is a professor emeritus at Princeton University. His work as an educator and author helped enhance quantitative understanding. He wrote or co-wrote many papers, books, and technical reports and is a founding editor of *Technometrics*.

Imai, Masaaki Made *kaizen*, a Japanese term that means gradual unending improvement by doing little things better and setting and achieving increasingly higher standards, familiar to American industry. See also *Kaizen: The Key to Japan's Competitive Success* (New York: McGraw-Hill, 1986).

Ishikawa, Kaoru Pioneer in quality control activities in Japan. In 1943, he used the cause-and effect-diagram (named in his honor) and initiated *quality circles*. Ishikawa, an ASQ honorary member, published many works, including *What Is Total Quality Control?, The Japanese Way*, *Quality Control Circles at Work*, and *Guide to Quality Control*. He is also credited with the term *company wide quality control* (CWQC), which involves the participation of workers from the top of the organization to the line worker. He is credited with the concept of "The next operation as the customer." He was a member of the quality control research group of the Union of Japanese Scientists and Engineers while also working as an assistant professor at the University of Tokyo. See also *What Is Total Quality Control? The Japanese Way*, trans. D. J. Lu (Englewood Cliffs, NJ: Prentice Hall, 1985), and *Guide to Quality Control* (White Plains, NY: Kraus International Publications, 1987).

Jaquard, Joseph-Marie Developed the weaving loom that used a punched card imprinted with the design to weave that design automatically into the fabric. Revolutionized the weaving industry from a cottage industry to one of the largest industries in the world.

Johanasson, Carl Edward   Generally credited with the development of precision gage blocks. Although gage blocks were used prior to Johanasson, he is the first recorded to have placed them in sets as we currently know them. His first set delivered in 1896 contained 102 blocks and covered all dimensions from .01 mm to 201 mm, for a total combination of 20,000 different dimensions.

Joiner, Brian   Advocate of process improvement, continuous improvement, and team building. In *The Team Handbook,* he identifies the concept of quality, the scientific approach, and all one team (all employees working as one). Originated the idea of the Joiner triangle. See also *The Team Handbook* (Madison, WI: Oriel, Inc., 2003).

Juran, Joseph M.   Chairman emeritus of the Juran Institute and an ASQ honorary member. Since 1924, Juran has pursued a varied career in management as an engineer, executive, government administrator, university professor, labor arbitrator, corporate director, and consultant. Specializing in managing for quality, he has authored hundreds of papers and 12 books, including *Juran's Quality Control Handbook*, *Quality Planning and Analysis* (with F. M. Gryna), and *Juran on Leadership for Quality.* Always stresses the importance of management involvement in solving quality-related problems by solving chronic problems, project by project. He feels that managing for quality requires the same attention as other operational functions. As such, he developed what is known as the Juran or quality trilogy, which includes quality planning, quality control, and quality improvement. He advocates the concept of "breakthrough" as a key to achieve quality improvements that significantly reduce chronic waste and achieve ever-higher levels of quality performance. See also *Juran's Quality Handbook,* 5th ed. (New York: McGraw-Hill, 1999).

Kano, Naritaki   Presents four levels of customer satisfaction known as the Kano model, defined as (1) satisfaction, (2) must be, (3) delighters, and (4) dissatisfaction.

King, Bob   Executive director of GOAL/QPC in Boston, King is the author of *Better Designs in Half the Time,* a quality function deployment (QFD) application. GOAL/QPC has contributed to the quality profession and to the collaboration of community, unions, and industry to education. GOAL/QPC publishes books and offers courses in quality tools and techniques. It was instrumental in translating case studies describing applications of the seven new tools or seven quality planning tools. GOAL/QPC may be best known for publishing *The Memory Jogger Plus* (Methuen, MA: GOAL/QPC, 1989).

Kirkpatrick, Donald Described four levels for evaluating training: (1) reaction, (2) learning, (3) behavior, and (4) results. He later added a fifth: ROI, or return on investment. See also **adult learning principles.** See also *Evaluating Training Programs* (Westport, CT: Greenwood Press, 1987). See also *Evaluating Training Programs: The Four Levels* (San Francisco: Berrett-Koehler, 1994).

Kotler, Philip Advocates marketing segmentation, that is, determining what customers in various markets want and then customizing products or services for them. See also *Marketing Management Analysis, Planning, and Control,* 2nd ed. (Englewood Cliffs, NJ: Prentice-Hall, 1972).

Kotter, John Defines the tasks of management as planning and budgeting, organizing and staffing, and controlling and problem solving. He defines leadership as establishing direction, aligning people, and motivating and inspiring, and lists strategies for dealing with change. See also *Leading Change* (Boston: Harvard Business School Press, 1986

Jim Kouzes and Barry Posner Define leadership as a shared responsibility and state that managers "get other people to do, but leaders get others to want to do." See also *The Leadership Challenge* (San Francisco: Jossey-Bass, 1987, pp. 27, 135).

Lewin, Kurt Proposed a generic model for change in *Force Field Analysis* and labeled it "unfreezing-movement-refreezing." See also *Leading Change* (Boston: Harvard Business School Press, 1966, p. 21).

Likert, Rensis L. Formulated a standard rating scale known as the Likert scale, used in recording responses to surveys such as "Strongly Agree," "Neutral," "Disagree," "Strongly Disagree." Similar scales may be used to rate management styles such as "Autocratic," "Benevolent," "Participative," and "Consultative." Many times used with numerical scales to rate degrees of agreement with a statement. See also *New Patterns of Management* (New York: McGraw-Hill, 1961).

Low, George M. George M. Low was the NASA administrator for nearly three decades. The George M. Low Trophy is presented by NASA to those NASA aerospace industry contractors, subcontractors, and suppliers who consistently maintain and improve the quality of their products and services. This award, formerly called the NASA Excellence Award for Quality and Productivity, is given in two categories: small business and large business.

Maslow, Abraham Sociologist credited with developing the hierarchy of needs: (1) physiological (eat, sleep, shelter); (2) safety (security, economic, and personal);

(3) belonging (accepted by family and friends); (4) esteem (to be held in high regard or status); and (5) self-actualization (to achieve one's best). See also *Motivation and Personality* (New York: Harper & Brothers, 1954).

Mayo, Etton Conducted the Hawthorne studies at the Western Electric Company in Chicago in 1924 to study the effect of employee fatigue and related efficiency by varying working conditions. The concept indicated that every change results (initially, at least) in increased productivity. The studies showed the importance of human factors in motivating employees.

McClelland, David Proposed three personal motivational needs: (1) need for *achievement,* (2) need for *affiliation,* and (3) need for *power* over others. These are acquired by our interaction with our environment. He also proposed four motivational theories: (1) A person who works well with others is motivated by *affiliation.* (2) A person who works to accomplish personal goals is motivated by *achievement.* (3) A person who works to contribute to the welfare of others is motivated by *altruism.* (4) A person who wants to have control over others is motivated by *power.* See also "Business Drive and National Achievement" (*Harvard Business Review* [July-August 1962]: 99–112).

McGregor, Douglas Proposed the Theory X and Theory Y managers. Theory X managers take a negative view of people: they are fundamentally lazy and self-centered. Theory Y type managers take a positive view, believing people want to do a good job. See also *The Human Side of Enterprise* (New York: McGraw-Hill, 1985).

Mintzberg, Henry In his book *The Rise and Fall of Strategic Planning: Reconceiving Roles for Planning, Plans, Planners,* he developed three levels of managerial planning: strategic, tactical, and operational. Also proposed that a manager's job involves "tacit" knowledge that relies on judgment and intuition. See also *The Rise and Fall of Strategic Planning* (New York: Free Press, 1994).

Nelson, Lloyd Founding editor of the *Journal of Quality Technology* and a longtime author of the journal's "Technical Aids" feature. An ASQ honorary member.

Ohno, Taichi Proposed the concept of "seven types of waste": the opposite of value is waste, and there are seven waste factors that affect productivity and quality: (1) overproduction, (2) waiting, (3) transporting, (4) inappropriate processing, (5) excess inventory, (6) unnecessary motions, and (7) defects. See also *Toyota Production System—Beyond Large Scale Production* (Portland, OR: Productivity Press, 1988).

Ott, Ellis R.   Educator who devoted his career to providing U.S. industry with statistical quality control professionals. In 1946, Ott became the chairman of the mathematics department at Rutgers University's University College, with one condition: that he could also consult on and teach quality control. His influence led the university to establish the Rutgers Statistics Center. Ott, an ASQ honorary member, developed the analysis of means (ANOM) procedure and published many papers. Best known for saying "Plot the data!" See also *Process Quality Control* (New York: McGraw-Hill, 1975).

Pareto, Vilfredo   Italian economist in the 1800s who noted that 80% of the wealth in Italy was held by 20% of the population. He is credited with the Pareto chart, a graphical tool for ranking causes from most significant to least significant. It is based on the Pareto principle, which was first defined by J. M. Juran in 1950. The principle suggests most effects come from relatively few causes; that is, 80% of the effects come from 20% of the possible causes. The Pareto chart is one of the seven tools of quality.

Pavlov, Ivan   Russian physiologist (1849–1936) who experimented with various stimulants to see what would make animals respond. He used food to make dogs respond and found he could condition dogs to salivate by providing various stimulants, inferring that people also respond to stimulants and this affects their behavior.

Pearson, Karl   Developed the "goodness of fit" tables and is credited with making statistics a science.

Peters, Tom   Wrote *Thriving on Chaos* in which he indicated it is a must to provide employees a chance to better themselves and have an opportunity for advancement. He also co-wrote *In Search of Excellence* in the early 1980s that helped accelerate the quality revolution in North America. See also *Thriving on Chaos* (New York: Alfred A. Knopf, 1987).

Romig, Harry G.   Honorary member and founder of ASQ who was most widely known for his contributions in sampling. At AT&T Bell Laboratories, Romig and Harold F. Dodge developed the Dodge-Romig sampling tables, operating characteristics for sampling plans and other fundamentals. Romig alone developed the first sampling plans using variables data and the concept of average outgoing quality limit. Later in his life, Romig was a consultant and taught quality-related courses at several universities.

Schein, Edger H.   Described paradoxes of leadership when stating that leaders of the future will be persons "who can lead and follow, be central and marginal, be hierarchical above and below, be individualistic and a team player, and, above all, be a perpetual learner." He also defined three levels of culture within an organization: (1) artifacts (architecture, decor, the way people behave toward others); (2) espoused values (strategies, goals, and philosophies of the company); and (3) shared tacit assumptions (values, beliefs, and feelings of the company, possibly from the founders). See also F. Hesselbein et al., eds., *Leadership and Organizational Culture.*

Scholtes, Peter   Author of *The Team Handbook* and many articles on continuous improvement. He proposed 10 ingredients for a successful team: (1) clarity of team goals, (2) an improvement plan, (3) clearly defined roles, (4) clear communications, (5) beneficial team behaviors, (6) well-defined decision procedures, (7) balanced participation, (8) established ground rules, (9) awareness of the group process, and (10) use of the scientific approach. In addition, in *The Team Handbook* he advocates eliminating employee performance reviews. He proposed using the multivoting technique, in a team environment, and uses the terms *forming, storming, norming,* and *performing.* With questioning techniques he proposed asking three questions: (1) What is the purpose of the project? (2) How do you know you are making a difference? (3) What methods are you using to achieve that purpose? He also proposed asking seven additional questions to get more detail: (1) Why (Japanese technique of asking why five times). (2) What is the purpose? (3) What will it take to complete the project? (4) Will someone care? (5) What are your thoughts on the subject? (6) What data do you have? (7) Where did your data come from? See also *The Team Handbook* (Madison, WI: Oriel, Inc., 2003).

Senge, Peter   Proponent of systems thinking and of organizational learning. Author of *The Fifth Discipline.* He advances the concept of three stages of commitment to customers: (1) compliance (follow the letter of the law or contract), (2) enrolled (free choice to follow the vision or mission), and (3) commitment (wants the vision or mission to come alive; a committed team will do what it takes to satisfy the customer). See also *The Fifth Discipline* (New York: Doubleday, 1990).

Shanin, Dorian   An honorary member of ASQ, Shanin developed the Red X Strategies as a technical problem-solving approach (in General Motors this discipline is called *statistical engineering*). He was in charge of quality control at a larger division of United Technologies Corp. and later did consulting for more than 900 organizations. Shanin also was on the faculty of the University of Chicago and wrote more than 100 articles and several books.

Shewhart, Walter A. Referred to as the "Father of Statistical Quality Control" because he brought together the disciplines of statistics, engineering, and economics. He described the basic principles of this new discipline in his book *Economic Control of Quality of Manufactured Product*. Shewhart was ASQ's first honorary member and best known for creating the control chart. He worked for Western Electric and AT&T Bell Telephone Laboratories, in addition to lecturing and consulting on quality control. See also *Economic Control of Quality of Manufactured Product* (Milwaukee: ASQ Quality Press, originally published 1931; reprinted 1980).

Shingo, Shigeo Japanese manufacturing leader who developed the *poka-yoke* mistake proofing concept and the single minute exchange of dies (SMED) and co-authored the Toyota Production System. The lean manufacturing "Shingo Prize for Manufacturing Excellence" is awarded annually by Utah State University. See also *Modern Approaches to Manufacturing Improvement* (Portland, OR: Productivity Press, 1990).

Simon, Leslie E. Used statistical quality control at Picatinny Arsenal. Gathered quality control experts to develop quality control courses during World War II.

Taguchi, Genichi Past executive director of the American Supplier Institute, the director of the Japan Industrial Technology Institute, and an honorary professor at Nanjing Institute of Technology in China. Combined engineering and statistical methods to achieve rapid improvements in cost and quality by optimizing product design and manufacturing processes. Taguchi is well known for developing a methodology to improve quality and reduce costs, which in the United States is referred to as the "Taguchi methods." He also developed the "quality loss function" and "signal to noise ratio." He is an honorary member of ASQ. See also *Introduction to Quality Engineering* (Dearborn, MI: American Supplier Institute, 1986).

Taylor, Fredrick W. Creator of the *scientific management* school of management; advocate of time and motion studies. He urged matching individuals to the job in order to be more efficient. He studied the way a job should be done by using time and motion studies as a means of increasing efficiency and productivity. See also *Principles of Scientific Management* (New York: Harper & Bros., 1911).

Vavra, Terry Studies and writes about customer satisfaction and the methods used in measuring and improving various aspects of customer satisfaction. His books include *Improving Your Measurement of Customer Satisfaction,*

Aftermarketing: How to Keep Customers for Life Through Relationship Marketing, and *Customer Satisfaction Measurement Simplified.* See also *Improving Your Measurement of Customer Satisfaction* (Milwaukee: ASQC Quality Press, 1997).

Weisbord, Marvin   Proposed the *six boxes* of organizational diagnosis as (1) purposes (does the company provide employees information?); (2) structure (how the company is organized); (3) relationships (how do people interact with each other?); (4) rewards (how are employees paid and rewarded?); (5) leadership (what is the character of the leaders—participative, visionary?); and (6) helpful mechanisms (is there a method to help and track progress as people work on projects?). See also *Organizational Diagnosis: A Workbook of Theory and Practice* (Reading, MA: Addison-Wesley, 1978).

Wescott, Mason E.   ASQ founder and honorary member. A professor emeritus at the Rochester Institute of Technology (RIT), Wescott has been teaching mathematics and statistics since 1925. He has taught at Northwestern University, Rutgers University, and RIT, where the Wescott Statistics Laboratory was dedicated in his honor in 1984. Wescott succeeded Martin A. Brumbaugh as the editor of *Industrial Quality Control* in 1947, a position he held until 1961.

Westcott, Russell T.   Wrote the book *Tapping the Many Voices of the Customer.* In it he describes the concept of LCALI: Listen, Capture, Analyze, Learn, Improve a process by establishing a listening post to collect and analyze customer satisfaction data. *See also* **listening post.** See also "Tapping the Many Voices of the Customer" (*The Informed Outlook* [June 2000]: 20).

Wheeler, Don   Defined the *brink of chaos* as an operation making products that conform to specifications but the process is out of control. See also *Understanding Variation: The Key to Managing Chaos* (Knoxville, TN: SPC Press, 1993) and *Understanding Statistical Process Control,* 2nd ed. (Knoxville, TN: SPC Press, 1992).

Whitney, Eli   Inventor of the cotton gin and generally credited with the development of interchangeability of parts (mass production). This required that all parts be made to the same dimension when nearly everything was still being made by hand.

Appendix B
Quality Acronyms

Note: The same acronyms may have different meanings from industry to industry. Acronyms listed here reflect those in use in the quality field.

AA	Arithmetical average
AACE	American Association of Cost Engineers
ABC	Activity-based costing
ACL	Acceptance control limit
ACSI	American customer satisfaction index
AGD	American gage design standards
AIAG	Automotive Industry Action Group
A2LA	American Association for Laboratory Accreditation
ANOM	Analysis of means
ANOVA	Analysis of variance
Ao	Operational availability

ANSI   American National Standards Institute

AOQ   Average outgoing quality

AOQL   Average outgoing quality limit (level)

APL   Acceptable process level

APQP   Advanced product quality planning

AQIP   Academic quality improvement project

AQL   Acceptable quality level/limit

AQP   Association for Quality and Participation

APICS   American Production and Inventory Control Society

ARL   Average run lengths

ASCII   American standard code for information interchange

ASME   American Society of Mechanical Engineers

ASN   Average sample number

ASNT   American Society for Nondestructive Testing

ASQ   American Society for Quality

ASQC   American Society for Quality Control (renamed ASQ in 1997)

ASTD   American Society for Training and Development

ASTM   American Society for Testing and Materials

ATI   Average total inspection

AV   Appraiser variation

BACM   Best available control measures

BACT   Best available control technology

BATF   Bureau of Alcohol, Tobacco, and Firearms

BB   Black Belt

BMP   Best management practices

BOK   Body of knowledge

BOM   Bill of materials

BPR   Business process reengineering

BSI   British Standards Institute

BSR   Board of Standards Review

BTU   British thermal unit

C/A   Corrective action

C of A   Certificate of analysis

C of C   Certificate of conformance/compliance

CAD   Computer-aided design

CAE   Computer-aided engineering

CAM   Computer-aided manufacturing

CAR   Corrective action request/report

CASE   Computer-aided software engineering

CAT   Corrective action team

CBT   Computer-based training

CCT   Certified Calibration Technician

CDC	Centers for Disease Control and Prevention
CE	Concurrent engineering
C & E	Cause-and-effect diagram
CE Mark	Conformité Européenne Mark
CEO	Chief executive officer
CFO	Chief financial officer
CFR	Code of Federal Regulations
CGMP	Current good manufacturing practices
CI	Continuous improvement
CL	Centerline
CLCA	Closed-loop corrective action
CMI	Certified Mechanical Inspector
CMM	Capability maturity model (software development)
CMM	Coordinate measuring machine (inspection)
COO	Chief operating officer
COPQ	Cost of poor quality
COQ	Cost of quality
C_p	Capability ratio (statistical formulas)
CP	Control plan
CPI	Continuous process improvement
C_{pk}	Capability index (statistical formula, centered)

CPM   Critical path method

CPN   Critical path network

CQA   Certified Quality Auditor

CQA-HACCP   Certified Quality Auditor—Hazard Analysis and Critical Control Point

CQE   Certified Quality Engineer

CQI   Continuous quality improvement

CQIA   Certified Quality Improvement Associate

CQMgr   Certified Quality Manager

CQT   Certified Quality Technician

CR   Capability ratio

CRE   Certified Reliability Engineer

CRM   Customer relationship management

CRS   Cold rolled steel

CS   Customer satisfaction

CSQE   Certified Software Quality Engineer

CSA   Canadian Standards Association

CSM   Customer-supplier model

CSR   Customer service representative

CSSBB   Certified Six Sigma Black Belt

CUSUM   Cumulative sum control chart approach

CWQC   Company wide quality control

DFA	Design for assembly
DFM	Design for manufacturability
DFMEA	Design failure mode and effects analysis
DFSS	Design for Six Sigma
DMADV	Define, measure, analyze, design, and verify
DMAIC	Define, measure, analyze, improve, and control
DOA	Dead on arrival
DOE	Design of experiments
DPMO	Defects per million opportunities
DT	Destructive testing
DU	Dobson unit
EARA	Environmental Auditors Registration Association (now IMEA)
e-business	Electronic business
ECN	Engineering change notice
ECO	Engineering change order
e-commerce	Electronic commerce
ECR	Engineering change request/release
EDI	Electronic data interchange
EI	Employee involvement
e-learning	Electronic learning
EMS	Environmental management system

EOCA   European Organization for Conformity Assessment

EPA   Environmental Protection Agency

ESD   Electrostatic discharge

e-signature   Electronic signature

ESOP   Employee stock ownership plan

EU   European Union

EVOP   Evolutionary operations

EWMA   Exponentially weighted moving averages

FAO   Finish all over

FCCA   Full cycle corrective action

FDA   Food and Drug Administration

FEA   Finite element analysis

FIFO   First in first out

FIM   Full indicator movement

FMA   Failure mode analysis

FMEA   Failure mode and effects analysis

FMECA   Failure mode effects and criticality analysis

FOB   Free on board

FSCM   Federal supply code for manufacturers

FTA   Fault tree analysis

FTY   First time yield

F/U	Follow up
GB	Green Belt
GD&T	Geometric dimensioning and tolerancing
GERT	Graphical evaluation and review technique
GIGO	Garbage in garbage out
GLM	General linear modeling
GLP	Good laboratory practices (GLP) or 21 CFR, part 58
GMP	Good manufacturing practice
GR&R	Gage repeatability and reproducibility
HACCP	Hazard analysis and critical control point
HALT	Highly accelerated life test
HASA	Highly accelerated stress audits
HASS	Highly accelerated stress screening
HPP	Homogeneous Poisson process
IAQ	International Academy for Quality
IAQG	International Aerospace Quality Group
ID	Inside diameter
IEEE	Institute of Electrical and Electronic Engineers
IEMA	Institute of Environmental Management and Assessment
IER	Independent evaluation report
ILS	Integrated logistics support

IQA   Institute of Quality Assurance

IQL   Indifference quality level

IRCA   International Register of Certified Auditors

IRR   Internal rate of return

ISO   International Organization for Standardization

IT   Information technology

JCAHO   Joint Committee for the Accreditation of Healthcare Organizations

JIT   Just in time

JUSE   Union of Japanese Scientists and Engineers

KISS   Keep it simple silly (or stupid)

KPI   Key performance indicator

LCL   Lower control limit

LIFO   Last in first out

LMC   Least material condition

LOE   Lack of objective evidence

LQL   Limiting quality level/limit

LSL   Lower specification limit

LTL   Lower tolerance limit

LTPD   Lot tolerance percentage defective

LURD   Left, up, right, down

MAV   Minimum acceptable value

MBB	Master Black Belt
MBNQA	Malcolm Baldrige National Quality Award
MBO	Management by objectives
MBTI	Myers-Briggs Type Indicator
MBWA	Management by walking around
MIL-STD	Military standard
MMC	Maximum material condition
MR	Moving range (in SPC charts)
MRB	Material Review Board
MRO	Maintenance, repair, and operations
MRP2	Manufacturing resource planning
MSA	Measurement system analysis
MSDS	Material safety data sheet
MTBF	Mean time between failures
M&TE	Measurement and test equipment
MTTR	Mean time to repair
NAFTA	North American Free Trade Agreement
NAICS	North American Industry Classification System
NASA	National Aeronautical and Space Administration
NBS	National Bureau of Standards
NCQA	National Committee for Quality Assurance

NDE   Nondestructive evaluation

NDT   Nondestructive testing

NGT   Nominal group technique

NIST   National Institute of Standards and Technology

NQM   National quality month

NPL   Natural process limits

NPV   Net present value

OC   Operating characteristic curve

OD   (Dimensional) = outside diameter

OD   (Management oriented) = organizational development

OEM   Original equipment manufacturer

OJT   On-the-job training

OSHA   Occupational Safety and Health Administration

PCI   Process capability index

PDCA   Plan-do-check-act

PDM   Precedence diagramming method

PDPC   Process decision program chart

PDSA   Plan-do-study-act

PE   Professional engineer

PERT   Program evaluation and review technique

PFMEA   Process failure mode effects analysis

PIG   Process improvement group

PIT   Process improvement team

PONCE   Price of nonconformance

PPAP   Production part approval process

PPB   Parts per billion

PPE   Personal protective equipment

$\mathbf{P}_{pk}$ Potential process capability

PPM   Parts per million

PRAT   Production and reliability acceptance text

PPMO   Parts per million opportunities

PSI   Pounds per square inch

QA   Quality assurance

QC   Quality control

QE   Quality engineer

QEDS   U.S. standards group on quality, environment, dependability, and statistics

QEIT   Quality engineer in training (former ASQ certification)

QFD   Quality function deployment

QIC   Quality Information Center

QLA   Quality level agreement

QM   Quality management/manual

QMS   Quality management system

QP   Quality plan or policy or procedure

QuEST   Quality Excellence for Suppliers of Telecommunications

RAB   Registrar Accreditation Board

RAM   (Quality related) reliability/availability/maintainability

RAS   Reliability, availability, and serviceability

RETAD   Rapid exchange of tooling and dies

RFS   Regardless of feature size

RMS   Root mean square

ROE   Return on equity

ROI   Return on investment

RONA   Return on net assets

RPN   Risk priority number (in FMEA)

RQL   Reject quality level

R&R   Repeatability and reproducibility

RTY   Rolled throughput yield

SAE   Society of Automotive Engineers

SCAR   Supplier corrective action request (report)

SDCA   Standardize do check act

SDWT   Self-directed/managed work team

SI   Metric system units of measure

SIC   Standard Industrial Classification

SIPOC Suppliers, inputs, processes, outputs, and customers

SMED Single minute exchange of dies

S/N Signal-to-noise ratio

SOP Standard operating procedure

SOW Statement of work

SPC Statistical process control

SQA Software quality assurance

SQC Statistical quality control

SQI Supplier quality improvement

SR Severity rating (in FMEA)

SRM Standard reference material

SWAG Scientific wild anatomical guess

SWOT Strengths, weaknesses, opportunities, and threats

TARP Technical assistance research programs

TE Tooling and equipment

TIR Total indicator reading (runout)

TOC Theory of constraints

TPM Total predictive/productive maintenance

TQC Total quality control

TQM Total quality management

TR Total runout

UCL   Upper control limit

UI   Ultrasonic inspection

UL   Underwriters Laboratories

USDA   United States Department of Agriculture

USL   Upper specification limit

UTL   Upper tolerance limit

VAE   Value added per employee

V&V   Verification and validation

WBS   Work breakdown structure

WIIFM   What's in it for me?

WIT   Work improvement team

Appendix C
Quality Control Formulas and Symbols

n Total number of items in a sample.

N Total number in population, denoting a census is taken.

X Individual sample (actual) value.

$\overline{X}$ Sample means.

$\overline{\overline{X}}$ Average of the means.

μ Mean or average of the population, based on a census.

Z Standard normal deviate equals the number of standard deviations away from the mean used in generating intervals.

σ Sigma: standard deviation of the population, based on a census.

S Standard deviation of the sample (used to estimate σ).

π Proportion of the population. (Population proportion based on a census or estimate.)

R Sample range (maximum value – minimum value).

$\overline{R}$ Average or mean range.

A_2 $\overline{X}$-chart factor used in SP control charts determined from sample size and assumption of normally distributed process. Used for LCL and UCL X-bar chart.

D_3 R-chart factor used in generating the LCL_R, determined from sample size and assumption of normally distributed process.

D_4 R-chart factor used in generating the UCL_R as in D_3.

Σ Sum of or summation.

ND Normally distributed or normal distribution.

P Probability or sample proportion depending on the context.

$\overline{P}$ Mean of the proportion of several samples or the proportion of a very large sample.

f Long-run relative frequency used to estimate the probability of an event.

$UCL\,/\,LCL$ Upper/lower control limit of a control chart.

$UTL\,/\,LTL$ Upper/lower tolerance limit. Same as USL/LSL specification limits. Identifies good and defect parts, products, or services.

$X = \mu \pm Z\sigma$ Confidence interval for a single actual observation assuming a large sample from the population (n>30): Population mean ± number of standard deviation $\times$ sigma (standard deviation). Consider small sample requirements given in the formula. ND (n ≤ 30)

$\overline{X} = \mu \pm Z\sigma / \sqrt{n}$ Confidence interval for sample mean = average of the sample ± number of standard deviation $\times$ sigma (standard deviation) over the square root of the number of items in the sample.

$ND(n \le 30)$
$S = \sigma \pm Z\sigma / \sqrt{2n}$ Confidence interval for sample standard deviation of the sample = sigma (standard deviation of the process) ± number of standard deviation of the process over the square root of 1 $\times$ the number of items in the sample.

$$P = \pi \pm Z \frac{\sqrt{\pi(1-\pi)}}{n}$$

Confidence interval for sample proportion = Proportion of the population ± number of standard deviation × the square root of [population proportion × (1 – population proportion) divided by the sample size].

$$Z \sim ND(0,1)$$

Denotes that Z is normally distributed (with a mean of zero and a standard deviation of 1).

$$\mu = \overline{\overline{X}} = \Sigma \overline{\overline{X}} / N'$$

The population mean can be estimated using the average of sample means, which equals the sum of sample means divided by the number of sample means.

$$N'$$

Number of sample means calculated.

$$\sigma = \overline{S} = \Sigma S / N'$$

Standard deviation of the population can be estimated by the mean of sample standard deviations = sum of standard deviation of the sample divided by the number of sample standard deviations.

$$Z_x = \frac{x - \mu}{\sigma}$$

Number of standard deviations an actual observation is away from its mean. The area under the normal distribution describes the probability of this Z value if X is from a ND with a mean of μ and standard deviation of σ.

$$Z_x = \frac{\overline{x} - \mu}{\sigma / \sqrt{n}}$$

Number of standard deviations a sample mean is away from the population mean and the mean of the distribution of sample means, based on the distribution of sample means. The area under the normal distribution describes the probability of this Z value if X is from a ND with a mean of μ and standard deviation of σ.

$$Z_x = \frac{S - \sigma}{\sigma / \sqrt{2n}}$$

Number of standard deviations a sample standard deviation is away from the population standard deviation based on the distribution of sample standard deviations. The area under the normal distribution describes the probability of this Z value if X is from a ND with a standard deviation of σ.

$$Z_p = \frac{P - \pi}{\dfrac{\pi(1-\pi)}{\sqrt{n}}}$$

Number of standard deviations a sample proportion is away from the population proportion as measured using the distribution of sample proportions. The area under the normal distribution describes the probability of this Z value if P is from a population with a proportion of π and the sample n is large, greater than 30.

$$Est\pi = \overline{P}$$

Estimated population proportion = mean of the sample proportions.

$$Z_p = \frac{\overline{P} - \overline{P}}{\sqrt{\frac{\overline{P}(1 - \overline{P})}{n}}}$$ Number of standard deviations the sample proportion is away from the estimated population proportion, based on the distribution of sample proportions.

$$\overline{X} = \overline{\overline{X}} \pm A_2 \overline{R}$$ Confidence interval for sample means, the basis of UCL and LCL of X-bar charts.

$$R = \left\{ \begin{array}{c} D_4 \overline{R}(UCL) \\ D_3 \overline{R}(LCL) \end{array} \right\}$$ Confidence interval for sample ranges on R chart.

$$MAD = \frac{\Sigma|x - \mu|}{n}$$ Mean absolute deviation = the sum of the absolute values of the sample minus the average of the sample over the total number of items in the samples.

$$MAD = \frac{\Sigma|A - F|}{n}$$ Mean absolute deviation = the sum of the absolute values of actuals less forecasts, divided by the number of observations.

$$MAD = 0.8\sigma$$ Approximate formula for the ND.

$$1.25 MAD = \sigma$$ Approximate formula for the ND.

$$\frac{UTL - LTL}{6\sigma}$$ Process capability ratio for a symmetrical process where the process average is centered between the UTL and LTL.

$$C_{pk} = \min\left[\frac{UTL - \overline{X}}{3\sigma} \text{ or } \frac{\overline{X} - LTL}{3\sigma} \right], \text{whichever is smaller}$$

The process capability index: =min.[UTL – sample mean over 3 sigma and sample mean – LTL over 3 sigma].

$$A_2 \overline{R} = 3\frac{\sigma}{\sqrt{n}}$$ Approximate identity useful in converting from different measures.

DISTRIBUTION	FORM	PROBABILITY FUNCTION	COMMENTS ON APPLICATION
Normal		$y = \dfrac{1}{\sigma\sqrt{2\pi}} e^{\frac{(X-\mu)^2}{2\sigma^2}}$ μ = Mean σ = Standard deviation	Applicable when there is a concentration of observation about the average and it is equally likely that observations will occur above and below the average. Variation in observations is usually the result of many small causes.
Exponential		$y = \dfrac{1}{\mu} e^{-\frac{x}{\mu}}$	Applicable when it is likely that more observations will occur below the average than above.
Weibull		$y = a\beta(x - \xi)^{\beta-1} e^{a(x-\xi)^\beta}$ a = Scale parameter β = Shape parameter ξ = Location parameter	Applicable in describing a wide variety of patterns of variation, including departures from the normal and exponential.
Poisson		$y = \dfrac{(np)^r e^{-np}}{r!}$ n = Number of trials r = Number of occurrences p = Probability of occurrence	Same as binomial but particularly applicable when there are many opportunities for occurrence of an event, but a low probability (less than 0.10) on each trial.
Binomial		$y = \dfrac{n!}{r!(n-r)!} p^r q^{n-r}$ n = Number of trials r = Number of occurrences p = Probability of occurrence $q = 1 - p$	Applicable in defining the probability of r occurrences in n trials of an event which has a probability of occurrence of p on each trial.
Negative Binomial		$y = \dfrac{r + s - 1)!}{(r-1)!(s!)} p^r q^3$ r = Number of occurrences s = Difference between number of trials and number of occurrences p = Probability of occurence $q = 1 - p$	Applicable in defining the probability that r occurrences will require a total of r + s trials of an event which has a probability of occurrence of p on each trial. (Note that the total number of trials n is r + s.)
Hypergeometric		$y = \dfrac{\dbinom{d}{r}\dbinom{N-d}{n-r}}{\dbinom{N}{r}}$	Applicable in defining the probability of r occurrences in n trials of an event when there are a total of d occurrences in a population of N.

Appendix D
Choosing an SPC Control Chart

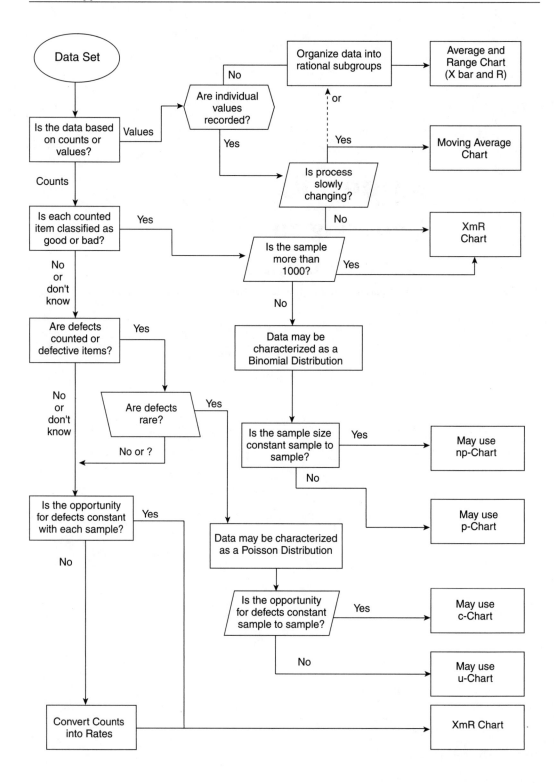

Appendix E
Common Types of Lines Used on Blueprints

Geometric Dimensioning and Tolerancing Symbols

Symbol	Description	Category
▱	Flatness	
—	Straightness	
○	Circularity	**Form Tolerances**
⌭	Cylindricity	
⊥	Perpendicularity	
∠	Angularity	**Orientation Tolerances**
//	Parallelism	
⌓	Profile of Surface	**Profile Tolerances**
⌒	Profile of Line	
⌰	Total Runout	**Runout Tolerances**
↗	Circular Runout	
⊕	Position	**Location Tolerances**
○	Concentricity	
⌀	Cylindrical Tolerance Zone or Feature	
Ⓛ	Least Material Condition	
Ⓜ	Maximum Material Condition	**Other Symbols and Definitions**
Ⓢ	Regardless of Feature Size	
— A —	Datum Feature Symbol	

Title Block of a Blueprint

XYZ Corporation	Name: Cam	Revision: 0
Tolerances: .X = .1 XX = .01 XXX = .001 Angles: ± .5	Date Drawn: 1/15/04	Drawing No. 1 of 1
	Scale: Full	Drawn By: C.J.
	Material: CRS	Checked By: B.D.

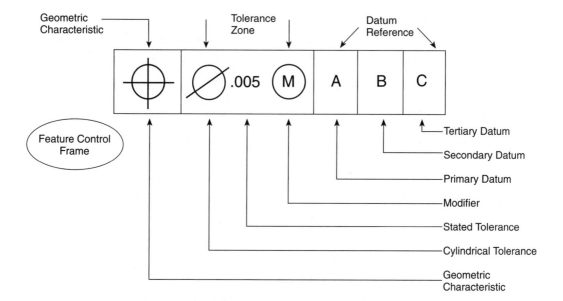

Feature: A feature is a physical portion of a part such as a hole, surface, or slot.

Tolerance Zone: All tolerance zones shown in a feature control frame are total. For example, the position within a .005 cylindrical tolerance zone means that the tolerance zone is a .005 cylinder where the actual centerline of the feature must lie within. The exact position lies in the center of the .005 zone.

Object line
(visible line) ———————— (heavy solid line)

Used to show the outer and inner boundaries of surfaces and features in a particular view.

Centerline —— — —— (light long and short dashed line)

Used to show the geometrical center of an object.

Hidden line – – – – – – – – (short dashes)

Used to show surfaces and features that exist, but cannot be seen in that particular view.

Leader line (solid medium line with an arrow)

Used to point (or lead) the reader from a dimension (or note) to the feature or surface where the dimension or note applies.

Extension line ———————— (light solid lines)

Used to extend a feature or surface from the view so it can be dimensioned.

Dimension line ◀————————▶ (light solid lines with arrows

Used to dimension the part or to show the distance between the extension lines.

Section lines ////////// (light solid lines at 45°)

Used to show the surfaces of a part that has been sectioned (cut) to show a cross-sectional view.

Phantom line —··—··—··—··· (one long and two short dashes)

Used in four main ways

1. To show an existing structure that needs modification. To show how something should fit on to something that is not yet assembled.

2. To show an alternate position of an object. A lever or lid that must move.

3. To avoid unnecessary detail. To show where coils in a spring would be without having to draw in all the coils.

4. To show the direction of a unilateral profile tolerance zone in geometric tolerancing.

Cutting plan   (thick broken lines with directional arrows)
Used to show where a part is to be cut or viewed by the reader.

Short break   (medium jagged line)
line   Used to break up a particular view and to show some of it in section.

Appendix F
Quality-Related Standards

ANSI/ASQ E4-2004: Quality Systems for Environmental Data and Technology Programs—Requirements With—Guidelines for Use

ANSI/ASQ Z1.13-1999: Quality Systems Guide for Research

ANSI/ASQ Z1.4-2003: Sampling Procedures and Tables for Inspection by Attributes

ANSI/ASQ Z1.9-2003: Sampling Procedures and Tables for Inspection by Variables for Percent Nonconforming

ANSI/ASQC B1-1996: Guide for Quality Control Charts

ANSI/ASQC B2-1996: Control Chart Method of Analyzing Data

ANSI/ASQC B3-1996: Control Chart Method of Controlling Quality

ANSI/ASQC C1-1996 (ANSI Z1.8-1971): Specifications of General Requirements for a Quality Program

ANSI/ASQC D1160-1995: Formal Design Review

ANSI/ASQC E1-1996: Quality Program Guidelines for Project Phase of Nonnuclear Power Generation Facilities

ANSI/ASQC E2-1996: Guide to Inspection Planning

ANSI/ASQC E4-1994: Specifications and Guidelines for Quality Systems for Environmental Data Collection and Environmental Technology Programs

ANSI/ASQC M1-1996: American National Standard for Calibration Systems

ANSI/ASQC Q3-1988: Sampling Procedures and Tables for Inspection of Isolated Lots by Attributes

ANSI/ASQC S1-1996: An Attribute Skip-Lot Sampling Program

ANSI/ASQC S2-1995: Introduction to Attribute Sampling

ANSI/ASQC Z1.11: Quality Assurance Standards—Guidelines for the Application of ANSI/ISO/ASQC Q9001 or Q9002 to Education and Training Inst.

ANSI B1.1–1990: Screw Threads—Sizes and Profiles

ANSI/IEC/ASQC D601070-1997: Compliance Test Procedures for Steady-State Availability

ANSI/IEC/ASQC D601078-1997: Analysis Techniques for Dependability—Reliability Block Diagram Methods

ANSI/IEC/ASQC D601123-1997: Reliability Testing—Compliance Test Plans for Success Ratio

ANSI/IEC/ASQC D601164-1997: Reliability Growth—Statistical Test and Estimation Methods

ANSI/IEC/ASQC D601165-1997: Application of Markov Techniques

ANSI/IEC/ASQC D60300-3-1-1997: Dependability Management—Part 3: Application Guide—Section 1—Analysis Techniques for Dependability: Guide on Methodology

ANSI/IEC/ASQC D60300-3-2-1997: Dependability Management—Part 3: Application Guide—Section 2—Collection of Dependability Data from the Field

ANSI/ISO 14001-1996: Environmental Management Systems—Specifications with Guidance for Use

ANSI/ISO 14004-1996: Environmental Management Systems—General Guidelines on Principles, Systems, and Supporting Techniques

ANSI/ISO 14010-1996: Guidelines for Environmental Auditing—General Principles on Environmental Auditing

ANSI/ISO 14011-1996: Guidelines for Environmental Auditing—Audit Procedures—Auditing of Environmental Management System

ANSI/ISO 14012-1996: Guidelines for Environmental Auditing—Qualification Criteria for Environmental Auditors

ANSI/ISO 14020-2001: Environmental Labels and Declarations—General Principles

ANSI/ISO 14021-2001: Environmental Labels and Declarations—Self-Declared Environmental Claims (Type 2 Environmental Labeling)

ANSI/ISO 14024-2001: Environmental Labels and Declarations—Type 1 environmental labeling—Principles and Procedures

ANSI/ISO 14031-1999: Environmental Management—Environmental performance evaluation—Guidelines

ANSI/ISO 14040-1997: Environmental Management—Life cycle assessment—Principles and framework

ANSI/ISO 14041-1998: Environmental Management—Life cycle assessment—Goal and Scope Definition and Inventory Analysis

ANSI/ISO 14042-2000: Environmental Management—Life cycle assessment—Life cycle impact assessment

ANSI/ISO 14043-2000: Environmental Management—Life cycle assessment—Life cycle interpretation

ANSI/ISO 17025-1999: General Requirements for the Competence of Testing and Calibration Laboratories

ANSI/ISO/ASQ Q9000-2000: Quality Management Systems: Fundamentals and Vocabulary

ANSI/ISO/ASQ Q9001-2000: Quality Management Systems: Requirements

ANSI/ISO/ASQ Q9004-2000: Quality Management Systems: Guidelines for Performance Improvements

ANSI/ISO/ASQ QE19011-2002: Guidelines for Quality and/or Environmental Systems Auditing

ANSI/ISO/ASQC A3534-2-1993: Statistics—Vocabulary and Symbols—Statistical Quality Control

ANSI/ISO/ASQC Q10006-1997: Quality Management—Guidelines to Quality in Project Management

ANSI/ISO/ASQC Q10011-1994 Series: Guidelines for Auditing Quality Systems

ANSI/ISO/ASQC A8402-1994: Quality Management and Quality Assurance—Vocabulary

ANSI/ISO/ASQC Q9000-1-1994: Quality Management and Quality Assurance Standards—Guidelines for Selection and Use

ANSI/ISO/ASQC Q9001-1994: Quality Systems—Model for Quality Assurance in Design, Development, Production, Installation, and Servicing

ANSI/ISO/ASQC Q9002-1994: Quality Systems—Model for Quality Assurance in Production, Installation, and Servicing

ANSI/ISO/ASQC Q9003-1994: Quality Systems—Model for Quality Assurance in Final Inspection and Test

ANSI/ISO/ASQC Q9004-1-1994: Quality Management and Quality System Elements—Guidelines for Service

ANSI/ISO/ASQC Q9004-3-1993: Quality Management and Quality System Elements—Guidelines for Processed Materials

ANSI/ISO/ASQC Q9004-4-1993: Quality Management and Quality System Elements—Guidelines for Quality Improvement

ANSI/ISO/ASQC Q10006-1997: Quality Management—Guidelines to Quality in Project Management

ANSI/ISO/ASQC Q10007-1995: Quality Management—Guidelines for Configuration Management

ANSI/ISO/ASQC Q10011-1994 Series: Guidelines for Auditing Quality Systems

ANSI/ISO/ASQC Q10013-1995: Guidelines for Quality Manuals

ANSI/ISO/ASQC Q10015-2001: Quality Management—Guidelines for Training

ANSI/NCSL Z540-1-1994: Calibration Laboratories and Measuring and Test Equipment—General Requirements

ASME Y14.5M-1994: Dimensioning and Tolerancing (on blueprints)

ASME Y14.5.1M-1994: Mathematical Definitions of Dimensioning and Tolerancing

ASQ Z1.11-2002: Quality Assurance Standards—Guidelines for the Application OF Ansi/Iso/Asq Q9001-2000 to Education and Training Institutions

ASTM E29-93A: Practice for Using Significant Digits in Test Data to Determine Conformance with Specifications

ASME Y14.5.1M-1994: Mathematical Definitions of Dimensioning and Tolerancing

ASTM E122-89: Practice for Choice of Sample Size to Estimate a Measure of Quality for a Lot or Process

BSR/ASQ E4-2001: Quality Systems for Environmental Data and Technology Programs: Specification with Guidance for Use—DRAFT

BSR/ASQ Z1.9-2000 Draft National Standard: Sampling Procedures and Tables for Inspection by Variables for Percent Nonconforming

BSR/ISO/ASQ QE19011-2002: Guidelines for Quality and/or Environmental Management Systems Auditing

FDIS BSR/ISO/ASQ Q9004 -2000 and Healthcare: Quality Management Systems—Guidelines for Process Improvements in Healthcare Organizations

IEC/ISO 17025: General Requirements for the Competence of Testing and Calibration Laboratories

IEEE Std 12207.0-1996: IEEE Standard for Industry Implementation of ISO/IEC 12207:1995

ISO 5725-1-1994: Accuracy (Trueness and Precision) of Measurement Methods and Results—Part 1: General Principles and Definitions

ISO 5725-2-1994: Accuracy (Trueness and Precision) of Measurement Methods and Results—Part 2

ISO 5725-3-1994: Accuracy (Trueness and Precision) of Measurement Methods and Results—Part 3

ISO 10012:2003: Measurement Management systems—Requirements for Measurement Processes and Measuring Equipment

ISO 10012-1-1992: Quality Assurance Requirements for Measuring Equipment—Part 1: Metrological Confirmation System for Measuring Equipment

ISO GUIDE 64-1997: Guide for the Inclusion of Environmental Aspects in Product Standards

ISO TR10014-1998: Guidelines for Managing the Economics of Quality

ISO/TR 10017:2003: Guidance on Statistical Techniques for ISO 9001:2000

ISO/TR 14025:2000: Environmental Labels and Declarations—Type III Environmental Declarations

ISO/TR 14032:1999: Environmental Management—Examples of Environmental Performance Evaluation

ISO/TR 14061:1998: Information to Assist Forestry Organizations in the Use of Environmental Management System Standards ISO 14001 and ISO 14004

ISO/TS 16048:2002: Environmental Management—Life Cycle Assessment—Data Documentation Format

ISO/TS 16949:2002: Quality Systems—Automotive Suppliers—Particular Requirements for the Application of ISO 9001:2000

IWA-1: 2001: Quality Management Systems: Guidelines for Process Improvements in Health Service Organizations

SAE AS9100: The International Aerospace Quality System Standard, Revision B

Appendix G
Quality Awards

To be included, awards must be quality-related, eligibility cannot be limited to members of a sponsoring organization, and they have to be based on past achievements. Awards in the form of grants and scholarships for future works are not included.

Contact information subject to change has been excluded. Visit www.asq.org to view the complete awards listing and most recent contact information, compiled annually by *Quality Progress* magazine.

U.S. AWARDS

Acclaim Award: American Medical Group Association.

Recognizes quality improvement efforts led by physician directed organizations that measurably improve health outcomes and the quality of life for patients.

Visit www.amga.org.

Armand V. Feigenbaum Medal: ASQ.

Recognizes the achievement of professionals under the age of 36 who have displayed outstanding characteristics of leadership, professionalism and potential in the quality field.

Accepts only electronic applications. Visit www.asq.org.

Malcolm Baldrige National Quality Award: National Institute of Standards and Technology (NIST) in a partnership with ASQ.

Award criteria are built on seven core values: leadership, strategic planning, customer and market focus, information analysis, human resource focus, process management, and business results.

Call NIST at 301-975-2036; e-mail nqp@nist.gov; or visit www.quality.nist.gov.

Three awards may be given in each category every year. Categories include small business, manufacturing, service, education, and healthcare.

Brumbaugh Medal: ASQ.

Presented for the paper published in an ASQ journal that made the largest contribution to the development of the industrial application of quality control.

No nomination form for this award. The award committee decides independently which paper should receive the award.

Philip B. Crosby Medal: ASQ.

Presented to the individual who has authored a distinguished book contributing significantly to the extension of the philosophy and application of the principles, methods, or techniques of quality management.

Deming Medal: ASQ.

Awarded to the leader who combined statistical thinking and management to achieve outstanding quality in product or services.

Deming Prize: The Union of Japanese Scientists and Engineers (JUSE).

Awarded to individuals or teams who have contributed significantly to the development and dissemination of total quality control. The prize has three categories: Application Prize, Prize for Individuals, and Quality Control Award for Operations Business Units.

Call the Deming Prize Committee at 81-3-5379-9812; e-mail juse@juse.or.jp; or visit www.juse.or.jp.

Award was established in 1951 to commemorate Deming's distinguished service.

Design News Engineering Achievement Awards: Design News.

Presented to individuals, teams and organizations whose work greatly improved function, lowered costs, increased reliability, or offered other customer benefits.

For more information call 617-558-4660.

Awards include Excellence in Design, the Engineering Quality Award, and the Global Innovation Award.

Distinguished Service Medal: ASQ

Recognizes the lifetime contribution of a person as a long-term enabler, catalyst, or prime mover in the quality movement. Granted only to those who have driven progress by promulgation of quality principles, methods, or science for the good of society.

Petitions should be submitted to the chairman of the board for deliberation by the Board of Directors. Call 800-248-1946 or read Policy G-60 on www.asq.org.

The Distinguished Service Medal represents the highest distinction that can be accorded by the American Society for Quality for service.

E. Jack Lancaster Medal: ASQ.

Awarded to an individual who has demonstrated exceptional leadership and contributions when promoting quality on an international front.

Nominees must be quality professionals with an international reputation.

E.L. Grant Medal: ASQ.

Presented to the individual who has demonstrated exceptional leadership regarding the development and implementation of educational programs in quality control.

Edwards Medal: ASQ.

Presented to the person who has demonstrated the most outstanding leadership in the application of modern quality control methods.

Candidates are evaluated on technical competence, management creativity, and development.

Freund-Marquardt Medal: ASQ.

Awarded to nominees who have applied quality principles to the development, implementation, and literature of management standards.

Golden Torch Awards: National Society of Black Engineers.

Recognize excellence among African-American engineers, scientists, and technologists, as well as organizations that have demonstrated a commitment to the recruitment, retention and promotion of minorities. For more information call 703-549-2207; or visit www.nsbe.org.

Categories include engineer of the year, diversity leadership in industry, woman in technology, and lifetime achievement in industry.

Hispanic Engineer National Achievement Awards: Hispanic Engineer Achievement Awards Conference.

Seeks, identifies, honors, and documents Hispanic excellence in science and technology nationwide.

Call the Hispanic Engineer National Achievement Awards Conference at 323-262-0997 or 323-262-5545; or visit www.henaac.org.

Categories include engineer of the year, executive excellence, and outstanding technical achievement.

Ishikawa Medal: ASQ.

Presented to the individual or team whose work has had a major impact on the human environment in the workplace and the quality of goods/services delivered to customers.

National Association of Home Builders Research Center Quality Awards: National Association of Home Builders Research Center and Professional Builder magazine.

Open to all U.S. home builders, recognizes the role customer focused quality plays in construction, business management, sales, design, and warranty service.

For more information call 800-638-8556; or visit www.nahbrc.org/awards.

Two awards: the National Housing Quality Award and the National Remodeling Quality Award.

Nova Awards: The Construction Innovation Forum.

Honor innovations that improve construction quality and lower costs.

Phone 248-409-1500; e-mail info@cif.org.

Nominations represent proven cost savings and quality improvement on actual projects.

Shewhart Medal: ASQ.

Based on a career of achievements, honors technical leadership in the field of modern quality control with emphasis on the development of theory, principles, and techniques.

Named for the "father of statistical quality control" and ASQ's first honorary member, Walter Shewhart.

Shingo Prize for Excellence in Manufacturing: Utah State University, College of Business.

Established in 1988 to promote an awareness of lean manufacturing concepts and to recognize companies that achieve world-class manufacturing status.

Contact the Shingo Prize for Excellence in Manufacturing at 435-797-2279; fax 435-797-3440; or visit www.shingoprize.org.

Applications are open to manufacturers in the United States, Mexico, and Canada and to researchers around the world.

Simon Collier Quality Award: Los Angeles Section of ASQ.

To honor, encourage and specifically identify outstanding individual or group leadership, accomplishment and ingenuity in organizing, promoting, operating or improving quality systems and programs in industry, government, education, business, healthcare, or service organizations, which fit the professional objectives of ASQ.

Collier was a founding member of ASQ, the first Edwards Medalist, and the fourth honorary member of ASQ.

Society of Plastics Engineers Award Program: Society of Plastics Engineers.

Recognizes individuals who are making outstanding contributions to the plastics field.

Visit www.4spe.org.

Includes categories such as engineering and technology, design, research, education, and business management.

SME International Honor Awards: Society of Manufacturing Engineers (SME).

Recognizes accomplishments in advancing the concepts of orderly production, education related to manufacturing, research leading to improved productivity, and successful integration of infrastructure and manufacturing process.

Call 313-271-1500; or visit www.sme.org.

Awards include the Eli Whitney Productivity Award, the SME Frederick W. Taylor Research Medal, and the Donald C. Burnham Manufacturing Management Award.

AUTOMOTIVE AWARDS

DaimlerChrysler Supplier Awards: DaimlerChrysler.

Uses a balanced scorecard concept to judge suppliers for the Commodity Award.

Interested suppliers should contact their DaimlerChrysler purchasing agent.

Program includes Gold Awards given to supplier sites that exceed DaimlerChrysler expectations.

Ford Motor Co. World Excellence Awards: Ford Motor Company.

Based on their performance regarding quality, delivery, and cost, Ford suppliers are honored with platinum, gold and silver awards.

For information call 313-390-5411.

Program also includes the Recognition of Achievement Award, honoring suppliers whose work supports Ford's consumer driven strategy.

General Motors Supplier of the Year Award: General Motors.

Recognizes GM supplier companies worldwide that exceed specific performance standards in the areas of quality, service, and price.

Interested suppliers should contact their worldwide purchasing buyer for more information.

Selected by a team of quality, engineering, manufacturing, and purchasing experts from GM operations around the world.

J.D. Power and Associates Award Program: J.D. Power and Associates.

The awards are based on responses from customers who have used the products and services being rated. This provides product quality and customer satisfaction data that enable people to make more informed purchasing decisions.

For more information e-mail information@jdpa.com, or visit www.jdpower.com/awards/about/.

J.D. Power and Associates surveys consumers and business customers to gather opinions and expectations about products and services. These research data are used to compile rankings based on product quality, customer satisfaction, or other industry-specific metrics that gauge company performance.

Total Quality Awards: Strategic Vision.

Based on car buyers' satisfaction with buying, owning and driving a vehicle.

Call 714-544-3466 or visit www.vision-inc.com.

More than 15 categories such as compact car, luxury car, and medium sports utility vehicle.

GOVERNMENT AWARDS

George M. Low Trophy: NASA's Quality and Excellence Award.

Follows criteria similar to the Baldrige criteria.

Visit www.hq.nasa.gov.

Award is in memory of George M. Low.

Innovations in American Government Awards: Ash Institute for Democratic Governance and Innovation at Harvard University's John F. Kennedy School of Government.

An annual awards competition recognizing and promoting excellence and creativity in the public sector.

For more information call the Ash Institute at 617-495-0558; e-mail innovations@harvard.edu; or visit www.excelgov.org.

President's Quality Award Program: Office of Merit Systems Oversight and Effectiveness, U.S. Office of Personnel Management.

Recognizes organizations within the federal government for exemplary performance in support of the initiatives identified in the President's Management Agenda.

Call 202-606-1875; e-mail quality@opm.gov; or visit www.opm.gov/pqa.

Public Service Excellence Awards: Public Employees Roundtable.

Recognize groups involving two or more public employees.

Call 202-927-4923; e-mail psea@theroundtable.org; or visit www.theroundtable.org.

Reward programs that reduce costs in government projects or services that improve the quality of community life or increase productivity.

INTERNATIONAL AWARDS

Akao Prize: Administered by the Quality Function Deployment (QFD) Institute.

Following the processes used for the Deming Prize. Awarded to individuals for expertise in practice and dissemination of the QFD method.

Visit www.qfdi.org.

Named for Yoji Akao, the co-developer of the QFD method. Presented at the International Symposium on QFD to recipients around the world.

Argentina National Quality Award Private Sector: Foundation for the National Quality Award.

There are three categories: large, medium, and small business, and two enterprises in each category are granted awards.

For information e-mail fpnc@mail.mya.com.ar; or visit www.premiocalidad.com.ar.

Argentina also has a quality award for the public sector.

International Asia Pacific Quality Award: Asia Pacific Quality Organization and the Walter L. Hurd Foundation.

Uses the Baldrige criteria. Candidates for the award must already have won their national quality award.

Only one award will be presented per classification to a country each year.

Australian Business Excellence Awards: Business Excellence Australia, a division of Standards Australia International.

Criteria are the Australian Business Excellence Framework.

Contact the Awards Manager at 61-2-82066568; e-mail awards@businessexcellenceaustralia.com.au; or visit www.businessexcellenceaustralia.com.au.

Mission is to promote, nurture, recognize, and celebrate organizational excellence in all its forms.

The Gold Award for Quality: Joint Accreditation Scheme of Australia and New Zealand.

Award criteria focus on eight critical quality management elements outlined in ISO 9004:2000.

In Australia call 61-2-62825840. In New Zealand call 64-4-4743348; e-mail admin@jas-anz.com.au; or visit www.jas-anz.com.au.

Established by the Australian Organization for Quality to recognize and encourage organizations in the pursuit of excellence and sound companywide quality management. Runners-up receive the Silver Award.

Austrian Quality Award: Austrian Association for Quality (ÖVQ)

Based on the European Foundation for Quality Management Excellence Model (EFQM) model.

Call the OVQ at 43-1-5333052; e-mail office@afqm.at; or visit www.oevq.at.

Belgian Quality Award: Belgian Association for Total Quality Management and Mouvement Wallon de Qualité.

Based on the European Foundation for Quality Management Excellence Model (EFQM) and awarded twice a year.

Call 32-3-201-1450; fax 32-3-232-4436.

A Quality Manager of the Year award is also offered. Co-sponsored by Vlaams Centrum voor Kwaliteitszorg (VCK).

National Quality Award of Brazil: Foundation for the National Quality Award.

Applicants must meet Brazil Award Excellence criteria, which can be downloaded from the website in Portuguese, English, and Spanish.

Visit www.fpnq.org.br.

Recognizes the best management practices for performance excellence throughout Brazil.

National Quality Award for the Public Transportation and Traffic Industry: Brazilian National Public Transport Association.

Uses the Baldrige model with some adaptations.

Visit www.antp.org.br.

Categories include rail rapid transit, buses, and transit and traffic authorities.

Regional Quality Award Brazil: Sponsored by Associação Qualidade RS/PGQP.

Rewards Brazilian organizations who meet Programa Gaucho da Qualidade e Productividade (PGQP) assessment criteria.

State of Rio de Janeiro Top Empresarial Quality Management Prize and Prêmio Qualidade Rio: State of Rio de Janeiro through the General Office of State Energy, the Naval Industry and Petroleum of the State of Rio.

Both prizes follow the criteria of the Brazilian National Prize of Quality (similar to Baldrige criteria).

Visit www.seinpe.rj.gov.br or www.premiotop.com.br.

Top Empresarial Prize is for small business. Each award has a bronze, silver, and gold category.

Canada Awards for Excellence: Administered by the National Quality Institute (NQI).

Organizations that complete NQI-PEP Level 4 are eligible to apply for the coveted Canada Awards for Excellence.

Call Canada Awards for Excellence adjudicator at 416-251-7600, x240; or 800-263-9648; or visit www.nqi.com.

NQI helps Canadian organizations improve performance (for both Quality and a Healthy Workplace) using NQI's innovative Roadmap to Excellence. The roadmap guides organizations through all processes of the Progressive Excellence Program (NQI-PEP).

Bob Cardno Award: ASQ Toronto Section 0402.

Available to graduates of the quality certificate program of ASQ and offered at eligible institutions in the greater Toronto area.

Education Institution Awards: ASQ Toronto Section 0402.

Open to students who have successfully completed three of the component courses of the ASQ Toronto Section quality certificate program.

London Chamber of Commerce Business Achievement Awards: London, Ontario, Canada, Chamber of Commerce.

Honor area businesses using criteria focusing on business achievements; management/employee relations; product, service and technology innovation; training; contribution to employment; and commitment to community.

Call the London Chamber of Commerce at 519-432-7551, x29; or visit www.chamber.london.on.ca.

Categories include environment, innovation, and business incubator.

Czech Republic National Quality Award: Czech Quality Award Association.

Has two categories: companies with up to 250 employees and companies with over 250 employees. Also awards the Czech Republic National Quality Prize.

Call Czech Quality Association at 420-2-66109811; fax 420-2-6848244; or visit www.czechmade.cz.

Danish Quality Prize: Danske Kvalitets Pris (Danish Quality Prize Committee).

Based on the EFQM model.

Call the Danish Quality Prize Committee at 45-86-720022; fax 45-86-720066; or visit www.kvalitetspris.dk.

Dubai International Award for Best Practices: Dubai Quality Group.

Best practices should demonstrate a positive and tangible impact on improving the quality of the living environment of people.

Call the Dubai Quality Group at 971-4-3431950; e-mail dqg@dqg.org; or visit www.dqg.org.

Groups are judged on their ability to bring about change in one of the various areas listed on the website.

The European Quality Awards: The European Foundation for Quality Management (EFQM).

Presented to European organizations that demonstrate excellence in managing quality as a fundamental process for continuous improvement.

For information call 32-2-7753525; e-mail info@efqm.org; or visit www.efqm.org.

Special awards are given to companies that demonstrate exceptional use of the EFQM model.

Finnish Quality Award: Finnish Society for Quality (Center for Excellence Finland).

Based on the EFQM criteria.

For information call 358-9-6224400.

French Quality Award: French Quality Movement (MFQ).

Award criteria are based on the French MFQ model, not the EFQM model.

Call the French Quality Movement at 33-1-46110240, fax 33-1-46110250; or visit www.mfq.asso.fr.

German National Quality Award: Administered jointly by Deutsche Gesellschaft für Qualität (German Society for Quality) and Verein Deutscher Ingenieure (Association of German Engineers). Based on the EFQM criteria.

Call the German Society for Quality at 49-69-954-24-0; fax 49-69-954-24-133. Call the Association of German Engineers at 49-211-6214-0; fax 49-211-6214-575; or visit www.dgq.de or www.vdi.de.

The German National Quality Award aims to promote business excellence.

Hellenic National Quality Award Greece: Ministry of Development.

Similar to Baldrige and EFQM criteria.

Call the Ministry of Development at 301-720-4600; fax 301-720-4500.

Hong Kong Award for Industry: Quality Trade and Industry Department.

Open to companies based and operating in Hong Kong with products wholly or partly manufactured in Hong Kong in the 12 months prior to closing date of entry.

Visit www.hkpc.org.

Hungarian Quality Development Center Award.

Based on the EFQM criteria.

Call European Organization for Quality at 36-12-12-88-03; fax 3612-12-76-38; or visit www.eoq.org.

Rajiv Gandhi National Quality Awards: Bureau of Indian Standards.

Honor Indian manufacturing and service organizations and individuals considered leaders in India's quality movement.

Visit www.bis.org.in.

Designed in line with the Baldrige Award, Deming Prize, and European Quality Award.

Northern Ireland Quality Awards: Northern Ireland Center for Competitiveness.
Use the EFQM model for their criteria.
Call 44- (0)28-9046-8362; or visit www.cforc.org.
Premier business prize in Northern Ireland recognizing role model organizations in different sectors.

The Q-Mark Irish National Quality Award and Irish Business Excellence Award: Excellence-Ireland.
The Q-Mark focuses on continuous improvement and customer satisfaction. The Irish Business Excellence Award is based on a nine-element model, similar to the Baldrige award.
Visit www.excellence-ireland.ie.
The Q-Mark was started in 1982 and is seen as a symbol synonymous with Irish quality.

IQA National Quality Award: The Institute of Quality Assurance (IQA).
Presented to the student or quality professional who submits the best synopsis from a dissertation, thesis or project report on any aspect of quality.
Call IQA at 44-0-20-7245-6722 (London); e-mail iqa@iqa.org; or visit www.iqa.org.

Israel Improvement Teams Association Award: Improvement Teams Association.
Given to the team winning the annual competition organized by the association. Criteria are based on real achievements.
Call Improvement Teams at 972-3-5752650; fax 972-3-5755265.
This award was first given in 1990.

National Award for Quality and Excellence in Industries: Israel Association of Electronic and Information Industries along with the Israeli government.
Allocated annually to small (fewer than 150 employees) and large companies. Its criteria were first based on the Baldrige award and have since been enlarged.
This award was started in the early 1990s.

National Award for Quality and Excellence in Public Service Israel:
Quality and Excellency Division of the Civil Service Commission of the Prime Minister's Office.
Based on the EFQM model.
This award was started in 1996.

The Quality Award of the Electronic and Information Industries: Israel Association of Electronic and Information Industries.
Allocated annually to small (fewer than 150 employees) and large companies. Its criteria were first based on the Baldrige award and have since been enlarged.
This was Israel's first quality award and was initiated in the early 1980s.

Italian Quality Award: Associazione Premio Qualità Italia.
Based on the EFQM model.
Call 39-50-541751; e-mail apqi@interbusiness.it.

Japan Quality Medal: Union of Japanese Scientists and Engineers (JUSE).

Deming Application Prize winning companies are invited to apply for this medal many times over.

Call International Relations Section of JUSE at 81-3-5378-9812; e-mail juse@juse.or.jp; or visit www.juse.or.jp.

Established in 1970.

Japan Quality Award: Japanese Quality Award Committee.

A maximum of six companies (two manufacturing, two service sector, and two medium/small business) are eligible.

Visit www.jqac.com.

Established in 1995.

Japan Quality Recognition Award: JUSE.

To contribute to the development of Japanese industry and the expansion and enhancement of quality improvement activities centering on total quality management.

Call International Relations Section of JUSE at 81-3-5378-9812; e-mail juse@juse.or.jp; or visit www.juse.or.jp.

Established in 2000 to commemorate JUSE's 50th anniversary. Has two awards: recognition of TQM achievement and quality system innovation.

The Nikkei QC Literature Prize: Established by the Nippon Keizai Shimbun (*Japan Economic Journal*) and JUSE.

Recognizes literature that contributes to the progress and further development of total quality control.

E-mail juse@juse.or.jp.

The work must be published in Japan.

Juran Medal: ASQ.

Recognizes chief executive of an organization that has received national or international recognition for business improvement based on the body of knowledge of quality management. Leader's tenure and performance improvement are five years or greater.

Medal commemorates Joseph M. Juran's 75-year career in quality.

Korea National Quality Management Award: Sponsored by the Ministry of Commerce, Industry and Energy, and the South Korean government.

Presented to the company scoring the highest in the following categories: leadership, strategic planning, customer focus, information and analysis, and process management.

The award is administered by the Korean Standards Association.

Latino Magnifico Quality Awards: International Latino Magnifico Quality Awards Foundation Inc.

Recognizes U.S. and international Latino owned, managed or operated businesses, institutions, organizations, and government entities that practice quality production and excellence in achievement.

Call International Latino Magnifico Quality Awards Foundation at 215-533-2629; fax 215-674-3314.

Mexican Quality Award: Fideicomiso del Premio Nacional de Calidad.
Based on the National Quality Model.
Based on continuous improvement and customer satisfaction criteria.

Netherlands National Quality Award: Dutch Institute for Quality (INK).
Uses the EFQM model for its criteria. (National model differs from the EFQM model only on minor issues.)
Call INK at 31-73-613-87-87.

New Zealand Quality Award Program: New Zealand Business Excellence Foundation.
Includes the Progress, Commendation, Achievement, and National Quality Awards.
Call 64-9-270-5164; e-mail info@nzbef.org.nz; or visit www.nzbef.org.nz.
Program evaluators are trained by Baldrige examiners.

Polish Quality Award: Polish Chamber of Commerce, Polish Center for Testing and Certification and Club Polish Forum ISO 9000.
Any company can apply for the PQA provided it has been operating in Poland for the last four years. Categories include large organizations, small/medium enterprises and public sector, manufacturing, and service organizations.
E-mail pnj@kig.pl; or visit www.pnj.pl.
The award is based on the European Quality Award.

Quality Control Circles and Teamwork National Contest: Teamwork Mexican Association.
Based on the accurate application of problem solving methodologies, statistical tools, and achievements.
Call Teamwork Mexican Association at 52 -55-8595-7610; e-mail amte@prodigy.net.mx; website www.amte.org.mx.

São Paulo State Award: Paulista Excellence Management Institute, São Paulo Industry Federation and São Paulo Government Quality Institute.
Follows a simplified criteria of the Brazilian National Quality Award and Baldrige award.
E-mail ppqg@ppqg.org.br.
There are four award recognitions: bronze, silver, and gold medals and one trophy (Governor Excellence Award) for the top applicant in each of the eight award categories.

Scottish Quality Award: Quality Scotland Foundation.
Uses the EFQM model for its criteria.
Call Quality Scotland Foundation at 44-131-5562333; e-mail info@qualityscotland.co.uk; or visit www.qualityscotland.co.uk.

The South African Performance Excellence Award: South African Excellence Foundation.

Recipients must have a system that ensures, through sound leadership, continuous improvement in the delivery of products or services and that provides a way of satisfying and responding to customers.

Call the South African Excellence Foundation at 27-12-349-2765; or visit www.saef.co.za.

Open to companies, small and medium-sized enterprises, and public sector organizations in South Africa.

Premio Príncipe Felipe a la Calidad Industrial (Prince Felipe Industrial Quality Award): Asociación Española para la Calidad (Spanish Association for Quality).

Uses the EFQM model for its criteria.

Call the Spanish Association for Quality at 34-1-575-27-50; or visit www.aec.es.

Swedish Quality Award: The Swedish Institute for Quality (SIQ).

Applicants can choose to use SIQ's Model for Performance Excellence, the Baldrige criteria, or the EQFM criteria.

Call SIQ at 46-31-723-1700; e-mail siq@siq.se; or visit www.siq.se.

The award is open to applications from all sectors (including businesses, education, healthcare, and government). More than 20 regional, local, and sectorial awards exist in Sweden.

Swiss Quality Award: Swiss Association for Promotion of Quality.

Uses the EFQM model for its criteria.

Call the Swiss Association for Promotion of Quality at 41-62-205-45-45; e-mail info@saq.ch; or visit www.saq.ch.

United Kingdom Quality Award for Business Excellence: The British Quality Foundation.

Uses the EFQM model for its criteria, with some adaptations.

Call the British Quality Foundation at 020-7654-5000; fax 020-7654-5001; or visit www.quality-foundation.co.uk.

Vietnam Quality Award: Directorate for Standards and Quality.

The program follows seven steps of criteria that are very close to the core values of the Baldrige award.

Call the Directorate for Standards and Quality at 84-4-9439731; fax 84-4-8252733; or visit www.moste.gov.vn.

Presented to Vietnamese manufacturing and service organizations that produce high quality products and services in Vietnam and foreign markets.

The Wales Quality Award: Administered by the Wales Quality Center.

Based on the EFQM model; it aligns with the European Quality Awards.

E-mail info@walesqualitycentre.org.uk; or visit www.walesqualitycentre.org.uk.

Award sponsors change each year. Application fee is 50 pounds.

U.S. STATE AWARDS

Alabama

Alabama Quality Award: Alabama Productivity Center.

The applicant's efforts must be implemented within the state of Alabama, but the organization may have affiliates, divisions, or headquarters in other states.

Visit http://proctr.cba.ua.edu.

Arizona

Arizona Quality Awards: Arizona Quality Alliance.

The Arizona Governor's Award for Quality recognizes organizations that have mature and fully deployed quality systems and demonstrate a commitment to continuous improvement.

Call 602-636-1383; or visit www.Arizona-Excellence.com.

The Arizona Pioneer Award for Quality recognizes organizations that deploy fundamental quality systems within their operations.

Arkansas

Arkansas Institute for Performance Excellence: Arkansas Institute for Performance Excellence..

A four-level award program, beginning with the Challenge Award through the Governor's Quality Award.

E-mail info@arkansas-quality.org; or visit www.arkansas-quality.org.

California

California Awards for Performance Excellence: California Council for Quality and Service.

Program features awards in three stages: the California Challenge (stage one), the California Prospect Award (stage two), and the Eureka Award for Performance Excellence and the California U.S. Senate and Productivity Award (stage three).

Visit www.ccqs.org.

Offers categories including service, nonprofit, and military and armed forces.

Colorado

Colorado Performance in Customer Service Award: Better Business Bureau of the Pikes Peak Region.

Focuses specifically on customer service as practiced by Pikes Peak businesses or organizations. Visit www.csbbb.org.

Colorado Performance Excellence Awards: Colorado Performance Excellence Inc.

Colorado state program modeled after the Baldrige award.

Visit www.coloradoexcellence.org.

Connecticut

Connecticut Award for Excellence

Three levels of recognition include Nutmeg, Chart Oak, and Genius Award, which is similar to the Baldrige award.

Call 860-285-2578 for more information.

Categories include education, government, and healthcare.

Connecticut Quality Improvement Award: The Connecticut Quality Improvement Award (CQIA) Partnership.

America's first state-level Baldrige award involves three levels of Baldrige based awards: the CQIA Innovation Prize, the Break-through Quality Award, and the Leadership Quality Award.

Visit www.ctqualityaward.org.

Delaware

Delaware Quality Award in honor of W.L. "Bill" Gore: Accolade Alliance LLC.

Three levels of recognition: the Gore Award for Performance Excellence, the Award of Merit, and the Quality Commitment Award. New awards for 2003 are the Accolade Award and the Genevieve W. Gore Lifetime Achievement Award.

Visit www.accoladealliance.org.

Organizations that have operated in Delaware for at least three years can apply.

Florida

Florida Governor's Sterling Award: The Florida Sterling Council.

Uses acknowledged international standards for a management system designed to achieve organizational excellence.

Visit www.floridasterling.com.

Georgia

Georgia Oglethorpe Award: Georgia Oglethorpe Award Process Inc.

Follows Baldrige criteria, but has included education and healthcare categories since its inception in 1996.

Visit www.georgiaoglethorpe.org.

Named after Georgia's founder, James Edward Olgethorpe.

Hawaii

The Hawaii State Award of Excellence: Hawaii Chamber of Commerce.

All organizations, including military and not-for-profit, can participate.

Call 808-545-4300.

Idaho

Idaho Quality Award: Idaho Department of Commerce.

Awards given in marketplace, workplace, community, and quality management systems categories.

Visit www.idahoworks.com.

The program is run entirely by volunteers.

Illinois

Illinois Lincoln Award for Business Excellence: The Lincoln Foundation for Business Excellence.

This three-tiered program offers several education and outreach services to help increase knowledge and awareness of quality practices.

Trains 120 examiners a year from all sectors.

Indiana

Baird, Kurtz and Dobson (BKD) Indiana Quality Improvement Award: BMT Corp.

Award recognizes businesses in Indiana that use quality to stay competitive and achieve third-party recognition for excellence in quality.

Call 317-635-3058; fax 317-231-7095; or visit www.bmtadvantage.org.

Iowa

Iowa Recognition for Performance Excellence: Iowa Quality Center.

A three-tiered process using the Baldrige criteria, which recognizes performance excellence practitioners at all levels.

E-mail info@iowaqc.org; or visit www.iowaqc.org.

Kansas

Kansas Award for Excellence: Kansas Award for Excellence Foundation.

Three-tiered program includes awards for beginning to advanced quality practitioners.

Kentucky

Commonwealth of Kentucky Quality Award: Kentucky Quality Council.

Offers the Governor's Quality Award as its highest of four award levels.

Visit www.kqc.org.

Other awards include quality interest, quality commitment, and quality achievement.

Louisiana

Louisiana Quality Award: Louisiana Quality Foundation.

Offers applications using the Baldrige business or education criteria.

Visit www.laqualityaward.com.

Has three levels of judging.

Maine

Margaret Chase Smith Maine State Quality Award: Margaret Chase Smith Quality Association.

Publicly or privately held organizations of any size located in Maine may apply.

Baldrige-based, using the previous year's Baldrige application and materials. Has three levels of recognition and awards.

E-mail MCQ@maine-quality.org; visit www.Maine-Quality.org.

Maryland

Maryland Governor's Quality Award: Center for Continuous Quality Improvement.

Visit www.dop.state.md.us/ccqi.

U.S. Senate Productivity and Maryland Quality Award: University of Maryland Center for Quality and Productivity.

Uses Baldrige criteria.

Visit www.umcqp.umd.edu.

Massachusetts

Massachusetts Performance Excellence Award: Mass-Excellence.

Three levels, with the top honor named after Armand V. Feigenbaum.

E-mail info@massexcellence.com; or visit www.massexcellence.com.

Michigan

Michigan Quality Leadership Award Program: Michigan Quality Council.

Recognitions include the Honor Roll (for improved quality and operation performance) and Navigator (for organizations that complete a seven category, Baldrige based self-assessment).

Visit www.michiganquality.org.

Also offers a Lighthouse Award for completing a self-assessment.

Governor's Quality Care Award: Michigan Department of Consumer and Industry Services.

Honors Michigan licensed day care, adult foster care, nursing homes, hospices, and before and after school programs with exceptional levels of quality care.

Visit www.cis.state.mi.us.

A team of health and child care experts evaluates the nominations before finalists are announced and site visits are scheduled.

Minnesota

Minnesota Quality Award: Minnesota Council for Quality.

Organizations can participate year round in assessment and training opportunities both within and outside the award process.

E-mail MC4Quality@aol.com.

Mississippi

Mississippi Quality Awards Program: Mississippi's State Board of Community and
   Junior Colleges.

Doesn't offer specific categories. Uses business, healthcare, and education
   criteria.

Visit www.sbcjc.cc.ms.us/progs.html.

Any organization can apply regardless of industry.

Missouri

Missouri Quality Award Program: The Excellence in Missouri Foundation.

Offers three awards: the Quality Award (for organizations), Team Quality Award
   (honoring team activity), and Governor's Quality Leadership Award (individual
   honor).

Visit www.mqa.org.

Nebraska

The Edgerton Quality Awards: Nebraska Diplomats and Nebraska's Department
   of Economic Development.

Offers a family of awards: Edgerton Award of Commitment, Edgerton Award of
   Progress, and Edgerton Award of Excellence.

Visit assist.neded.org/edgerton/about.html

Nevada

Nevada Governor's Award for Performance Excellence (APEX): Nevada Quality
   Alliance.

Uses the Performance Excellence criteria of the Baldrige award. Companies
   and organizations may chose from four application levels differing in
   complexity.

Visit www.nvqa.org.

A tiered series of four awards are provided for leadership, customer service,
   community support, and workforce development.

New Hampshire

New Hampshire Granite State Quality Award: Granite State Quality Council.

Five tiers of awards including overall, achievement, commitment, interest, and
   category.

Visit www.gsqc.com.

New Jersey

Governor's Award for Performance Excellence: Quality New Jersey.

Given at three levels: gold, silver, and bronze.

Visit www.qnj.org.

Formerly known as the New Jersey Quality Achievement Award.

New Mexico

New Mexico Quality Awards: Quality New Mexico.

All organizations are eligible regardless of industry, as long as they employ at least five full-time employees.

Visit www.quality-newmexico.org.

There are no categories for the awards.

New York

New York Empire State Advantage (ESA) Award Program: Excellence at Work Program.

The ESA program is based on a Framework for Leadership and Management Excellence that expands on the Baldrige criteria and is tailored to and provides best practices for each sector.

Call 866-RING-ESA; e-mail office@empirestateadvantage.org; or visit www.EmpireStateAdvantage.org.

The five sectors (business, education, government, healthcare, and not-for-profit) can receive assessments, mentoring, and training in management systems and processes. Opportunities to also earn recognition for excellence in leadership and management through ESA certifications and the Governor's Award for Excellence.

Ohio

Ohio Award for Excellence

A four-tiered program recognizing Performance Excellence and Continuous Improvement. Uses Baldrige criteria for Performance Excellence.

All applicants receive a site visit.

Ohio Team Excellence in the Public Sector: Ohio Office of Quality Services.

Award demonstrates the value of teamwork and employee involvement in the public sector.

Teams showcase accomplishment through the use of quality tools and improvement processes.

Oklahoma

Oklahoma Quality Award: Oklahoma Quality Award Foundation Inc.

A three-tiered program including the quality awards for excellence, achievement, and commitment.

Visit www.OklahomaQuality.com.

Oregon

Oregon Excellence Award: Oregon Partnership for Excellence.

Visit www.oregonexcellence.org.

Pennsylvania

Greater Pittsburgh Total Quality Award: Greater Pittsburgh Chamber of Commerce and Q-NET.

Organizations from all sectors can apply, but headquarters must be in Allegheny, Beaver, Butler, Washington, or Westmoreland counties.

Winners are selected from each Baldrige category.

Pennsylvania's Keystone Performance Excellence Award.
   Call 717-560-2910; fax 717-581-5261.

Pennsylvania's Lancaster Chamber Performance Excellence Award: Lancaster Chamber of Commerce and Industry.

This four-tiered award program recently began accepting applications on a statewide basis.

Visit www.lcci.com.

Pennsylvania's Quality Valley USA Awards: Quality Valley, USA Regional Quality Council.

Open to any publicly or privately held organization of any size in the Lehigh Valley region.

Has three award levels: highest achievement, significant progress, and serious commitment.

Rhode Island

Rhode Island Quality Award Program: The Rhode Island Center for Performance Excellence.

Offers two awards: Governor's Award for Competitiveness and Performance Excellence and Performance Excellence Achievement Award.

Visit www.ricpe.org.

South Carolina

South Carolina Governor's Quality Award: The South Carolina Quality Forum.

Based on Baldrige criteria.

Visit www.scquality.com.

Forum also administers the Milliken Medal, awarded to individuals for their accomplishments in the area of quality management.

South Carolina Trident Area Quality Award: ASQ Section 1122 (Carolina Low Country).

Based on Baldrige criteria. Recognizes team efforts in addition to organizationwide endeavors.

Visit www.taqac.org.

South Dakota

South Dakota Business Excellence Award (ABEX): South Dakota Chamber of Commerce and Industry.

Awards given every two years in eight categories.

Visit www.sdchamber.biz.

Tennessee

Tennessee Quality Award: Tennessee Quality Award Inc.

Baldrige-based education and assessment program. Has four levels of recognition with open eligibility and 100% site visit opportunity.

Visit www.tqa.org.

Pyramid of Excellence: Greater Memphis Association for Quality.

Organizations in the northern Mississippi, eastern Arkansas, and western Tennessee regions can apply for this award.

Visit www.gmaq.org.

Texas

Northwest Texas Quality Award: Sponsored by ASQ Section 1412 and Northwest Texas Quality Award.

Recognizes achievements of organizations in Northwest Texas who are committed to continuous quality improvement.

Visit www.qualityamarillo.org.

While there is no guarantee of a site visit, most of the organizations applying for the award receive one.

Texas Award for Performance Excellence: Quality Texas Foundation.

Focuses on continuous improvement and customer satisfaction to drive job creation and retention and on improvements in the quality of life in Texas.

E-mail quality-info@texas-quality.org; or visit www.texas-quality.org.

Houston Awards for Excellence: Houston Awards for Excellence.

Any business in Harris County or in the seven surrounding counties can apply for this award.

Greater Austin Quality Awards: Quality of Life Foundation of Austin and Austin Chamber of Commerce.

Baldrige-based, but an addendum based on the Carnegie Mellon Capability Model is included for software companies.

Call the Austin Quality Council's executive director at 512-322-5603; or visit www.utexas.edu/courses/kincaid/gaqc.

Utah

Utah Quality Award: Utah Quality Council.

In addition to the Quality Award and the Governor's Award, program includes the Continuous Improvement Award, given to the organization that demonstrates the most improvement during prior years.

Visit www.utahqualityaward.org.

Vermont

Vermont Program for Performance: Vermont Council for Quality.

Includes four award levels: interest, commitment, achievement, and the Governor's Award for Excellence.

Visit www.vermontquality.org.

Virginia

U.S. Senate Productivity and Quality Awards: Virginia Senate Productivity Quality Award Board.

One of the oldest quality award programs in the country. Started 20 years ago.

Washington

Washington State Quality Award: Washington State Quality Award.

In addition to the award, certificates of merit are presented to organizations for outstanding commitment and significant progress in quality performance.

Visit www.wsqa.net.

Wisconsin

Wisconsin Forward Award: Wisconsin Forward Award Inc.

Uses the Baldrige criteria. Focuses on recognizing continuous improvement through a tiered award system.

Visit www.forwardaward.org.

Bibliography

Albrect, Karl. *At America's Service.* New York: Warner Books, 1988.

ANSI/ISO/ASQ. *American National Standard Quality Management and Quality Assurance—Vocabulary.* Milwaukee: ASQC Quality Press, 1994.

ASQC Quality Cost Committee. *Principles of Quality Costs,* 3rd Edition. Milwaukee: ASQ Quality Press, 1999.

ASQ Statistics Division. *Glossary and Tables for Statistical Quality Control.* Milwaukee: ASQC Quality Press, 1996.

Bennis, Warren. *The Strategy for Taking Change.* New York: Harper & Row, 1985.

———. *The Planning of Change,* 3rd ed. New York: Holt, Rinehart and Winston, 1986.

Berry, Leonard. *On Great Service.* New York: Free Press, 1995.

Blanchard, Ken. *The Power of Ethical Management.* New York: Ballantine Press, 1988.

Bloom, Benjamin S. *Taxonomy of Educational Objectives: The Classification of Educational Goals.* New York: Longman Group, 1999.

Box, George. *Statistics for Experimenters.* New York: John Wiley & Sons, 1978.

Breyfogle, Forrest W., III. *Implementing Six Sigma Smarter Solutions Using Statistical Methods.* New York: John Wiley & Sons, 1999.

Carlzon, Jan. *Moments of Truth.* New York: Harper Business, 1997.

Cartin, Thomas J. *Principles & Practices of TQM.* Milwaukee: ASQC Quality Press, 1993.

Ciampa, Dan. *Total Quality: A User's Guide for Implementation.* Reading, PA: Addison-Wesley, 1992.

Covey, Stephen R. *The 7 Habits of Highly Effective People.* New York: Simon & Schuster, 1989.

Crosby, Philip B. *Quality Is Free.* New York: McGraw-Hill, 1979.

———. *Quality Without Tears: The Art of Hassle Free Management.* New York: McGraw-Hill, 1984.

———. *Leading: The Art of Becoming an Executive.* New York: McGraw-Hill, 1990.

Deming, W. Edwards. *Quality, Productivity*, and *Competitive Position*. Cambridge: Massachusetts Institute of Technology, Center for Advanced Engineering Study, 1982.

———. *Out of the Crisis*. Cambridge: Massachusetts Institute of Technology, Center for Advanced Engineering Study, 1988.

———. *The New Economics*, 2nd ed. Cambridge: Massachusetts Institute of Technology, Center for Advanced Engineering Study, 1996.

Drucker, Peter. *Management: Tasks, Responsibilities, Practices*. New York: Harper & Row, 1974.

Feigenbaum, Armand V. *Total Quality Control*, 3rd rev. ed. New York: McGraw-Hill, 1991.

Goldratt, Eliyahu. *Theory of Constraints*. Great Barrington, MA: North River Press, 1990.

Dettmer, H. William. *Theory of Constraints: A Systems Approach to Continuous Improvement*. Milwaukee: ASQ Quality Press, 1997.

Goodman, John. "Maximizing the Value of Customer Feedback." *ASQC Quality Progress* (December 1996): 35–39.

Grant, Eugene L., and Levenworth, Richard S. *Statistical Quality Control*, 6th ed. New York: McGraw-Hill, 1988.

Hammer, Michael, and Champy, J. *Reengineering the Corporation: A Manifesto for Business Revolution*. New York: Harper Business, 1992.

Harrington, James H. *Business Process Improvement: The Breakthrough Strategy for Total Quality, Productivity, and Competitiveness*. Milwaukee: ASQC Quality Press, 1991.

Hayes, Bob. *Measuring Customer Satisfaction: Survey Design, Use, and Statistical Analysis Methods*, 2nd ed. Milwaukee: ASQC Quality Press, 1997.

Herzberg, Fredrick. *The Motivation to Work*, 2nd ed. New York: John Wiley & Sons, 1959.

Imai, Nasaski. *Kaizen: The Key to Japan's Competitive Success*. New York: McGraw-Hill, 1986.

Ishikawa, Kaoru. *What Is Total Quality Control? The Japanese Way*. Trans. D. J. Lu. Englewood Cliffs, NJ: Prentice Hall, 1985.

———. *Guide to Quality Control*. White Plains, NY: Kraus International Publications, 1987.

Juran, Joseph M., and Godfrey, A. B., eds. *Juran's Quality Handbook*, 5th ed. New York: McGraw-Hill, 1999.

Juran, Joseph M., and Gryna, Frank M. *Quality Planning and Analysis*. New York: McGraw-Hill, 2001.

Kirkpatrick, Donald. *Evaluating Training Programs: The Four Levels*. San Francisco: Berrett-Koehler, 1994.

Lewin, Kurt. *Leading Change*. Boston: Harvard Business School Press, 1966.

Likert, Rensis L. *New Patterns of Management*. New York: McGraw-Hill, 1961.

Maslow, Abraham. *Motivation and Personality*. New York: Harper & Brothers, 1954.

McClelland, David. "Business Drive and National Achievement." *Harvard Business Review* (July-August 1962): 99–112.

McGregor, Douglas. *The Human Side of Enterprise*. New York: McGraw-Hill, 1960.

Mintzberg, Henry. *The Rise and Fall of Strategic Planning*. New York: Free Press, 1994.

Okes, Duke, and Westcott, Russell T. *The Certified Quality Manager Handbook,* 2nd ed. Milwaukee: ASQ Quality Press, 2001.

Ott, Ellis R., and Shilling, Edward G. *Process Quality Control.* New York: McGraw-Hill, 1990.

Peters, Tom. *Thriving on Chaos.* New York: Alfred A Knopf, 1987.

Peters, Tom, and Waterman, R. A., Jr. *In Search of Excellence.* New York: Harper & Row, 1982.

Pyzdek, Thomas. *What Every Engineer Should Know About Quality Control.* New York: Marcel-Dekker, 1989.

Pyzdek, Thomas, and Berger, Roger W. *Quality Engineering Handbook.* Milwaukee: ASQC Quality Press, 1992.

Schein, Edgar H. *Leadership and Organizational Culture,* 2nd ed. San Francisco: Jossey-Bass, 1997.

Scholtes, Peter, Joiner, Brian L., Braswell, Bill, Finn, Lynda, Hacquebord, Heero, Little, Kevin, Reynard, Sue, Streibel, Barbara, and Weiss, Lonnie. *The Team Handbook.* Madison, WI: Oriel, Inc., 2003.

Senge, Peter. *The Fifth Discipline.* New York: Doubleday, 1990.

Shewhart, Walter A. *Economic Control of Quality of Manufactured Product.* Milwaukee: ASQC Quality Press, 1980.

Shiego, Shingo. *Modern Approaches to Manufacturing Improvement.* Portland, OR: Productivity Press, 1990.

Taguchi, Genichi. *Introduction to Quality Engineering.* Dearborn, MI: American Supplier Institute, 1986.

Vavra, Terry. *Customer Satisfaction Measurement Simplified.* Milwaukee: ASQ Quality Press, 2002.

Weisbord, Marvin. *Organizational Diagnosis: A Workbook of Theory and Practice.* Reading, MA: Addison-Wesley, 1978.

Wheeler, Don. *Understanding Statistical Process Control,* 2nd ed. Knoxville, TN: SPC Press Inc., 1992.

About the Author

Don Siebels is a senior member of ASQ and has been a member since 1983. He is an ASQ certified quality manager, ASQ certified quality engineer, ASQ certified quality auditor, and Six Sigma Green Belt. Don holds a bachelor of science in business administration from Mount Mercy College, Cedar Rapids, Iowa. He has worked in the quality profession in various positions over the last three decades as senior quality engineer and quality manager with a Fortune 500 company. He now holds the position of quality systems manager for a major transportation company. Don is the section chair for the local ASQ section. He serves on the panel of judges and is a senior examiner on the board of examiners for the Arkansas Institute for Performance Excellence (formerly Arkansas Quality Award).

6/05
B
26.40

For Reference

Not to be taken

from this library